ALEX MACGILLIVRAY writes about global issues. He has a degree in Modern History from Oxford University and a masters' degree in Environmental Science from Imperial College London. He has written a history on the birth of the environmental movement: *Rachel Carson's Silent Spring*.

Alex is a senior associate of the New Economics Foundation – and the Institute for Social and Ethical Accountability. He has worked with all the major players in globalization, from UN agencies and national governments to multinational companies and radical campaigning groups. Before this, Alex worked for a multinational company printing banknotes for half the countries of the world.

Other titles in this series

A Brief History of 1917: Russia's Year of Revolution
Roy Bainton

A Brief History of The Birth of the Nazis
Nigel Jones

A Brief History of British Kings & Queens
Mike Ashley

British Sea Power
David Howarth

The Celts: A History
Peter Berresford Ellis

Christianity: A History
Bamber Gascoigne

The Circumnavigators: A History
Derek Wilson

The Crusades
Geoffrey Hindley

A Brief History of The Druids
Peter Berresford Ellis

The Dynasties of China: A History
Bamber Gascoigne

A Brief History of Fighting Ships
David Davies

A Brief History of The Great Moguls
Bamber Gascoigne

A Brief History of the Hundred Years War
Desmond Seward

Infinity
Brian Clegg

A Brief History of Medicine
Paul Strathern

A Brief History of Mutiny
Richard Woodman

Napoleon in Russia
Alan Palmer

A Brief History of Painting
Roy Bolton

A Brief History of Science
Thomas Crump

A Brief History of The Tudor Age
Jasper Ridley

A Brief History of The Vikings
Jonathan Clements

A BRIEF HISTORY OF

GLOBALIZATION

THE UNTOLD STORY OF OUR INCREDIBLE SHRINKING PLANET

ALEX MacGILLIVRAY

CARROLL & GRAF PUBLISHERS
New York

Carroll & Graf Publishers
An imprint of Avalon Publishing Group, Inc.
245 W. 17th Street
11th Floor
New York
NY 10011–5300
www.carrollandgraf.com

AVALON
publishing group incorporated

First published in the UK by Robinson,
an imprint of Constable & Robinson Ltd, 2006

First Carroll & Graf edition, 2006

ISBN-13: 978–0–78671–710–1
ISBN-10: 0–7867–1710–6

Printed and bound in the EU

For Lilli, Megan and Alba

CONTENTS

ACKNOWLEDGEMENTS

First thanks go to Becky Hardie, my editor at Constable Robinson, and *Brief History* series editor Saul David. I'm very grateful for intellectual support and the chance to see globalization in action around the world to many colleagues and friends at the London think tanks New Economics Foundation and AccountAbility and the international Alliance 21. A wealth of ideas, favourite dates and other suggestions came flooding in from Kripa Ananthpur, Christian Bertonnier, Kai Bethke, John Cavanagh, Adrian Clarke, Sarah Burns, Elna Kotze, Sanjiv Lingayah, Jonathan Loh, Tim Jackson, Nic Marks, Ed Mayo, Pete Raynard, Bernardo Reyes, Nick Robins, Brian Shaad, Hetan Shah, Andrew Simms, Françoise Wautiez and Simon Zadek. Susie Dent of *Countdown* clarified the meaning – and spelling – of the word globalization. David Boyle, John Sabapathy and Felipe Fernández-Armesto deserve special thanks for ploughing through the text, and for their careful but always positive comments.

I am indebted to a host of hitherto unknown experts, who responded to sometimes bizarre questions with alacrity: Tyler Cowen at George Mason University for comments on the global reach of spaghetti westerns; Daniel Lemin at Google Inc. for explaining the ins and outs of the Zeitgeist exercise; Bonnie Ward at World Watch Institute; Grazia Ietto Gillies at London's South Bank University and Alan Rugman at the Kelley School of Business, Indiana University for insights and data on the global reach of transnational corporations; Fuat Sezgin of the Institute for the History of Arabic-Islamic Science at the Johann Wolfgang Goethe University in Frankfurt, Germany for papers and posters of the Al-Mamud world map; Ken Alder of Northwestern University for filling me in on the French attempt to measure the meridian; Allen Palmer at Brigham Young University for the low-down on the International Meridian Conference of 1884; Linda Champanier for details and the image of Nellie Bly; Keisuke Nakashima, research associate at the CSIS Global Aging Initiative for steering me to statistics on median ages worldwide; Rebecca Dubs at UEFA Media Services for data on home-grown footballers; Stephen V. Marks, Professor of Economics at Pomona College for his knowledge of the Indonesian nutmeg trade; and Robin Dunbar at Liverpool University and Duncan Watts at Columbia University for their ground-breaking work on how we network in a small world.

Though I am a little sceptical about claims that the internet is a transformative global technology, I could not have researched so much of this book from home without four invaluable tools: the google search engine, the wikipedia encyclopaedia and Project Gutenburg transcripts of out-of-copyright books. The fourth tool is France Telecom's commitment to providing high-speed internet access in rural areas, and for replacing the fibre-optics whenever cable-rustlers strike.

My father Ian MacGillivray's encyclopedic first-hand knowledge of the world, his massive 1960s world map and his uncanny ability to take the strategically important Kamchatka in the board game *Risk* first got me interested in global history. We often discuss and occasionally agree on what to make of that history. Meanwhile Norman Matson instilled in me the duty of a son-in-law to get the message to García without asking dumb questions. Most of all, this book could not have been written without the patient intellectual and emotional support of Lilli Matson, and close questioning from our children Megan and Alba. They also helped me build a massive wall-sized bookcase to house a growing library of books on globalization. But like the Great Wall of China or Berlin Wall, erecting a Great Wall of Books can be no defence against internal mistakes, for which I readily accept responsibility.

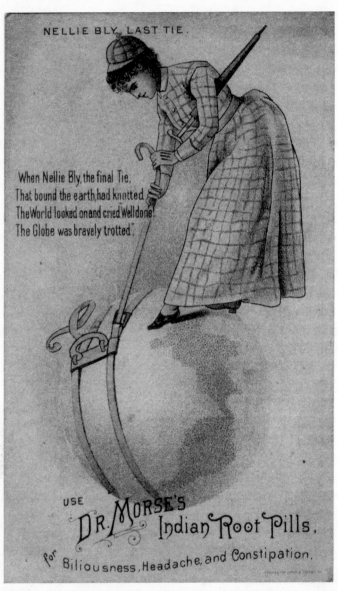

Nellie Bly's 1889 circumnavigation epitomized
the late nineteenth-century global contraction

I

INTRODUCTION

'The multitude of books is making us ignorant.'
François-Marie Arouet
('Voltaire,' 1694–1778)

There are 3,300 books in English in print on the subject of globalization. Add to these 700 recent French titles on *mondialisation*, 670 on *globalisierung* in German, and hundreds more in Russian, Arabic, Hindi, Chinese, Spanish and other languages. In all, there are over 5,000 titles in print on globalization.[1] It's a crowded field. There are two books called *Empire*, one Marxist, the other capitalist. Four books are called *Globalization and its Discontents*. There are pro- and anti-globalization books by Michael Moore and Mike Moore – the first an award-winning, subversive documentary maker, and the second the former head of the World Trade Organization.

I don't claim to have read all these books, but with a bit of training, I have at least learnt how to sort them into one of four genres. First come the academic books by sociologists and political scientists. Many of these books claim that the phenomenon is something new, rather exciting and utterly complex. Some writers were tempted to see globalization as an epic 'Clash of Civilizations' between Western capitalism and Islam: McWorld vs. Jihad or the Lexus against the Olive Tree.[2]

From the late 1990s came a wave of popular books by activists and journalists, again warning that globalization was new, but taking a more negative view and identifying multi-national corporations as the culprits. The anti-globalization movement was an unlikely coalition of greying academics, glamorous anti-corporate activists, Indian peasants and French cheese-makers. With no apparent irony, glossy cof-fee-table books on anti-globalization started to appear.[3]

Why, the proponents of global free trade asked themselves, should the devil have all the best tunes? In response to the amazing sales and high media profile of the photogenic 'anti-globalizers', came a spate of books by economists announcing that globalization is in fact good news for everyone – if only we would embrace it fully. Even writers for *The Economist*, who normally guard their journalistic anonymity jealously, began revealing themselves in print. You know things have got out of hand when historians start muscling in. Globalization, we were told by Niall Ferguson, made goods cheaper, people freer, economies stronger and cultures richer. And the British, by jingo, got the whole global process going. According to Ferguson, it is now high time the USA took on the colossal task of global imperialism.[4]

Meanwhile, a plethora of individual commodity histories, with titles like '*X: the y that changed the world*', began to appear. It is hard to imagine a commodity, invention or singular event obscure enough not to merit this genre's earth-shattering treatment. On my desk now is the fascinating *Brazilian Popular Music and Globalization*.[5] Could balsamic vinegar, Minitel and the Cold Winter of 1963 be next? Many of these books maintain a sense of proportion, and situate their chosen commodity in the broader context of global economic, cultural and social history.

But among all these titles, there was almost nothing written on the history of globalization.[6] What is missing is a balanced history for the general reader, to find out where globalization came from, and what that tells us about where it might be going next. The story, in short, of the incredible shrinking planet. Inspired by Voltaire, possibly the most voluminous writer ever, I took up my pen to add to the multitude of books on globalization. In this book, I address five important questions:

- In what ways does a history of globalization differ from a history of the world?
- Is globalization really a new way of looking at the world, or is it simply a new word for imperialism, colonialism, modernism or capitalism?
- Who is behind globalization? Is it really an American phenomenon?
- How far has globalization progressed? Will it reach a 'tipping point', when the world is fully globalized? If so, when?
- Is globalization a good thing or a bad thing? Who are the winners and losers?

In 1752, Voltaire wrote *Micromégas*, a short story in which two giant visitors from Outer Space visit Earth and try to make sense of humankind's global obsession with scientific measurement and propensity for pointless warfare at the cost of genuine happiness. *Micromégas* was one of the first works of science fiction. Too many writers on globalization borrow from this genre, relying more on technocratic fantasy, conspiracy theories and bold economic assertions than a careful assessment of the historical record. 'I will relate honestly what occurred, without adding anything of my own invention,' promised Voltaire in *Micromégas*. As he well knew and I soon discovered, this is 'a task which demands no small effort on the part of a historian.'

Defining globalization – scope and intent

> *'Globalisation is, indeed, a staggering concept.'*
> *Spectator*, 5 October 1962

For Bill Clinton globalization was the 'world without walls'. Tony Blair says it is 'inevitable and irresistible'. George W. Bush calls it the 'ties of trade and trust.' For George Monbiot, globalization allows companies to hold 'a gun to government's head'.[7] Political leaders and polemicists alike thrive on such alliterations.

Other writers have eased themselves and their readers into what can be a heavy subject by visual imagery and anecdote: a man at the Wailing Wall holding up a mobile phone so that a distant friend can commiserate; or a video still of Osama Bin Laden carrying a Kalashnikov rifle and wearing a Timex wristwatch. John Micklethwait and Adrian Wooldridge amusingly reincarnate and walk an astonished Karl Marx from his grave in Highgate Cemetery through modern-day London. 'Nearly swept off his feet by a passing Rolls-Royce', write the two *Economist* journalists, 'he might be more surprised to discover that the vehicle, like the rest of Britain's car industry, was now owned by a German company.'[8]

Sloganeering and imagery don't get us far in defining globalization, though. There are two basic types of definition around: the tight economic definition and the broader social definition. When his parents asked him to explain his work, economist Paul Krugman would tell them 'Oh, global schmo-bal, you know.' To everyone else, he said 'globaloney'. Nowa-days, he is more forthcoming as a leading proponent of a narrow economic definition of globalization. For Krugman, globalization is 'a catchall phrase for growing world trade, the growing linkages between financial markets in different coun-tries, and the many other ways in which the world is becoming a smaller place'.

Ex-World Bank economist Joseph Stiglitz focuses even more specifically on 'the removal of barriers to free trade and the closer integration of national economies'. Many opponents as well as proponents of globalization favour a narrow defini-tion. For example the International Forum on Globalization, one of the leading groups promoting alternatives to globaliza-tion, defines it as 'the present worldwide drive toward a globalized economic system dominated by supranational cor-porate trade and banking institutions that are not accountable to democratic processes or national governments.' Explicit in these definitions is the central role of trade and finance.[9]

Others reject the economic focus as too narrow. In a recent 'very short introduction' to globalization, Manfred Steger of Illinois State University reviews half a dozen broader defini-tions by academics. He concludes that globalization is 'a multidimensional set of social processes that create, multiply, stretch, and intensify worldwide social interdependencies and exchanges while at the same time fostering in people a growing awareness of deepening connections between the local and the distant'.[10] Professor Steger's definition may not be very short, though it certainly stresses the social aspect.

But what about religion, war, sport, terror, the environ-ment? Are they social, or economic? In the debate, ulterior motives have been ascribed to these competing definitions. A narrow economic focus is 'pro-capitalist'; a broader social perspective 'anti-capitalist'. 'Globalisation is neither new nor a folly', the brilliant Indian economist Amartya Sen told a Mumbai theatre packed to bursting point in 2001, 'but a global movement of ideas, people, technology and goods from one region to others, benefiting the people at large.'[11] Sen is unusual in making a beneficial motive part of the definition.

Perhaps the debate about what globalization covers is a reflection of genuine uncertainty about what we're experiencing and why it matters. A history of globalization must accept that this is an idea whose novelty we are still getting to grips with. For this reason, I reject a thematic economic-or-social definition in favour of the broadest possible coverage. But don't worry, I won't call *everything* globalization.

The Oxford English Dictionary (OED) – itself a powerful global authority – reminds us to refocus on the geographical scope of the word 'globe'. In its broad sense, says the OED, 'global' means 'embracing the totality of a number of items' and more specifically 'pertaining to or involving the whole world; worldwide; universal'. To Kate Galbraith of *The Economist*, globalization 'at its simplest, means crossing borders.'[12] But to my mind, when two newly independent neighbouring Baltic countries trade peat for potatoes, this is not global trade. City currency traders hedging between sterling and the euro are not global financiers. A Parisian woman taking a mini-break to Brussels is no more a globalizer than if she goes to more distant Marseilles. Using the world-wide-web to find a local hairdresser is not global fashion.

Like politics, most history is local – or at least national. Readers looking for a good history of the world are spoilt for choice.[13] It is my focus on global scope and global intent that distinguishes this history of globalization from yet another history of the world. This book tries to untangle the processes, interconnections and exchanges that are *global* from those that are merely cross-border, regional, international or even long-distance. In a world where the tag 'global' is slung around, I have found amazingly few researchers prepared to grapple with the challenge of an operational definition of what is means to be truly global. We should be especially wary of using the word global as aggrandizing shorthand for big or 'world-class', as many corporations, business magazines – and charities – are tempted to do.

What is to come

It would be pedantic, however, to restrict globalization to only those processes that occur in every single place on the planet. It would also make this a very brief history indeed. Some global events certainly progress in incremental fashion, one frontier at a time. The Black Death was a devastating case in point. As a rule of thumb, though, an exchange involving three participants on three different continents is more convincingly global than a one-to-one exchange. I explore the development of this 'global intent' in the next chapter. This is a brief history, but brief does not mean recent. Global intent is the world-encompassing mental process that began with Pythagoras in the fifth century BC, and reached a culmination of sorts with the sea voyages of Columbus and da Gama in the fifteenth and sixteenth centuries AD. Our understanding of the globe continues to evolve today.

Globalization needs tighter definition not just in terms of scope (*global-*) but of motive (*-ize*). In other words, we are interested not just in the *how much* and *where* but want to know the *who* and the *why*. Reserving globalization for players and events that deliberately and consciously embraced the globe helps invest the term with meaning. Again, an overly tight interpretation on intention would disqualify AIDS as a global phenomenon. But this focus helps sift through a mass of detail to find those who acted globally – the real planet-shrinkers covered in Chapter Three. This is the story of how individuals and nations struggled – and competed – to encompass the newly-imagined globe, from the first circum-navigations to the age of satellites and cheap air travel in the 1970s.

The spice trade is an early manifestation of global scope and global intent coming together. In the sixteenth century, Portuguese mariners gained direct sea access to the Moluccan Spice Islands and Malabar coast of India. In doing so they managed to cut out the Venetians, who had previously enjoyed a monopoly on the European trade. This business was far-flung, exotic and profitable. But it was not yet, as I argue in Chapter Four, a fully global trade.

The spice trade became global when Dutch, British and French entrepreneurs destroyed the Portuguese-dominated supply-chain by purloining seeds and started growing spices in promising locations all across the tropics, from Mauritius and Réunion to Grenada and Brazil. They also created demand for spices among the middle and then working classes, and outside Europe, too. Chapter Four charts this development of the global commodities trade, beginning with spices in the fifteenth century and following the transformation from three East India Companies through to today's 60,000 multina-tional corporations. Brazilian pepper is now sold to Indian immigrants under a British brand with a German name by a US company with an Irish name. That is globalization in a nutshell. But how prevalent is global trade? Is it improving labour standards or consigning more and more workers to a sweatshop planet?

Globalization is not just the story of goods on the move.

Muscle, the next chapter, also became a global commodity. The seventeenth- and eighteenth-century Atlantic slave trade, and the great migrations of the nineteenth century, both provide important insights into today's mass movements of refugees and migrant workers. Many analysts stress the astonishing growth of business travel and short-haul holidays, but are these really the key trends in modern global migration? Two hundred years after the slave trade was banned, how is it that there are still tens of millions of slaves in the world?

Chapter Six tackles the juice of globalization, tracking the transition from gold to the dollar as global reserve currency. The key challenge for a global currency has always been the balance between scarcity and abundance. This has not just been a concern for bankers and speculators, but has major impacts on the income levels of ordinary people worldwide. Oil, rather than the dollar, yuan and euro, is perhaps the *de facto* global reserve currency, a position it began surreptitiously to assume in the 1970s. Not for nothing are three of the world's largest 50 economies oil companies. But with a warming planet now a certainty, will carbon dioxide replace oil as the global juice of the twenty-first century?

In the penultimate chapter, we turn to the broad world of ideas: global religion, language, culture, sport and communication. Technological potential and fads have run ahead of the real social impact of global cultural exchange, from the telegraph and world fair right through to the internet and sushi. Global culture is better understood as a tense dynamic between local identity and global ambition, whether in religion, art, film, music or football.

These four chapters cover the main global exchanges – trade, labour, finance, ideas – in turn, with a strong focus on global scope and global intent. The history of globalization in many ways defies a traditional chronological treatment.

Although there are long-run trends, globalization is a jerky process of conflict between the local and the universal. Some historians describe broad 'waves' of globalization, but it is possible to identify the key developments more precisely – as a series of global contractions. These overlapping episodes of exploration, trade, migration, conflict and creativity progress from chapter to chapter, and are brought together in the concluding chapter, The Incredible Shrinking Planet. This panorama gives us a richer understanding of where globalization has come from, and where it might be taking us next.

Globalization: the biography of a word

Many people assert that globalization is another word for imperialism, colonization, Americanization. One textbook tells us the term was invented by US academics in the 1960s. In fact, the earliest use of the adjective 'global' I have been able to find dates back to 1892, and appears in the pages of *Harper's Magazine*. But it was not coined by an American.

The *Harper's* article describes a Monsieur de Vogüé, a Frenchman who 'loves travel; he goes to the East and to the West for colors and ideas; his interests are as wide as the universe; his ambition, to use a word of his own, is to be "global".'[14] 1892 was an eventful year around the world, with British and French invasions in Nigeria and Dahomey bringing the European 'Scramble for Africa' to a new pitch of imperialism. But there is something different about Vogüé's ambitions. They are not quite imperial, not simply modernist, broader than colonial.

Vogüé's quest for inspiration and novelty is startlingly voracious. It is globe-encompassing. 1892 was also the year Ellis Island opened to immigrants; the year when Edison patented the two-way telegraph and General Electric was founded. It saw the birth of two very different politicians – Wendell Wilkie and Haile Selassie – both with global vision. Globalization was alive and well in the late nineteenth century.

Globalization predates the American Century, then. Nor was it exclusively the creation of the British Empire (what Niall Ferguson has memorably called 'Anglobalization'). As we'll see, many of the building blocks of globalization turn out to be French: *laissez-faire* economics, *pommes frites*, the passport, the metric system, the Suez canal, the round-the-world trip, FIFA and the Olympics, Minitel, Louis Vuitton. Maybe not Minitel, but not matter how the French decry 'coca-coloniza-tion', their fingerprints are all over globalization. And it's not just the French who have had global ambitions: we find unique contributions from many other cultures and nations – Greek, Mongol, Islamic, Chinese, Dutch, Irish – in the history of globalization.

In the twentieth century, the term 'global' rapidly caught on, according to the OED. Newspapers like London's *The Times* were using it in the context of international trade discussions by the late 1920s. It was taken up to describe the new 'global warfare' – both in terms of its unprecedented geographical expanse and lethal intensity – in the early 1940s. In the immediate post-war years, globalism was being used in coun-terpoint to isolationism and nationalism. By the 1950s it had again been pressed into service to explain the Cold War. B-36s became 'global bombers'.

In 1961, globalization made it into *Webster's Dictionary*, an important rite of passage. It was used by economics journals in discussions about the European Common Market. Interest-ingly, though, *The Economist*, *New Scientist* and other jour-nals were equally happy using the French-inspired alternative

'mondialization' in the early 1960s. In the 1970s, mondialization gradually died out – a symbol perhaps of waning French
influence on the shape and size of the planet.

The only deviant synonym to survive is 'worldization'. But
this today has a highly specific meaning: a technique for
recording multiple film soundtracks in a range of outdoor
environments to deliberately capture background noise and
varying sound perspectives. Worldization was pioneered by
Orson Welles in *Touch of Evil* and first used extensively by
sound designer Walter Murch in the soundtrack to *American
Graffiti* (1973). There is as much background noise in globalization, not all of it so easy on the ear.

Globalization the word carried all before it. The phrase
'global village' made its appearance in the title of a 1968
book by bestselling media pundit Marshall McLuhan, ably
assisted by graphic artist Quentin Fiore. McLuhan's thesis
was that new electronic communications media, especially
the telegraph and radio, enabled or forced events to be
shared simultaneously around the world. 'Tribalism is our
only resource since the electro-magnetic discovery. Moving
from print to electronic media we have given up an eye for
an ear,' wrote McLuhan with characteristic hyperbole.
'The globe has contracted, spatially, into a single large
village.'[15]

According to language expert Susie Dent, throughout the
1960s and seventies, normal usage of the term still required
elaboration – 'the globalization of' production, quotas and so
on – to explain it. Veteran *New York Times* journalist Soma
Golden Behr, for example, used it in an article called 'Grappling with Multinational Corporations' in December 1974.
Eighty years after the appearance of the term, there was still
uncertainty about what exactly it meant.

'Only in the late 1980s do we start to see the free-standing

word as shorthand for the process of global market capitalism', says Dent. 'Finally, you get the first evidence for
"anti-globalization" in 1995.' 1995 was the 'Year of the
Sweatshop,' when companies like Gap and Nike were regularly in the news, accused of poor labour standards in
factories in Indonesia and elsewhere. Wal-Mart was starting
to attract criticism for its aggressive sourcing, expansionary
plans and employment practices. McDonald's was in the
midst of suing two London campaigners for libel. Globalization became irrevocably associated with US multinational
corporations.

But using globalization as shorthand for US capitalism was
misleading. In the Year of the Sweatshop, a brutal Nigerian
military government under the late Sani Abacha hanged nine
Ogoni activists, including the playwright Ken Saro-Wiwa. This
sparked worldwide protests against the alleged complicity of
Anglo-Dutch oil company Shell. The same year Greenpeace
shamed the company over its plans to dispose of the North Sea
oil storage buoy Brent Spar. Criticism of the self-appointed
group of world leaders called the G7 (another French invention) had been rumbling for years, but reached a new pitch at
the G7 Halifax Summit that year.

Over the next five years, the word globalization was
seldom seen in public without the prefix 'anti-'. Protesters
began to gather alongside annual get-togethers of global
organizations like the World Trade Organization (WTO),
International Monetary Fund, World Bank, World Economic Forum and G7. The protests in Seattle, Washington,
Davos and elsewhere were often violent and always high-
profile. In Genoa, birthplace of planet-shrinker Christopher
Columbus, a young protestor was shot dead by police. By
2000, journalists were writing about globalization on a
daily basis, as the graph shows for the *New York Times*.

Journalists like Naomi Klein detected a new worldwide movement in the making, forged from an unlikely coalition of student activists, labour organizers, radical academics and peasant movements. Increasingly, these groups were turning the tools of globalization (the internet, mobile phones) against corporate power.

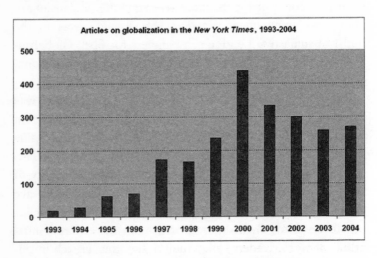

In the process, globalization was being redefined as a far less benign process than Monsieur de Vogüé's all-encompassing thirst for the exotic – the sights, sounds, smells and colours of the whole world. Judging by the *NYT*, interest in the globalization debate may have dipped somewhat from its peak in 2000, but the word globalization looks set to enjoy an eventful second century.[16] Although protests over corporate abuse have been a recurrent feature in the history of globalization, never before has there been such concern from so many quarters about the dangers of quenching our thirst for everyday luxury on a shrinking – and overheating – planet.

The global tipping point?

'Globalization is nothing new. We have always had globalization.'

Arriel Salvador, Workers
Assistance Center, Philippines[17]

'[Globalization] is now in a genuinely new phase.'
Felipe Fernández-Armesto,
Queen Mary, University of London[18]

When did globalization begin? Most commentators insist it is a process that got under way only after 1950. For many, the turning point was after the internet began to work in the early 1990s. But as we'll see, there is plenty of evidence that the period from 1870 to 1913 – M. de Vogüé's era – marked a heyday of genuine globalization. Other historians plausibly trace the birth of the modern world back further, to 1780. In the period from 1600 to 1800, some argue, came a phase of 'proto-globalization'.

Still others detect a prior era of 'archaic globalization', stretching back thousands of years and driven not by the West, but by China and Islam. 'The West first bought itself a third class seat on the Asian economic train, then leased a whole railway carriage,' wrote the late André Gunder Frank, 'and only in the nineteenth century managed to displace Asians from the locomotive.' German historian Arno Peters wrote a 'synchronoptic' history of the world (1952) that gave every century exactly equal column inches. In this subversive book, the Inca civilization was given as much coverage as Medieval Europe; the twenty-ninth century BC as much as the twentieth century AD. It has never gone out of print in German – but has never been translated into English.

'The chronology of globalization,' argues historian Felipe Fernández-Armesto, 'has generated the most sterile controversy in history today . . . For some historians, it is a point of professional honour to insist that all processes are gradual, all changes cumulative, all apparent novelties rooted in precedent.'[19] Fernández-Armesto is no enemy of a little controversy himself. With all due respect to the person who taught me global history in the mid-1980s, if previous experiences of global exchange can tell us about where modern globalization is heading, then this debate may be controversial but it is far from sterile.

The tale begins in sixth-century BC Crotone and continues through to the Gleneagles Summit of the G8 in July 2005. But this history is not from the synchronoptic school. It does not attempt to give equal play to every period – nor to every civilization.[20] World history is the history of long-run trends, but at times the globe contracted dramatically. 'The discovery of America, and that of a passage to the East Indies by the Cape of Good Hope', wrote the gifted Scottish economist Adam Smith in 1776, 'are the two greatest and most important events recorded in the history of mankind.' Many historians have taken his lead, seeing 1492 as the starting date for globalization.

When bestselling historian Mark Kurlansky turned his attention from cod and salt to the date, his agent must have wondered whether he would find enough to say about the fruit of the Saharan oasis. In fact he was after a year that rocked the world, and Kurlansky picked not 1492 but 1968. He makes a fascinating case, peopled with TV-watching, college-occupying radical peaceniks from the USA and Paris to Mexico and Prague. As a result of civil rights, a new post-war generation, hatred of the Vietnam war and the growth of TV, 1968 saw an unprecedented and shocking shrinking of the globe. 'We will never again feel the thrill of the first moon shots or the first broadcasts from outer space,' Kurlansky argues. 'We now live in a world in which we await a new breakthrough every day.'[21] Every minute, he might have said.

New York Times journalist Thomas Friedman disagrees. For him, the key stage of globalization started in the year 2000, when a package of modern information and communication technologies – Windows, internet, web browsers, open-source software – came together with an aggressive drive by companies and individuals to seek new opportunities around a world made more open by the fall of the Berlin Wall. 'Globalization 3.0', Friedman writes, 'is shrinking the world from a size small to a size tiny and flattening the playing field at the same time.'[22]

Can all three be right? Certainly not, but they *are* right to focus in. Globalization may have started a long time ago, but there is little to be learned by dividing it up into two-hundred-year chunks. Globalization develops in a jerky, not gradual, fashion. There have been just a handful of short pulses of hyper-globalization. These were the critical planet-shrinking moments when people from all walks of life seized new opportunity and others complained that 'the world is going so fast'.

Academic historians shudder at efforts to pin planet-shrinking pulses to a single year. But arbitrary cut-off dates are hard-wired into the discipline. When I studied 'modern' history at Oxford University, the course finished in the year 1964, the year of my birth. Think what we students missed in the year after modern history 'ended'. 1965 saw 400,000 US combat troops in Vietnam; the independence of The Gambia, Singapore and Rhodesia; India, Pakistan and China engaged in border skirmishes; the invention of the term nuclear 'escalation' by writer Herman Kahn; and Sergio Leone's bleak vision of globalization in a poncho, *For A Few Dollars More*.

European and American historians have to be careful not to write global history from personal reminiscence, though. This is a young person's planet. Most people in the world simply weren't alive for earth-shattering events like the death of Elvis Presley in Tennessee, the murder of Steve Biko in a South African prison, the last football match of Pelé at the Giants Stadium in East Rutherford, New Jersey, or the death in Switzerland, in self-imposed exile from both Britain and the USA, of Charlie Chaplin at the age of 88. Most Asians and Latin Americans are close to the world median age – 27 years old according to the United Nations – but half of all Europeans are 39 or over, and the typical African is under 19 years of age. These disparities in average age make for major differences of perspective in what are the key developments of globalization. Young people are at once the most pro-global, and the least.[23]

In an effort to avoid both needless controversy and faulty perspective, this book identifies five globalizing decades over the past five centuries. In each of them, a concatenation of commercial, social, financial, cultural and technological events markedly and rapidly shrank the globe. Historical chance and local factors played as strong a hand as global intent in the build up to these planet-shrinking contractions. There have been frequent pulses of worldwide activity that did *not* generate globalization, like the Braxton Hicks tightenings of a false labour. In contrast, the decades of global contraction have been immediate and unmistakeable. Here, then, are five planet-shrinking contractions that stand out in the long history of globalization.

Contraction 1:
the Iberian carve-up (1490–1500)

In this decade, the shape and size of the globe finally became known, thanks to technical innovation, commercial ambition and strategic intent. The superpower Spain and the innovator Portugal spearheaded the process. Using their inside track to the global government of the day, the Papacy, these two countries agreed to carve up the globe between them. Middlemen were rapidly cut out of the supply-chains of long-distance trade. The period of global competition between rivals – nation-states, gold and silver, civilized and savage, land and sea – began. This was the point when printing began to spread knowledge and literacy widely.

Contraction 2:
the Britannic meridian (1880–90)

The British Empire, already *de facto* the leading imperial power, cemented its global reach. In addition to a favourable deal over the 'legal' partition of Africa and enforcing a global Gold Standard, London rode roughshod over alternative voices and dictated the position of the international meridian. Round-the-world trips became a practical possibility for wealthy Westerners, as did one-way trips for millions of working-class migrants. Modern corporations like Vestey's began to expand their global reach, using refrigerated steamships and telegraph. Consumers changed their shopping habits, and became more voracious for luxury. But this was also a decade of innovation for international institutions and rising concern over the negative impacts of global trade.

Contraction 3: Sputnik World (1955–65)

Winston Churchill's 1946 speech was not the first time the term 'Iron Curtain' had been used, but the erection of the Berlin Wall (1961) set a bi-polar world in concrete. The Soviet space programme galvanized the US from complacent isolationism into the Cold War. Rapid decolonization gave the superpowers a domino set to fight over. Far from being a brake on globalization, Sputnik World was a golden age for economic growth and trade in many parts of the world. The corporation began to flex its multinational muscles, while technical and cultural innovations, from the satellite to the jet airplane to the transistor radio and rock'n'roll had worldwide impacts. But this decade also saw the birth of the worldwide green movement, which formed non-governmental organizations to challenge government and corporations.

Contraction 4:
the global supply-chain (1995–2005)

The fault-lines of the previous contractions ran North-South. In this decade, they were reorientated East-West, dictated not by main force or by international negotiation, but by the supply-chains of giant multinationals. The new global meridian runs along lines of latitude like 36 degrees North, which connects Wal-Mart in Bentonville, Arkansas with the Haier Corporation in QingDao, Shandong. The globe was criss-crossed with a fibre-optic web and mobile telephone masts, allowing one billion people to communicate, collaborate and compete as never before. This was a heated decade in the globalization debate – from the Year of the Sweatshop to the Battle in Seattle. Worldwide movements questioned the free global market as never before. It was also the hottest decade since climatic records began.

Contraction 5: thermo-globalization

I must confess I can't give the dates of the fifth planet-shrinking decade. But it won't be not far off and we'll know it when it comes. The economic cake will continue to grow, but not as fast as the mounting appetite of the world's people. In this decade, the first crumbs will be visibly picked from the plates of rich nations, and they won't like it. Social networks will reach their greatest feasible extent, and virtual consumerism will supplement diminishing commodities. The dominant fault-line will be drawn not by explorers, traders or diplomats, but by climate change. The global 'isotherm' will be an unpredictable line of intolerable temperature rise traced onto the world map. It will encircle many Pacific island states, but also draw a red line through inhabited areas across all continents.

This fifth global contraction could be another 20 or more years in the coming. It could follow directly from the current period of supply-chain contraction and the hurricanes of 2005. 'It's not just happening in the Arctic,' says Inuit hunter John Keogak, on the front line of global warming. 'It's going to happen all over the world. The whole world is going too fast.'[24] The first four planetary contractions were largely unpredicted. What is different this time is that we *already know* that global contractions on a heating planet will present huge economic, social, cultural and environmental challenges. It could make all previous experiences of globalization look like a false labour.

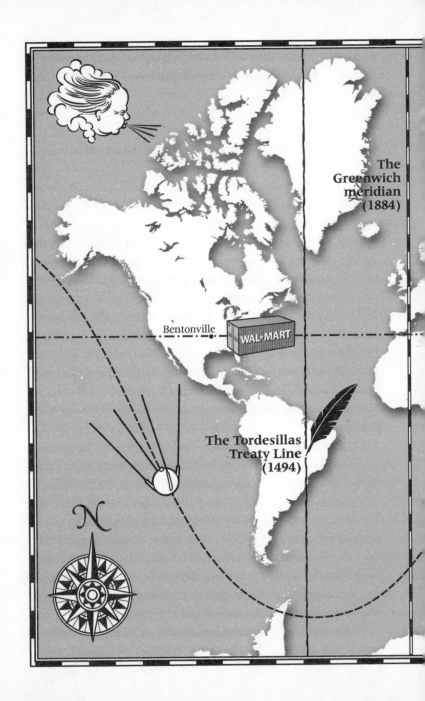

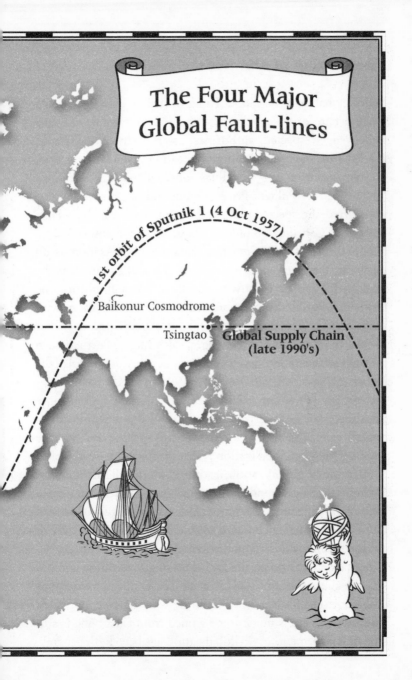

The Four Major
Global Fault-lines

1st orbit of Sputnik 1 (4 Oct 1957)

Baikonur Cosmodrome

Tsingtao Global Supply Chain
(late 1990's)

The nature of the beast

So, is globalization a Good Thing or a Bad Thing? This is a fierce debate, and it's far from settled yet. Voltaire would have approved. Respected authorities assert 'why globalization works' and 'the truth about globalization', while others write 'despatches from the frontlines' and tell us why we must 'defuse' it.[25] A Pulitzer-Prize winning journalist says it's just got started; a respected philosopher announces that it has just collapsed. Can they be talking about the same animal?

Supporters of unfettered free trade see globalization as an elephant, massively and undeniably there. It's a force to be exploited if you know how to handle it. Through history, the elephant has literally been pressed into service by those with global intent. The gift of an elephant clinched the deal that divided the world up between the Spanish and the Portuguese in the early sixteenth century. It later became a potent symbol of the British Raj in India. The period 1870–1913 was in some senses the 'woolly mammoth' version of globalization – even more impressive but sadly driven to extinction. Pro-global histories tend to exaggerate how far the process has gone to date. The elephant view of globalization is irresistible and unstoppable.

For critics of globalization, it is more like a gorilla in the closet. It's huge, destructive and about to get out of control. The gorilla view of globalization also has a tendency to exaggeration, and has sometimes being co-opted to lend topicality and novelty to the long-running anti-capitalist critique.

Both elephant and gorilla as images of globalization empha-size the sheer size and power of the beast. But the history of globalization shows us we should be wary of accepting such assertions. There is much to be gained from classifying it and studying its behaviour.[26] Globalization has been both progressive and destructive. It is a contradictory, even perverse, process. Like M. de Vogüé, it can draw in the exotic and luxurious, spreading diversity and wealth. But it is also Yum Corporation, pushing out the uniform and bland. It is like the 'push-me pull-you', that strange beast with a head at each end pulling in opposite directions. Much depends on how it is handled.

As we will see, history challenges claims by pundits on both sides of the debate about how far the process has gone. To my mind, globalization is more Tasmanian Devil than elephant or gorilla. Not the likeably naughty Looney Tunes character, but the real Tasmanian Devil. It certainly exists. But it is hard to classify: it looks like a dog, smells like a skunk, howls like a hyena but has a pouch like a wallaby. Like globalization, it was almost driven to extinction in the 1930s Great Depression, but then bounced back. It is noisy, vicious, and it smells awful. It may be smaller than you expected. But it's tenacious, rather impressive, and a little scary.

Like the Tasmanian Devil, globalization is fascinating and merits our study. In trade, finance, mobility and culture, globalization brings benefits and problems in equal measure. The good news is that we are *not* dealing with some beast so huge as to be unmanageable. But when you come face to face with a Tasmanian Devil, you need to handle the situation carefully. This is a far better strategy than putting it in your lap and stroking it – or running like hell.[27]

Photo by Wayne McLean (Wikipedia)

2

GLOBAL INTENT

*'It is not easy to see how the more extreme forms of nation-
alism can long survive when men have seen the Earth in its
true perspective as a single small globe against the stars.'*
Arthur C. Clarke (1917–)

The development of global intent is the essential prelude to
globalization. The transition from mysterious flat earth to
small, encompassable globe was a slow process requiring
massive intellectual, technological and commercial leaps. First
the flat earth had to be inflated into a sphere, and then it had to
be shrunk to manageable proportions. Far from blunting the
extremes of nationalism, as Arthur C. Clarke hoped, global
intent ushered in a period of extremely nationalistic competition. Nations competed first to conceive of the globe and
explore it – the subject of this chapter – and then to circum-
navigate it, claim it, and finally straddle it – the subject of the
next chapter. As we'll see, Greek galleys, Viking longboats,
Chinese junks or Arab dhows all had some of the components
of global intent. But globalization came instead in the wake of
Spanish galleons and Portuguese caravels.

Global thinking

Global intent is the ambition to encompass the whole planet. Identifying the emergence of a global world-view is a complex matter, however. Global intent required technical, mental and commercial breakthroughs to overturn flat earth thinking. Christopher Columbus, Vasco da Gama and Ferdinand Magellan conventionally take the credit, but a European victory was no foregone conclusion. Other power centres in the world could – may – have developed global intent before the Europeans.

The Inuit, the indigenous peoples of the Arctic, apparently believed they were the only people on earth, until their first contact with European explorers. Other isolated peoples, such as MesoAmerican civilizations and tribes in Papua New Guinea, may also have been living in a complete 'world system'. Does this mean they were, to the best of their knowledge, fully globalized?

Did conquerors and empires like Alexander the Great, Chandragupta Maurya, the Song Dynasty, Genghis Khan or the Ottomans – who straddled vast slices of an incompletely known globe – have globalizing ambition? What about St Paul's expansionary Christianity or the Buddhist faith that entered China and laid the foundations of the Silk Road in Asia in the first century AD? These religions used universalizing language even if their ideas spread incrementally.

I argue that global intent should be understood literally – as the emergence of awareness that the world is spherical in shape and not too big. This is a story that begins in ancient Babylon, moves to Italy and Egypt and is battled out in the cloisters of medieval England, on Venetian galleys, and in the rival courts of Spain and Portugal. Along the way, intelligence is secretly assembled by a Baghdad potentate; vast Chinese fleets set sail under eunuch admirals; and a Turkish octogenarian finds a long-lost treasure in a dusty Istanbul archive.

Inflating the globe

'The bulk of the earth must not only be spherical, but not large in comparison with the size of other stars.'

Aristotle (384–322 BC)[28]

In prehistoric times migrants from Africa gradually peopled the planet. Early migrants edged into the unknown at a snail's pace – on average one or two kilometres a year.[29] We will return to these migrations in Chapter Five. To these migrants, the world must have seemed flat and limitless. The first known map portraying the whole world suggests this. It comes from Babylon (in modern-day Iraq) and has been dated to 600–500 BC. The clay tablet on which it is drawn is in fairly good condition and is now in the British Library in London. Although remnants of local maps and cosmic diagrams have been found dating back 5,000 years and more, this tablet is the first artefact to show the whole flat earth. Babylonia is at the centre, with seven unnamed lozenges surrounded by an ocean, and seven offlying islands depicted as triangles radiating from the ocean.

The cuneiform text on both sides of the tablet has been deciphered. It describes these mysterious lands, which connect the earth with the heavens. On one island lives a horned bull that attacks on sight; on another there is no daylight. Some of the islands, the Babylonians believed, were inhabited by people. Although it is not clear how wide the ocean was thought to be, the text states quite specifically that the islands lie seven miles beyond it, between six and nine miles from each other. The Babylonians believed that ancient heroes had visited these lands. The Babylonian world of 2,500 years ago – as gleaned from this tablet – was flat and mysterious.

The sleepy Calabrian town of Crotone, on the heel of Italy, may sound an unlikely birthplace for globalization. Even the town's tourist website can't claim much has happened there for 2,500 years. But while the Babylonians were carving their stylized map of the flat world on clay, Kroton was a thriving Greek colony and home to a mystical scientific community set up by Pythagoras (c.569–475 BC). Widely considered the father of mathematics and a great lover of numbers, music and geometry, little else is known for certain about Pythagoras. His academy relied on oral teaching and a cult of personality.

In addition to his mathematical and musical prowess, Pythagoras is perhaps best known for warning his followers to abstain from eating beans. This may have been simply a practical injunction to make communal life less flatulent. However, some modern scholars believe he was in fact advising his group to keep out of politics: elections of the day used black and white beans as ballot cards. Sound advice for mystical mathematicians, but Pythagoras himself may not have followed it. As a leading figure in Kroton society he appears to have been dragged into the town's commercial and military rivalry with neighbouring Sybaris, and one story has Pythagoras driven into exile by a thuggish and jealous local grandee.[30]

More crucial than the Pythagorean bean debate was their belief that the earth was a sphere. Before this time, most Babylonian, Egyptian and Greek thinkers seem to have envisaged the earth as a flat disc, sometimes floating in a watery dish of unknown dimensions like a block of wood. Pythagoras and his followers devised their spherical view from aesthetics: the sphere was a perfect form and it was pleasing to think of the earth, sun and visible planets as a set of harmonious, musical spheres. The Pythagoreans' view of the world as a spherical planet – a complete, closed system – pinpoints a starting point for global ambition in the mid-sixth century BC.

It took over two hundred years for this belief to find practical expression, though. Overlooked among the many achievements of the philosopher and scientist Aristotle were his proofs that the world was not just spherical, but *small*. Like Pythagoras and other philosophers, Aristotle's view of a spherical earth was dictated by his spiritual belief in the harmonious arrangement of heavenly spheres. But as usual, he backed up his ideas with half a dozen practical arguments. Careful observation of the shape of lunar eclipses was one strong indication of earth's spherical shape, but Aristotle's clincher came from an everyday sight in coastal Greece. As boats sailed out to sea, the tops of their masts were the last thing to disappear, evidence that the earth slopes away gradually towards the horizon. Combining his spiritual, astronomical and maritime observations, Aristotle believed in a spherical planet of no great extent. It should therefore be as possible to sail west as it was to travel east from Europe to reach Asia.

How small was 'not large', though? The first mathematical effort to measure the circumference of the world was by Eratosthenes (276–194 BC). Born in Cyrene (in modern Libya), Eratosthenes was based in Alexandria. Almost as much a polymath as Aristotle, he found time to make calculations of the noon-time altitude of the sun in Syene (modern-day Aswan) and Alexandria. Knowing roughly how far apart they were, and assuming a spherical world divided into 360 portions around an equator, he was able to calculate the length of one of these portions and thus the earth's circumference. His answer: exactly 252,000 *stadia*.

This was a brilliant calculation. The only trouble is, we don't actually know the length of the *stadion* – the widely used measure linked to the size of sports arenas. Athletic time trials must have been a nightmare for sprinters in those days, because depending on where it was used in the classical world, the *stadion* ranged in length from 157 to 211 modern metres. If Eratosthenes was using the 'short' *stadia*, he was dead right (to within a few hundred kilometres). The circumference of the Earth around the poles is actually 40,008 kilometres. If his was a 'long' *stadion*, though, his sums said that the world was over 53,000 kilometres around – way out. He probably had in mind the medium *stadion*, most used in Attica, and reckoned the girth of the earth was about 47,000 kilometres. This sounds pretty close, but the result was to overestimate the surface of the earth by over a third: an off-putting 7.3 billion square kilometres.

The dimensions suggested by Eratosthenes, far from confirming Aristotle's view of the earth as 'not large', must have seemed huge to classical thinkers and explorers alike. This was hardly the small planet envisaged by the Babylonians. What could possibly occupy so much unknown space? At least five Greek scholars set out to try to fit the small portion of known world onto a sphere of large size, using grid systems similar to our present system of longitude and latitude. Marinos of Tyre, Dicaearchus, Hipparchus and Eratosthenes himself all had a go, but none of their efforts survives. It is the Alexandrian Claudius Ptolemaeus (who we call Ptolemy), active around AD 140, who now is credited with this global breakthrough.

Ptolemy painstakingly gleaned the coordinates of all places in the known world – some 8,000 of them – from a wide range of sources. He studied the work of other geographers, military and administrative gazetteers, and the reports of seafarers. Some of this information was reliable; some was dodgy. He battled heroically to reconcile the coordinates onto flat paper according to a systematic degree-based grid system. The result, more obsession than hobby, was the first world atlas.

Ptolemy's world stretched from the westerly 'Fortune Islands' (possibly the Canary Islands, though these were not formally discovered until 1336) to China and Malaya in the east, and from the Arctic Circle in the north to well below the equator into Africa in the south. Despite its vast extent, Ptolemy realised he had mapped just a quarter or third of the globe. From around this time, serious debate began about what could be in the completely unknown southern half or hemisphere. Could it contain new lands which people called the Antipodes (because the soles of its inhabitants' feet would point towards the soles of ours)?

Ptolemy was well aware of the patchiness of some of his data. For example, his mapping of Great Britain was reasonably sound until he got north of Hadrian's Wall. At this point, beyond the safety of the Roman Empire, he was relying on sketchy reports from sailors. The result is that Scotland looks as though it has toppled east into the North Sea. More importantly, Ptolemy's work showed the Indian Ocean as a land-locked sea, providing no incentive for eastwards maritime exploration. Even the Atlantic appears to be an inland sea.

Ptolemy made another error that was to prove crucial. Despite all his hard work, he decided not to use Eratosthenes's estimates for the distance of each degree. Instead, he backed the more recent, fashionable calculations of Posidonius (c.135 BC–c.51 BC). Posidonius was well-connected, multi-talented, had travelled widely, and even taught Cicero, but for all that he stuck his equator in the wrong place – running through Rhodes. As a result, his circumference was far too short where

Eratosthenes' had been too long. Ptolemy used these less reliable calculations in good faith but screwed up his gridlines as a result. The result was that his globe was over six billion square kilometres smaller than it really is.[31] This was a mess for mathematicians but would be quite encouraging for explorers with westwards ambitions.

Most unusually for an academic, Ptolemy fully described his methodology and listed all his data so that future researchers could replicate and build on his atlas. This is the first recorded instance of open source software. It was a fortunate decision, because Ptolemy's original maps – if he drew any – disappeared in the following centuries.

Back to Babylon

'Maps were practically unknown in the middle ages.'
Paul Harvey, *Medieval Maps* (1991)

The Romans were excellent map-makers, provided the maps served practical applications. They were less interested in idle speculation about the unknown world or *terra incognita*. In the fourth century they produced a detailed road map of the entire Roman Empire. A medieval copy known as the Peutinger table, now in the Vienna National Library, shows it was nearly seven metres long, more detailed than many modern road atlases. They also carved in stone a vast 1:240 scale map of Rome some 13 by 18 metres – an early A-Z that would have been invaluable for chariot drivers if only it hadn't been permanently fixed to the side of a public building. There is even a mention of a more speculative Roman world map based on Ptolemy's work, apparently hung in the town of Autun in France, but long since vanished.

How big was the Roman world, though, and was it spherical? Julius Caesar is known to have ordered a majestic-sounding 'survey of the world' in 44 BC. Marcus Vispanius Agrippa, son-in-law of Augustus, is thought to have used it to compile a world map.[32] Although it hasn't survived, there is one piece of evidence about how the Romans saw the world. A strange map came to light in the collections of Sir Robert Cotton, a seventeenth-century enthusiast of Anglo-Saxon documents. Known as the 'Cotton Map', it is so unlike other early medieval maps that it may be a copy of Agrippa's – or a similar Roman world map – made in England in the tenth or eleventh century.

In the Cotton Map, the known Roman world is represented as a squared off continent, perhaps squashed to fit the page. The land mass is penetrated by the Mediterranean and Black Sea, with a dozen or so offlying islands. One of these is Britain, shown at the bottom left of the page. The Roman world-view that emerges was flat and constrained, with a truncated Africa, foreshortened Asia and absolutely no space left over for anything fanciful like unknown continents. Not just Ptolemy's maps and software (the instructions in the *Geography*) but the entire concept of the globe appears to have drifted into obscurity during the Roman era and the Dark Ages.

So the European world-view that resurfaced in late antique and early medieval Europe was Babylon all over again: a flat disc of land floating in water. It was not that early Christian churchmen were unaware of spherical thinking – indeed Bede wrote that the earth was round. But many scholars ruled out the Antipodes as pagan gibberish, flatly contradicted by numerous biblical references to the four corners of the earth. How could there be an unknown hemisphere that Noah's descendents could not have reached from Mount Ararat? Didn't the Bible clearly state that the apostles had preached across the whole wide world? There were practical objections too. If there *was* an Antipodes underneath the known world, how could its inhabitants avoid falling off? 'It is too absurd', wrote St Augustine, 'to say that some men might have taken ship and traversed the whole wide ocean, and crossed from this side of the world to the other.'[33]

Flat-earth thinking was prevalent in the early middle ages, according to the controversial 1896 thesis of Andrew Dickson White, co-founder of Cornell University.[34] The prevalence of flat-earthers has recently been challenged by Jeffery Russell, who argues that most educated people in medieval times already believed in a spherical earth. This debate can't be resolved conclusively, given the patchy evidence and the fact that religious and philosophical texts were written and read by a tiny elite in Europe. Whether medieval intellectuals favoured flat-earthism or sphericity in a theological sense, the medieval world-view as expressed in maps did little to encourage the development of global intent.

Early medieval world maps are based on simple two-dimensional diagrams known as T-O maps, because they depict a circle trisected by a T into three continents. Asia occupies the top half, Europe the bottom left quarter and Africa the bottom right quarter with Jerusalem in the middle. These T-O or trisected flat disc maps date back at least to the seventh-century encyclopedist Isidore, Bishop of Seville, and continue as the organizing principle of even the most elaborate medieval wall hangings known as the *mappae mundi* (literally cloths of the world). These 'world maps' became something of an obsession among religious institutions, especially in England.[35] The *mappae mundi* are filled with fascinating anthropological, moral and religious information as well as geographical content. Here are one-footed monsters and beautiful mermaids. The largest and arguably most impressive was rediscovered in the convent at Ebstorf, Germany, in 1832. This huge map, almost Roman in its scope, measured over ten square metres (it was destroyed in Hanover by allied bombing in 1943, but has been reconstructed from copies). On the Ebstorf map, the head, hands and feet of Jesus Christ literally encompass the known world – though this is unmistakably a flat disc.

Limits to the early medieval world-view are equally clear from the oldest original map in the family, a medium-sized map drawn by Richard of Holdingham in the 1280s, and now housed in Hereford Cathedral. Like the other *mappae mundi*, the Hereford 'world' map shows Asia at the top of the page, with Britain at bottom left. The Hereford map was generously saved for Britain by a donation from the late billionaire Sir Paul Getty, but there is no suggestion on the Hereford map that the world could be big enough to contain Getty's native California. The early medieval *mappae mundi* are evidence of a faith that was embracing the world theoretically, just as Christian crusaders were increasingly driven to expand or reclaim the faith geographically by crossing the Mediterranean. But no medieval visitor to Hereford cathedral could have gazed at the map and formed the desire to sail west. For all their beauty, these maps were more suited for universal exegesis than global exploration.

The world through other eyes

Genghis Khan (c.1165–1227) and his son Ogödei created the largest contiguous land empire the world has ever seen, stretching from Korea to near Kiev, and south to the Indus. He was a military leader of ruthless genius and huge ambition.

Recently, he has also been rehabilitated as an astute politician and capable administrator.

But to what extent was he engaged in a global venture to dominate the world's peoples? It was once claimed that the name Genghis Khan meant 'oceanic ruler' – certainly evidence of broad ambition. Recently, most scholars believe the title actually means 'true or just ruler'. Even if the Mongols did have global ambitions, however, they lacked not just time but the practical naval expertise to expand much further. This constraint limited the global ambitions of other impressive regimes in the Americas and Africa.[36]

Maritime civilizations – in Scandinavia, China and the Arabic world – were better placed to grapple with the un-known half of the planet. Controversy has surrounded the sagas recounting tenth-century Viking voyages to Greenland and Vinland since the idea was first raised by Danish historian Carl Christian Rafn in *Antiquitates Americanæ* (1837). In 1960, a small Viking colony identified by archaeologists in Newfoundland seemed to confirm the broad story, although these colonists only lasted a couple of years at Anse aux Meadows. Many details remain unresolved, such as the ex-istence of other more southerly sites for the first Vinland colony that would have produced grapes more plentifully than icy Newfoundland.

Most controversial of all is the Vinland map, revealed to the world in the late 1950s and now at Yale University. It appears to show an oblong island, 'Vinlanda Insula,' far out into the Atlantic on a 1440s German map. Researchers were fascinated to find that Viking explorations deep into the Atlantic had become part of the European database at a time when many maps showed the ocean as a thin margin. The trouble is, 40 years on, experts are still arguing about whether the map is a forgery or not. Is it medieval ink – or from the 1920s? Are the stains for real? Probably not, but even if it is genuine, the Vinland map is not convincing evidence of global ambition on the part of the Viking explorers. The tenth-century Vikings had the technical means to reach North America, but these were incremental and probably very dangerous westwards foraging expeditions, entirely without global intent.

China is a far stronger candidate for early global ambition. Outstanding cartographers like Phei Hsui in the second century AD independently developed techniques of mapping to scale by grid, and this tradition continued right through to the twelfth century, from which period a carved stone map of the whole of China survives in Changan. These maps were probably intended for military, administrative and irrigation purposes. For this purpose, China was challenge enough. But there is evidence that Chinese rulers also saw themselves in the centre of a wider world well worth exploring.

The Kangnido is a Korean version of state of the art Chinese cartography dating from 1402, and now in Japan. 'The world is very wide', its preface begins, although 'we do not know how [far it is] from China in the centre to the four seas at the outer limits'.[37] In this map, China and India utterly dominate the known world, as they did economically. But far from being a stylized representation, as were most contemporary European maps, this is clearly an effort to put together a comprehensive geographical and political world-view drawing on the best information available from Korean, Chinese and Arabic sources. Whether its purpose was diplomatic or strategic, it strongly suggests the development of a truly global vision in the early fifteenth-century Far East.

The magnetic compass, one of many Chinese discoveries such as printing, silk, gunpowder and mass-production iron, had been developed in the eighth century and possibly long before. Initially used in *feng shui*, it was gradually adopted for navigation over the next three hundred years. By the late fourteenth century, maps, compasses and industrial-scale shipyards enabled the Ming dynasty to build fleets of massive ocean-going ships to explore the Indian Ocean under Chinese eunuch admiral Zheng He. One voyage assembled 317 ships and 28,000 men; another voyage report was titled *Marvels Discovered by the Boat Bound for the Galaxy*.[38] These technical achievements and the strategic view evidenced in the world map show strong global ambition, irrespective of sensational recent claims by retired Royal Navy submarine commander Gavin Menzies that the fleet not only discovered the Americas, but actually settled thousands of colonists.

In one of history's most abrupt reversals, the Chinese suddenly pulled the plug on their naval 'space race' in 1433. This was part of a major retrenching exercise to marshal resources for building massive irrigation canals and the Great Wall.[39] Historians continue to debate whether this introspection was sound domestic policy or evidence of a 'silk ceiling' on their global ambitions. The result was that China more or less turned its back on the globe for 550 years. The country only started to reopen to the outside world in 1985. By 2001, it was ready to join the World Trade Organization, and in 2005 the country celebrated the 600th anniversary of Zheng He's epic voyage. With the 2008 Olympic Games in Beijing, it is hard to believe that the country once withdrew from the globalization race in such a strong position.

Far from a steady progression towards global intent, the Greek global view had been punctured by the Romans and ironed flat by Early Medieval churchmen. The tenth-century Vikings had the navigational means but not the motive. China had the technical means *and* strategic motive in the early fifteenth century before the opportunity was closed down by imperial decree. Did anyone else have such global ambitions? There is one other convincing candidate: the ninth- and tenth-century Arabic world.

In Baghdad and elsewhere, Islamic scholars brought their considerable mathematical skills and the findings of maritime trade to bear on translations of Ptolemy's *Geography* that had survived from Alexandria. Eminent among these scholars was the mathematician Mohammad Ibn Musa Al-Kwarizmi (d.840–845). Among his numerous achievements was the science of algebra – indeed the name comes from one of his books. Al-Kwarizmi also produced an atlas based on Ptolemy but adding more accurate latitudes and longitudes for places in Africa and the Far East, based on Islamic seafarers' accounts. By the ninth century, Arab dhows were regularly reaching China.[40]

Rumours of an Islamic world map from this period have long circulated in cartographic circles. Arab histories related that the map had been drawn up on the orders of the Caliph al-Ma'mum of the Abbasid dynasty, who reigned in Baghdad from 813 to 833 AD. A team of astronomers and geographers had supposedly been assembled to build intelligence for the Abbasid strategic plan for eastwards commercial and political expansion. In Europe, old maps or copies of them have a habit of reappearing in the most unlikely of places – for example as impromptu dust-jackets for farm estate accounts books. But the fabled Baghdad wall map never came to light and few Western academics seriously investigated the possibility of Islamic global ambition.

Until 2004, that is, when a Turkish octogenarian made a sensational claim at the Frankfurt Book Fair. He had found a copy of the Baghdad world map. Fuat Sezgin has a working knowledge of Arabic and Persian in addition to Latin and Greek – the basic requirements to pull off this feat. He also has Turkish, German and English. He runs one of Germany's least known museums – the Institute for the History of Arabic-Islamic Science at Johann Wolfgang Goethe University in Frankfurt.

For over 50 years Sezgin has been painstakingly assembling evidence of what he calls the Golden Age of Islamic Science, between the eighth and sixteenth centuries. He has reconstructed scientific instruments from written descriptions – often paid for out of his own pocket – and has published his findings in 15 volumes.[41] His work shows that Muslim navigators in this Golden Age began to undertake long sea voyages eastwards and explorations deep into Africa. There was ample evidence of mathematical and geographic expertise in Islam. 'Why not try to find the map?', Sezgin asked himself. After years of searching, he finally unearthed a medieval copy of the Baghdad world map in an encyclopedia in Topkapi Sarai, the Istanbul museum. From this copy, it is clear that the team assembled in The House of Wisdom in Baghdad borrowed openly and without prejudice from Ptolemy as well as Jewish and Persian technical sources. 'Many geographers, many astronomers, many mathematics scholars made this map,' says Sezgin.

Sezgin has assembled enough evidence to reconstruct a globe based on the Baghdad world map. The outline of much of Europe, Asia and Africa is depicted with remarkable accuracy and the recreation of Caliph al-Ma'mum's map also shows a good understanding of the oceanic expanses surrounding the continents. The project was not a one-off. From around 995, Al-Baruni worked out with remarkable precision, on the difference in longitude and latitude between Ghazni in Afghanistan and Mecca. He went on to calculate the dimensions of the spherical earth with impressive accuracy – and this at a time when practical investigation of the globe was out of favour in Christian Europe.

Ptolemy's work was a personal hobby, the Viking voyages were foraging trips, and state backing for the Chinese adventures was withdrawn at a crucial moment. The Baghdad world map was commissioned by a powerful ruler with strategic commercial, military, religious and cultural ambitions. The project potentially opened over half the world to Islamic trade, and showed more clearly that ever before that the other half was there for the taking. In the end, the Abbasid dynasty's global ambitions unravelled through doctrinal infighting. They lost control of Mediterranean trade to Venice, and the overland route to China was disrupted by the Mongol invasions of the thirteenth to fifteenth centuries. The creation of the Baghdad world map in the 820s could easily have been the starting point of a different history of globalization. Instead, its influence was to filter across to Europe in the thirteenth and fourteenth centuries, giving fresh impetus to the development of European global ambitions.

The strange emergence of European global intent

> 'They all laughed at Christopher Columbus
> When he said the world was round . . .
> But – ho, ho, ho! – who's got the last laugh now?'[42]

Compared to the Mongols, Abbasids or Chinese, late thirteenth-century Europe appeared to lack the means, motive *and* opportunity for global ambitions. Despite the universalist rhetoric of Christianity, its territorial ambitions extended no further than Jerusalem. Europe, in short, was peripheral, fragmented, and apparently happy to stay that way. But from the early fourteenth century, European global intent began to emerge rapidly, not despite but because of its fragmentation. There was no central state with a stranglehold on technical, intellectual and commercial resources as had happened in China or Baghdad. Piecemeal innovations started to accumulate and spread through informal networks, until they quite suddenly reached a critical mass.

The key technological innovations were increasingly sophisticated Mediterranean coastal maps, aided by the arrival of the magnetic compass from China, and the development of better ships. The motivation was supplied by a renaissance in theoretical geography, abetted by the arrival of Aristotle and the later chance recovery of Ptolemy. The opportunity arose from periods of rapid growth and stagnation of maritime trade in the Mediterranean, leading to the search for commercial opportunities outside the Mediterranean and into the Atlantic.

From the late thirteenth century, Venetian and Genoese sailors began to compile detailed sets of sailing instructions for the Mediterranean and Black Sea. At the same time, landlubbers were drawing up increasingly accurate charts known as Portolans. Portolan charts were works in progress, added to as new information came to light – the medieval equivalent of dog-eared and annotated 1970s editions of *South East Asia on a Shoestring*. These charts sometimes included over a thousand coastal settlements. Meanwhile, magnetic compasses had begun to trickle westwards into Europe from China by the late twelfth century. The Chinese compass was improved en route, for example in Amalfi and in the Islamic world. By the early fourteenth century, both portolan chart and compass were being taken up by entrepreneurial Mediterranean mariners.[43]

In the Mediterranean, sea travel had traditionally been uncommon between October and April because cloudy skies made celestial navigation too dangerous. The key advantage of the new technologies was that they enabled almost year-round sailing. Venetian convoys could now make not one but two round trips a year on their seven principal trade routes in the eastern Mediterranean. Sailing outside the Mediterranean also became less hazardous, leading to a growth in maritime trade with northern Europe that was increasingly competitive with overland transport, not just in terms of cost but also speed.

Maritime technologies and commerce reinforced each other. The Northern market for bulky goods forced ships to become larger and so cheaper to run; navigation technology made them safer and extended their range. Genoese carracks doubled in size in just 100 years, reaching 2,000 tonnes by the fifteenth century. They could sail from Asia Minor to Southampton with just one stop, in Málaga or Seville.[44] On its own, the growth of medium distance sea trade in Europe gave no advantage over other maritime commercial cultures based around the Indian Ocean, or overland trade links based on the Silk Road.

But alongside trade goods trickled in translations of Greek philosophy. In the mid thirteenth century, Aristotle arrived; the *Summa theologica* of St Thomas Aquinas, written 1266–74, contains some 3,500 quotations from 'The Philosopher'. Inspired by Greek philosophy, medieval scholars like Aquinas increasingly accepted the Aristotelian reasoning for a spherical globe. As important was Ptolemy's *Geography*, bits of which trickled into Europe during the crusades. By 1397, the complete text was available in Florence.[45] When Pierre d'Ailly (1350–1420), French Cardinal and Chancellor of the University of Paris, wrote the *Imago Mundi*, he drew heavily on the rediscovered Ptolemy, and emphasized the small Atlantic and long Eurasian landmass.

Over the next fifty years, Ptolemy's methodology for charting the globe was slowly integrated with mariners' logs and annotations on portolan maps. This allowed more accurate renderings of the Mediterranean, Black Sea and Atlantic coastline. New information was also coming in for areas not covered by Ptolemy – for example from Marco Polo's epic Eastern journeys by 1375, from Scandinavia in the 1420s, and from Portuguese explorations of the Atlantic Islands and West African coastline in the 1420–80s. This new knowledge was assimilated slowly and piecemeal, and some aberrations – like the wonkiness of Scotland – persisted.

A handful of brilliant map-makers based in maritime centres like Venice managed to assemble a global overview from all the confusing information. By the 1460s, their world maps finally shook off Ptolemy's errors and the constraints of the *mappae mundi* format. A key development is the 1459 world map made by Fra Mauro and Andrea Bianco in Murano, the island off Venice. The commission came from King Alfonso of Portugal, and was top secret. A copy shows that Mauro successfully combined three disparate sources of information: the accurate Mediterranean coastal outlines from portolan charts, the Ptolemaic awareness of circumnavigable oceans, perhaps via copies of the Baghdad world map, and the latest findings from Portuguese explorations down the African coast. Mauro dares to depart from Ptolemy's erroneous measurements and greatly expands Asia. This pushes Jerusalem – traditionally the centre of medieval world maps – way to the west, and makes the globe look navigable. 'The whole basis of [this] map, its raison d'être, is geographic', according to cartographic historian Paul Harvey.

To European eyes, this spherical and navigable portrayal was a revolutionary way of seeing the world, and it spread thanks to the advent of printed atlases from about 1475. As it spread, it was improved upon. In 1589, Welsh student Richard Hakluyt was visiting his cousin in Middle Temple, London.

Hakluyt was riveted when he saw lying on his cousin's desk a new world map using the projection system recently devised by Flemish map-maker Gerardus Mercator (1512–1594). Mercator's projection, later refined by the calculations of English mathematician Edward Wright, was ideal for navigation. Any straight line drawn on the map was a line of constant bearing. One oddity of Mercator's method was that it made landmasses near the equator much smaller than they really were, while preserving their shape. This quirk, already evident in Mauro's map, made Africa and India look appetizing to the increasingly ambitious inhabitants of colder climes.

The carve-up

'This world is small, and experience has now proved it.'
Christopher Columbus, 1503/4[46]

Why was the Mauro map commissioned by the Portuguese crown in the first place? Without much fanfare, the remote village of Sagres, on the south-westerly tip of Europe, had become *the* centre of European maritime excellence under the patronage of the Infante Dom Enrique (only later nicknamed The Navigator, 1394–1460). Prince Henry had joined a Portuguese incursion on the North African coast in 1415 and become obsessed with tapping into the riches of Saharan trade routes. Henry became governor of the fabulously wealthy Order of Christ, and used its resources to establish an informal academy. Henry had more than commercial motives. Increasingly devout, he was desperate to make contact with the legendary Prester John, Christian ruler of the East. And Portugal itself was feeling the geopolitical pinch as its western neighbour Spain grew stronger.

Among the technical innovations developed at Sagres were a flexible hybrid ship, the caravel, improved navigational aids, naval weaponry and map-making. Henry's obsessions soon bore fruit, as Portuguese navigators charted the Madeira Islands (1420), the Azores (1427), Cape Blanco (1441), and Cape Verde Islands (c.1455). By Henry's death in 1460, dozens of ships a year were being sent south. Both gold and slaves were coming to Portugal from Africa in significant numbers, and sugar production had been established in the Azores.

Almost without anyone noticing, the Portuguese had established an important technical and commercial lead, and jealously guarded the intelligence that came in from these expeditions. Among Portugal's most prized resources must have been Mauro's world map, which made clear that it was possible to reach the southern tip of Africa, and thence sail on to India. All that remained was to do it; and in 1488 Bartolomeu Dias rounded the Cape of Good Hope. There was little now standing in the way of a maritime expedition to the Christian kingdom of the East – and its delirious riches.

Alongside faith, it was spices, slaves and gold that to varying degrees motivated European entrepreneurs with global ambitions. Each is addressed in detail in the middle chapters of this book. Genoese mariner and self-educated cartographer Christopher Columbus (1451–1506) was obsessed by all four. Columbus stands out from other explorers in an unmistakably global vision – and the ambition to act on it. His opportunity – and abiding problem – was that he had convinced himself from a selective reading of the available authorities that the globe was much smaller than conventional wisdom suggested. 'The world', he insisted, 'is not as big as the common crowd say.' Despite all the incremental southerly progress the Portuguese

had made, to Columbus the best route to the East was by
sailing west.

Columbus first looked for funding for his westwards venture at the Portuguese court. But with their expertise in
cartography, the Portuguese knew that Columbus – or any
one else – could never survive an immensely long westwards
crossing to the Indies. It was only after Portuguese rejection
that Columbus took his plan to the court of Ferdinand and
Isabella in Spain. The epic story of Columbus arguing for a
spherical earth against sceptical flat-earth churchmen at the
Spanish court is one of the most compelling of the European
'age of discovery'. It is also a pure myth, invented by Washington Irving, the US's first man of letters, in his novel, the
History of the Life and Voyages of Christopher Columbus
(1828).

More convincing is the image of Columbus as one of
hundreds of lobbyists peddling a pet project to monarchs with
more pressing matters on their minds. In 1492 they eventually
agreed to part-fund Columbus' harebrained but relatively
inexpensive project. This was more out of funding fatigue
than religious or territorial zeal. Having just expelled the last
Moors from Granada, Ferdinand and Isabella were not much
interested in finding more Christians, and had headaches
enough subduing their new and unruly possessions in the
Canary Islands. But the possibility of bullion and spices was
always interesting, no matter how faint the chance. Since the
Portuguese had a stranglehold on the eastwards route to the
Indies, the Spanish monarchs felt they had little to lose and
perhaps much to gain.

Shortly after Columbus got the go-ahead and started to
assemble his ships and crew, the Portuguese began making
careful preparations for a better-resourced push on the eastwards route to the Indies, but this took longer to assemble.

Columbus, on his final westwards effort to reach the Indies, actually hoped to rendezvous with Portuguese commander Vasco da Gama (c.1469–1524), known to be setting off eastwards for the same destination.[47] Columbus never got his chance to say 'Captain da Gama, I presume?' But the precise details, intellectual fumblings and moral failings of Columbus' four voyages to the Americas between 1492 and 1504, and the three expeditions by da Gama to the Indies (1497–1524), are less important for the history of globalization than the fact that between them these voyages implanted a global world-view into the European consciousness. Maritime technology, experimental cartography, religious zeal, military ambition and commercial opportunism had all been pioneered separately outside Europe. It was their combination in the late fifteenth-century Iberian Peninsula – part by design, part by chance – that enabled truly global ambitions.

In 1892, the 400th anniversary of Columbus' discovery was marked by rival adulation among Italian and Hispanic communities in New York. A few years later, Canadian sailor Joshua Slocum (1844–1909) was attempting to sail around the world single-handed. 'It sounds odd to hear scholars and statesmen say the world is flat,' reported Slocum; 'but it is a fact that three Boers favored by the opinion of President Kruger prepared a work to support that contention. While I was at Durban they came from Pretoria to obtain data from me, and they seemed annoyed when I told them that they could not prove it by my experience . . . [Two days later] I met one of the party in a clergyman's garb, carrying a large Bible, not different from the one I had read. I bowed and made curves with my hands. He responded with a level, swimming movement of his hands, meaning "the world is flat." A pamphlet by these Transvaal geographers, made up of arguments from sources high and low to prove their theory, was mailed to me before I sailed from Africa on my last stretch around the globe.'[48]

The modern world would probably be very different if a non-European had created a projection of the world, rather than Mercator. While New Yorkers were celebrating Columbus and Slocum was arguing with flat-earthers, Scottish Reverend James Gall proposed an alternative projection of the world that sacrificed shape in favour of area. Would European mariners ever have developed their global ambitions if they had appreciated the sheer size of Africa and Asia? By the time Gall devised his projection, between 1855 and 1885, the world had long been mentally encompassed, and its physical dominance by Europeans was nearing completion.

When German historian Arno Peters (1916–2002) proposed his 1974 World Map, correctly showing Africa as much bigger than Greenland, the West was fast building its financial and cultural hegemony. Peters' iconoclastic map itself became an icon for 1980s critics of global inequality between North and South, from German chancellor Willy Brandt and the United Nations to *New Internationalist* magazine. It sold 80 million copies and was used in the popular 1989 Longman atlas. But it never reversed our ingrained mental image of an over-sized Europe poised to straddle the rest of the globe.[49]

By the 500th anniversary of Columbus' landfall in 1992, people were increasingly drawing attention to his disastrous legacy on indigenous people in the Americas, and the traditional Columbus Day celebration of 12 October is now controversial. In Venezuela it has been renamed the Day of Indigenous Resistance and in 2004, supporters of populist president Hugo Chavez pulled down a statue of Columbus in Caracas.

The flat earth as a way of seeing the world – literally and metaphorically – has taken a long time to disappear. It was only in 2001 that Charles K. Johnson, the vociferous president of the International Flat Earth Society, died in Lancaster, California. 'Women have been taught that, for us, the earth is flat. If we venture out, we will fall off the edge,' radical feminist Andrea Dworkin (1946–2005) would proclaim. Best-selling *New York Times* columnist Thomas Friedman has recently announced that the world is flat again.[50] To his dying days, Columbus was convinced he had made the world small single-handedly. As we've seen, the global perspective was only slowly and haltingly acquired over the two thousand years separating him from Pythagoras. And in 1492 the real process of making the globe small was yet to begin. This planet-shrinking period, which unleashed five hundred years of intense individual and nationalistic competition, is the subject of the next chapter.

3

THE PLANET-SHRINKERS

The little apple

'Be it known that on this apple here present is laid out the whole world according to its length and breadth.'

Martin Behaim, maker of the
oldest surviving globe, 1493

'I concluded that [the earth] was not round in the way they say, but is of the same shape as a pear, which may be very round all over, but not in the part where the stalk is, which sticks up.'

Christopher Columbus, 1498[51]

In the late fifteenth century Europeans began to talk of the world as a piece of fruit. The process of carving it up began in 1494, ushering in an intense period of imperial rivalries and then nation-building. People today judge the world by its countries, not by its shape, and there are more and more nations on the shrinking planet. The United Nations has, at latest count, 191 members.[52] If we take as our guide the international football federation FIFA, which dubs itself the 'United Nations of Football', there are 205 national affiliates.[53] If we count dozens of territories and colonies like Puerto Rico and Bermuda that are governed to varying degrees by other countries, as the CIA does in its World Fact Book, we arrive at 266 countries. Whether you favour diplomacy, espionage or football as your benchmark of nations, we take it for granted that the world is made up of nation-states.

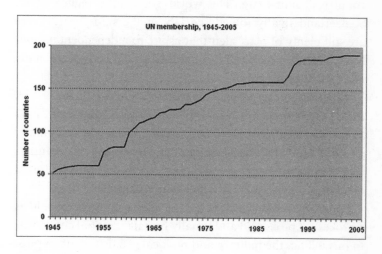

UN membership, 1945-2005

Political scientists say that globalization poses a major challenge to the sovereignty of the nation-state – the dominant system established in Europe at the Treaty of Westphalia in 1648. In fact, the first major pulses of globalization predated the Westphalian model and while they obliterated the concept of sovereignty for the peoples of the Americas, Africa and Asia, they enormously strengthened the European protagonists.

It is only more recently that global contractions have gone hand in hand with new state formation. The fastest sustained period of growth in the United Nations was in the decade after 1955, when European countries like Austria, Ireland and Italy were joined by many newly-independent African and Asian nations and some others such as Japan and Singapore. A second pulse of growth for the UN occurred in the 1990s, when the countries of Eastern Europe and the former Soviet Union joined *en masse*, alongside a number of Pacific island states.

On 20 May 2002, East Timor, a Portuguese colony from 1515 to 1975 and thereafter brutally occupied by the Indonesians, was finally granted its wish to become an independent country, Timor-Leste. The world got a little bigger again. Switzerland finally joined the UN in the same year. There are still plenty of places left that aspire to independent nationhood and a seat in the UN – or at least a qualifying place in the Football World Cup.

The process can go into reverse, too. On 1 January 1979, the US Government recognized the People's Republic of China as the sole legal government of China. The world got smaller as Taiwan – the *Ilha Formosa* in Portuguese or beautiful island, and a Dutch colony from 1624 to 1662 – ceased officially to exist as an independent country.

The story of how we have carved up the apple can be told as a process of piecemeal and usually brutal territorial conquests. In this telling, the military and political acquisition of empires was often incremental, almost accidental. This chapter focuses instead on the planet-shrinkers who deliberately and self-consciously set out to establish intellectual and institutional dominion over the globe. It is a story of line-drawers and deal-makers. The global fault-lines they created affect Timor, Taiwan and every other country to this day.

Planet-shrinking was galvanized by our obsessive competition to get round the world first and fastest. The first global fault-line was traced on the new globe by the 1494 Treaty of Tordesillas between Spain and Portugal. This was followed by an acrimonious 200-year contest between France and Britain about the shape and size of the earth and where the prime meridian should be, not finally resolved until 1884. The third global fault-line was created by the Space Race between the USA and Soviet Union beginning in 1957, a celestial manifestation of the Iron Curtain that split the world below. But this was not the final frontier in the history of globalization.

Split down the middle

In the late 1480s, the Portuguese stranglehold in charting the African coastline right down to the Cape of Good Hope gave them a monopoly on new discoveries, confirmed by a 1481 Papal Bull – a legally and morally binding decree – granting them all lands south of the Canary Islands. By 1493, their fortunes had been radically reversed by Columbus' first voyage, and Spanish-born Pope Alexander VI decreed an imaginary line running north and south through the Atlantic Ocean some 500 kilometres west of the Cape Verde islands. Not surprisingly given Alexander's Spanish origins, the papal decree was blatantly favourable to Spain, which would possess all unclaimed territories to the west of the line, leaving for Portugal anything to the east.

However, the Portuguese had ambitions west of the Papal line and had also begun to think about what would happen on the other side of the globe. It was a sign of continuing Portuguese leadership in navigation and commerce under King João II that the Spanish monarchs eventually agreed to discuss a new line pushed far to the west at the Treaty of Tordesillas. Recognizing, with lawyerly understatement, that 'a certain controversy exists . . . as to what lands, of all those discovered in the ocean sea up to the present day . . . pertain to each', the treaty announced that 'a boundary or straight line be determined and drawn north and south, from pole to pole, on the said ocean sea, from the Arctic to the Antarctic pole . . . at a distance of three hundred and seventy leagues west of the Cape Verde Islands.'[54]

The treaty was signed on 7 June 1494. João had laid the groundwork carefully at the Spanish Court, and his three negotiators were better informed and prepared than their opponents.[55] Portugal won its Brazilian foothold. The result was the first truly global empire, spanning Europe, North Africa, the Americas and Asia. The sheer arrogance of the Treaty of Tordesillas – eight men in a dusty village in Castille carving the apple into just two pieces – makes it a milestone in globalization. Few international treaties before or since have shown such ambition. It was greeted with outrage by other European powers. Francis I of France famously asked to be shown the clause in Adam's will that excluded him from the New World. The English and Dutch also objected to this duopoly, but their response was piracy rather than appeals to biblical law.

The practical implications of the treaty rapidly emerged. The Iberians had not just the legal right but the religious duty and commercial hunger to convert their paper possessions into reality. They soon made fresh discoveries, notably Cabral's 1500 landfall in Brazil, just to the east of the line, for Portugal. The Spanish were busy in the Americas too. Exploration soon turned to domination, first in the Caribbean and then the American mainland, with astonishingly rapid and brutal conquests in Mexico (1519–21) and Peru (1530–33). New discoveries were rapidly portrayed on maps and globes by mapmakers like de la Cosa and Waldseemüller. It was the latter who made the decision to name the emerging new continent America after explorer Amerigo Vespucci (rather than, say, Columbia after Columbus).

Iberian rulers and explorers 'saw themselves not only as powerful enough to split the world like an apple,' writes Arthur Crosby, 'but as being able to do so in a way that was precise in theory and before long could be precise in fact.'[56] A crucial building block for Portugal's global empire was the capture of Malacca in 1511 and Goa the following year. These conquests not only cemented their strategic grip of the Spice Islands but also enabled King Manuel to send Pope Leo IX a most pleasing gift: a performing elephant. This gift was rapidly followed by a new papal Bull, *Praecelsae devotionis* (1514), giving Portugal full rights to any and all heathen lands which could be reached by sailing eastwards. Effectively this papal decree restricted the Tordesillas line to the Atlantic and cut the Spanish out of the east.

But need to agree to a 'antimeridian' line in Asia became much more pressing with the epic three-year westwards circumnavigation of the globe by an expedition led by Fernão de Magalhães (Ferdinand Magellan, 1480–1521). Magellan was Portuguese and had served in the Indies and Africa with some distinction, but after a number of disputes with Manuel – and having formed a strong desire to attempt a westwards passage to the Indies, which was far from being in Portugal's interests – he offered his services to the Castilian crown. In the sixteenth century, national loyalties were somewhat fluid but Magellan's move was not far from outright treason.

Magellan was a brilliant navigator but an overbearing and foolhardy commander. He was killed in a skirmish with the indigenous people on Mactan – a small island later to be part of the Philippines. In the end, only 18 of the original group of 270 mariners made it back to Seville under the command of Juan Sebastián del Cano – though another 17 stragglers did eventually return to Spain. The news of Magellan's discovery of the south-west passage through the Americas did not go down well in Portugal.

The returning circumnavigators were accompanied by a large consignment of spices from the fabled Spice Islands of the Moluccas. Tradition recounts that the expedition, despite its terrible losses, actually turned a profit, though the organizers did not pay the survivors their full wages or any compensation to the families of the 250 crew members who lost their lives. Del Cano at least was awarded a coat of arms with the motto 'Primus circumdedisti mihi' (literally 'You went around me the first'). The coat of arms was decorated with three nutmegs, two sticks of cinnamon and 12 cloves – a modest recompense for his labours.[57] This coat of arms, a combination of naked competitiveness and commercialism, could stand as an emblem of sixteenth-century planet-shrinking.

Del Cano's status as the first circumnavigator has recently been disputed by Asian historians. Magellan's long-serving indentured Malay interpreter Enrique entered service in the early 1510s in the Indies, travelled back eastwards with Magellan to Portugal, left Spain in 1519 eastwards and finally arrived home in 1522. Enrique has a strong claim to be first person to get the whole way round the world in this patchwork of journeys.

The Portuguese were in a strong global position, because they had the foothold in Malacca. Although Portuguese adventurers advanced their own commercial agendas at the expense of the national interest, this was nothing compared to the losses endured by the Spanish in attempting to find their own foothold. Of 15 Spanish ships despatched to the Spice Islands in a decade, only one made it back. Another agreement was needed. Initial discussions had been opened on symbolic neutral ground: a bridge over the River Caya, the frontier between the two countries. But these discussions had broken down in mid-1524 and there had been bloody if ineffectual skirmishes in the Spice Islands themselves in 1527. Both countries reluctantly concluded that an understanding would be necessary to clarify where the Tordesillas line ran. Who owned the Spice Islands?

In negotiations at Zaragoza in 1529, the Spanish offered to suspend their claim to the Moluccas – temporarily at least – for 1,000,000 gold ducats. John III offered 200,000; the two countries finally shook hands on 350,000. As a result of Zaragoza, Spain was technically out of the spice race. This didn't stop it later grabbing the Philippines, a missing jigsaw piece for its own globe-spanning empire, even though the islands were clearly on the Portuguese side of the line. Zaragoza completed the global process begun in Tordesillas. The entire world had now been carved into two pieces – with substantial sums of money changing hands into the bargain.

At no point did the inhabitants of the contested lands get to challenge the European carve-up. One of the few protagonists who publicly asserted his belief in the rights of the conquered was Spanish friar Bartolomé de Las Casas (c.1470s–1566). Las Casas witnessed at first hand and then published a chilling account of the devastating impacts – death from disease, massacre and overwork – the Spanish conquests were having on indigenous peoples in the Americas. If his *Short Account of The Destruction of the Indies* (1539) was slightly exaggerated, it had a profound impact on the Spanish court.

In 1550, Las Casas squared off against polemicist Juan Ginés de Sepúlveda in Valladolid for a heated debate in front of a junta of policy-makers. The debate, convened by King Charles V, the most powerful man in Europe, was to settle the rumbling controversy about the juridicial status of the native Americans. Until the matter was resolved, further conquests were to be put on hold. Was it acceptable to wage war on them and enslave them, as Sepúlveda argued, with the full backing of Spanish settlers?[58] Or was this an infringement of their natural rights, as Las Casas maintained?[59]

Las Casas should not be seen as a prototype anti-globalization protester: he believed the Spanish presence in the Americas was justified. The argument was that the mission should be purely spiritual, not economic or political. In the event, the Valladolid debate was inconclusive. Both sides claimed victory, and while treatment of natives was regulated from Spain, there was little or no improvement in the lawless colonies. The English and French quoted Las Casas at every opportunity, not in defence of Indians but as a way of bashing the hated Spanish superpower.

Getting round in one piece

Magellan's voyage, more than any other discovery of the era, was a global event. It gave the Spanish–Portuguese global carve-up a new sense of urgency, with devastating consequences for non-Europeans. But planet-shrinkers still faced a major obstacle. It took three years to get round the globe – if you survived the attempt.[60]

Martin Frobisher's repeated searches for the North-West Passage in the 1570s were among the few relatively safe expeditions of the times. John Cabot and his entire fleet disappeared without trace on his second voyage. Sir Francis Drake's circumnavigation (1577–1580) for England's Queen Elizabeth proved the commercial viability of piracy, but only one of the five departing ships made it back. In 1586, Thomas Cavendish 'the Navigator' set off with three ships with the goal of making Drake's piracy less opportunistic and more strategically anti-Spanish. His circumnavigation was marginally faster than Magellan/Del Cano's and Drake's, and he managed to get two ships back, but his second expedition in 1591 ended in disaster and death. In 1594 the Venetian trader Francesco Carletti embarked on a westwards circumnavigation that took ten years.

These circumnavigations became a potent emblem of competition as European rulers sought to strengthen their nations by finding speedy routes to new trading posts. Views about sovereignty, which had been a fluid mixture of geography, religion and culture, began to coalesce around the concept of the nation-state in this period. The trend was epitomized by the 1648 Treaty of Westphalia, which brought the bloody Thirty Years War to an end. Holy Roman Emperor Ferdinand II is described in the text as 'King of Germany, Hungary, Bohemia, Dalmatia, Croatia, Slavonia, Arch-Duke of Austria, Duke of Burgundy, Brabant, Styria, Carinthia, Carniola, Marquiss of Moravia, Duke of Luxemburgh, the Higher and Lower Silesia, of Wirtemburg and Teck, Prince of Suabia, Count of Hapsburg, Tirol, Kyburg and Goritia, Marquiss of the Sacred Roman Empire, Lord of Burgovia, of the Higher and Lower Lusace, of the Marquisate of Slavonia, of Port Naon and Salines'. But the treaty actually strengthened France and Sweden and made the German states more independent. It enfeebled any authority higher than the nation-state governing the 'Christian world'; in effect it was the obituary of the Holy Roman Empire.

The 'Westphalian system' was the key development in the emergence of national sovereignty – in Europe, that is. The Treaty officially recognized the Dutch United Provinces, but the Dutch needed no such recognition on the other side of the world and had been aggressively probing the Indies for over 50 years. The amalgamation of Portugal into Spain in 1580 left

Holland at war with Spain and with no option but to seek their own sources of spices. The first Dutch circumnavigator, Olivier van Noort was more pirate than entrepreneur. His journey (1598–1601) is a catalogue of unprovoked attacks on indigenous people as well as sea battles with the Spanish in the Philippines. He lost three of four ships into the bargain.

Later Dutch efforts at circumnavigation ended in equally serious losses: de Cordes lost three ships and von Spilbergen (1614–1617) lost four of six. The Dutch expedition by Jacob LeMaire and Willem Cornelius Schouten in 1615–17 was the first to make it round the world without the loss of a ship, and in a little over two years. The Dutch record was not beaten until John Byron's circumnavigation of 1764–66 – a symbolic event for the emerging English maritime global empire. Even now, safety and speed could not be taken for granted. Circumnavigation was only for the most patriotic or piratical.[61] In 1740–44, when England was starting to depend on reliable long-distance shipping, an expedition led by Lord George Anson took well over three years to complete, and of 941 crewmen setting out, only 200 returned. Both circumnavigations by James Cook (1768–75) took around three years. Almost uniquely, he suffered no losses from scurvy.

This disease was the major danger of early voyages, far more than war, wrecks or starvation. Of the 160 men who sailed with Vasco de Gama in 1497, 100 probably died of scurvy. The slow progress in tackling the disease tells us much about the priorities of pre-modern globalization. European navies were not averse to innovations: there was rapid diffusion of technologies relating to navigation, gunnery and ship design, for example. But this was not the case for the health of crews. As early as 1601, English captain James Lancaster undertook an experiment to test the effectiveness of citrus fruit on a voyage to India. Lemon juice was administered to the crew of one of the four ships in the convoy, and it minimized the disease. But of the 278 sailors on the other three boats who did not receive vitamin C, nearly half had died by the midway point.

These results seemed clear enough, but it was only in 1747, almost 150 years later, that naval physician James Lind decided to test Lancaster's results again, onboard HMS *Salisbury*. Crew members were given citrus fruits or one of five other treatments, including nutmeg, cider, vinegar or – surely the short straw this – half a pint of sea water. Lind found without a shadow of a doubt that citrus fruits worked best, but he was not an eminent physician and it was not until 1795 that the Royal Navy finally adopted Lancaster and Lind's innovation, almost 200 years after it had first been discovered. It took another 70 years, until 1865, for the British Board of Trade to follow suit, eradicating scurvy from the merchant marine.[62]

Surprisingly, from 1519 right through to the mid nineteenth century, technological improvements and a massive increase in long-distance seaborne trade produced no general trend towards more rapid or safer circumnavigations. 100 years ago, Joshua Slocum on his vessel *Spray* took as long as Magellan for his 1895–98 single-handed circumnavigation, he was still having the same sorts of problems with the Patagonians as many seventeenth- and eighteenth-century circumnavigators. Slocum disappeared on a subsequent voyage to the Orinoco in 1909. The second solo circumnavigator, Harry Pigeon, has the distinction of performing the feat twice, the first time in four years and the second in five.

Major improvements in sailing speeds only took place with the rapid introduction of the streamlined clipper for the tea trade on the route from China to London and North America.

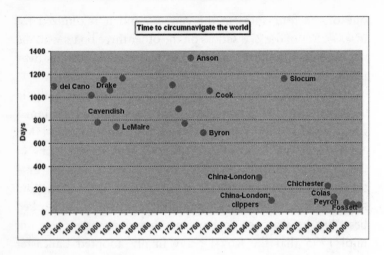

A journey that could take up to 300 days in the 1850s had
been whittled down to under 100 in 1869. The steamship then
began making its contribution to intercontinental trade, especially after the opening of the Suez Canal in 1869. The world
that Magellan encompassed finally began to shrink.

Today, sailing has been consigned to a less strategic form of
geopolitical competition. In 1966–67, English sailor Francis
Chichester for the first time made a significant improvement
on the time achieved by Dutch crews of the seventeenth
century. Thus began a new era of competition to encircle
the globe – an obsession shared equally by old antagonists
France and Britain, as well as the USA. As Ellen MacArthur on
B&Q-Castorama showed in 2005, beating a circumnavigation record – crewed or single-handed; with or without stops –
is still a cause for national celebration, echoed by the purchase
by sponsoring DIY store B&Q of its French rival.

These days, a circumnavigation which returns safely in under
72 days is an impressive achievement, but if it takes much
longer, the sponsors won't be happy. In 2004, a US team led
by Steve Fossett took the record for fastest circumnavigation in

58 days. However, in February 2005, Frenchman Bruno Peyron and a crew of 12 aboard the catamaran *Orange II* rounded the Cape of Good Hope and entered the Indian Ocean just two weeks after leaving the Channel. When Peyron returned to Brest in mid-March after a record-breaking 50-day circumnavigation, he became the second most famous French globe-trotter ever. Passepartout – the dependable servant of Englishman Phileas Fogg in Jules Verne's classic 1872 novel – still holds that honour. In many ways, Fogg's £20,000 bet that he could get round the world in less than 80 days remains a defining moment in globalization, whoever holds the Jules Verne Trophy for sailing round faster today.

The figure of the globe

"The world is big enough," [opines Stuart]
"It was once," said Phileas Fogg, in a low tone.
"What do you mean by 'once'? Has the world grown smaller?" [asks Stuart]
"The world has grown smaller, since a man can now go round it ten times more quickly than a hundred years ago," [confirms Ralph.].
"You have a strange way, Ralph, of proving that the world has grown smaller. So, because you can go round it in three months . . ." [quizzes Stuart]
"In eighty days," interrupted Phileas Fogg.'

Jules Verne, *Around the World
In Eighty Days*, 1873

Ralph was right. Captain James Cook's 1770s round-the-world voyages filled in many of the blanks on the globe. Before Cook's explorations geographical knowledge was limited. 'There was not', says Eric Hobsbawn '*one* world.'[63] By the mid-1770s, most of the gaps had been filled in and the concept of a single interconnected world was becoming widespread. 'When has the entire earth ever been so closely joined together, by so few threads?' asked Johann Gottfried Herder in 1774.[64] This question would echo down the following century, but for most Europeans it would remain largely rhetorical. In the early nineteenth century, the Europeans expatriated remarkably few people to run their far-flung empires. In 1805, there were just 31,000 British people in India.[65] Globe-trotting was mainly for armchair travellers.

The opportunities for global travel changed dramatically in the 1870s, when Jules Verne saw an advertisement in *Le Siècle* newspaper and realised that it could be possible to get around the world in 80 days – if the journey went without a hitch. Slowly from the 1820s, a range of new transport and communications technologies – railways, steamships, canals, telegraphs, accurate time-keeping and timetables – came into widespread use, not just in Europe but in North America, the Middle East and Asia. From 1840 to 1910, the cost of crossing the Atlantic fell by 70 per cent. On the eve of the First World War, there was 170 million tonnes of shipping capacity plying the oceans, almost all steam-powered, and over a quarter of it British.

The international railway system grew dramatically, though it was far from seamless. In the 1880s, Belgian entrepreneur Georges Nagelmackers' 'Express d'Orient' ran only to Giurgiu, where a ferry crossed the Danube to Bulgaria. A second train took passengers to Varna on the Black Sea, where they boarded an Austrian steamship for the final 14-hour leg to Constantinople. German efforts to construct a Berlin to Baghdad railway, de Lesseps' plan to link Europe to Bombay and Peking, and Cecil Rhodes' dream of a Cape Town to Cairo line never succeeded. The Russian Trans-Siberian, built with convict labour between 1891 and 1916, was partly laid over ice until engineers learnt the hard way just how heavy a locomotive is. For years, its few wealthy passengers and goods had to detrain on one side of Lake Baikal, take a special ice-breaking ferryboat imported from England, and retrain the other side. The patchy European rail network was hardly up to shipping French troops to Italy in 1917.[66] British railway construction in Argentina was dramatic – from 1,000 kilometres in 1871 to 12,000 kilometres two decades later, but entirely commercial in motivation: to move meat and wheat to ports.

Patchy as they were, these transportation innovations shrank the planet more rapidly than at any other time in history, and made Phileas Fogg's exploit possible. Nevertheless, Fogg suffered all sorts of setbacks and was only just on schedule when a wrongful arrest in Liverpool made him miss the express train to London. Luckily for him and his companions Passepartout and Aouda, he still won the wager with his friends in London's Reform Club. This is because of a curious fact beloved of suspense writers ever since. By travelling eastwards around the world it is possible to 'gain a day' compared to the people who stay at home. Circumnavigators from Del Cano onwards had been puzzled about what to do about the International Date Line. Fogg relied on agreed international methods of accurate timekeeping and navigation by latitude and longitude for his voyage – something he could not have taken for granted a hundred years earlier.

Resolving the shape of the earth – its figure, size and time zones – was a major scientific preoccupation of the mid eighteenth to late nineteenth century. What was the exact circumference of the globe? Where should the prime meridian and date line be? Was the earth really a sphere? Was a degree of latitude the same everywhere? Should new units of measurement be linked to the size of the globe? These were far from academic issues – they lay right at the heart of efforts to establish intellectual, military and political hegemony over the planet. 'Geodesy' – the measurement and mapping of the earth – attracted the finest brains and lavish funding. This was potentially an opportunity to create a shared intellectual understanding of the globe. In practice it became a source of intense national conflict between the leading intellectual powers of the day, France and England.

Navigation remained perilous well into the eighteenth century. After a particularly devastating multiple shipwreck in 1707, the British government offered a generous reward – about two and a quarter million pounds in today's money – to anyone who could devise a method of determining longitude accurately enough to avoid further tragedy. Yorkshire carpenter turned watchmaker John Harrison battled heroically against the English elite to solve the problem of how to measure longitude. He was up against an establishment inspired by the experiments of Jean Dominique Cassini, the gifted Italian-French mathematician who devised an astronomical method for fixing longitude drawn directly from Galileo.[67]

From 1728 to 1761 Harrison devoted his life to building more and more accurate chronometers, only to be dismissed by Sir Isaac Newton and other scientists still convinced that the best way to establish longitude was by astronomy – despite the mounting evidence that it was nearly impossible to take accurate star observations and perform four hours of complex calculations on a ship at sea. Eventually Harrison's watch *H4* was tested on a trip to the Caribbean and proved remarkably accurate. Still the establishment refused to pay him the full prize money. Eventually, George III interceded on his behalf and he got the prize in 1772. Harrison was by now a bitter old man, and not surprisingly. As a result of inflation, the prize money by 1772 was worth £600,000 less than it would have been in 1714.

For Columbus, the earth was pear-shaped, but in the age of circumnavigation most people believed it to be perfectly spherical. Doubts began to appear in France and Britain in the mid to late eighteenth century. The contested story of latitude is as important for globalization as the search for longitude. In theory, a degree of latitude is the same at the equator as at the pole. However, apple-obsessed Isaac Newton believed that the earth was 'oblate' or slightly flattened at the poles. If he was right, the length of a degree at the poles would be longer than it was at the equator.

Newton's apple-shaped notion was flatly rejected by the leading French mathematicians of the day, the Cassini. The post of director of the Paris Observatory had been held by the extraordinary Cassini family continuously for four generations. This was a classic case of nepotism or genetic intelligence, depending on your point of view. Giovanni Domenico Cassini (1625–1712) moved from his native Italy to France and through a grant from Louis XIV helped to set up the Paris Observatory in 1671. He was succeeded as director consecutively by his son Jacques (1677–1756), his grandson César François (1714–1784), and by his great-grandson Jacques Dominique (1748–1845). They were unique family participants in the 200-year Anglo-French battle for global hegemony.[68]

Never to be outdone by the French, King Charles II of England set up the Royal Greenwich Observatory in 1675. And when the English Royal Academy was founded in 1661, the French *Académie des Sciences* rapidly followed suit (1666). The competitiveness of these learned societies caused tension despite a growing international trend towards greater collaboration between scientists. This productive cross-fertilization came about not just in the new learned societies but through a rapid growth of personal correspondence – now possible thanks to Europe's new postal services – and by the trend towards open publication of results in peer-reviewed and circulated scientific journals.[69]

Expectations of collaboration, then, but with vicious national and personal rivalry, was the context for a series of detailed measurements of latitude, extending from Dunkerque in the North to the fishing village of Collioure near the Spanish border in the South. The Cassinis found that a degree of latitude was shorter near the poles than near the equator, suggesting that the globe was not round, but rather egg-shaped. Across the channel, Sir Isaac Newton (1642–1727) fulminated. The effect of gravity on the spinning globe should be to flatten it at the poles, making it apple-shaped. Moreover, said Newton, 'if our earth were not a little higher around the equator than at the poles, the seas would subside at the poles and, by ascending in the region of the equator, would flood everything there.' He may have wished the Cassinis were on the equator at the time.

In 1735, the French *Académie Royale des Sciences* decided to settle the matter. It despatched two expeditions, one to the Equator and another to the Arctic Circle. If the length of a degree of latitude was longer at the Arctic Circle than at the Equator, the earth would be egg-shaped, confirming the French position. In the unpalatable event that it was vice versa, it would be apple-shaped. If both degrees were equal, the globe would be a perfect sphere. France was making a clear statement here: it had the scientific, logistical, diplomatic and financial clout to mount such a complex and costly exercise. The expedition to Lapland (1736–37) by Pierre Louis Maupertuis went quite smoothly. The one to Peru, under Pierre Bouguer, Charles Marie de La Condamine and Louis Godin, was fraught with difficulties and took almost ten years (1735–44). La Condamine fell out so badly with his companions that he chose to travel home alone by descending the entire length of the River Amazon to Cayenne, thereby undertaking the first scientific exploration of the river.[70]

The results from both expeditions were clear: the earth was not a perfect sphere. It was flattened at the poles. Newton had been right and the Cassinis wrong.[71] The egg versus apple debate was far from just an intellectual defeat. There was a lot at stake, because a strong French-led movement had emerged to devise a new universal system of measures and weights, based on the shape and size of the globe. This was part of the growing Enlightenment movement to discover, or dictate, norms for the world, from weights and measures to universal human rights. An embodiment of these complex currents was the author of *The Spirit of the Laws*, Charles de Secondat, Baron de Montesquieu (1689–1755), at once a critic of slavery, an admirer of the British form of government and ardent Francophile who believed the French climate the most propitious in the world for breeding civilization.

One of the key projects of Enlightenment absolutism emanating from France was to establish units of length and weight based not on arbitrary measures differing from country to country – often from town to town – but on the immutable globe. Over the preceding century, the European powers had been busily suppressing rival systems of measurement in Asia, Africa and the Americas. But there were said to be 250,000 different weights and measures in use in France alone in the eighteenth century. No one outside the capital wanted the Parisian system imposed. The proposed unit of length, the metre, would be based on the diameter of the globe. The clarion call was 'ten million metres from the north pole to the equator.' The motive of the French scientists was an intention

to create a new set of universal, logical measures and weights
free of national pride and muddle. This was in part a well-
intentioned contribution to global standardization. France,
with its long north–south landmass, was uniquely placed to
measure the meridian and so establish the metre. But narrow
chauvinism played its part, too. France was to be the centre of
a rational globe.

The goal of universal measures for all times and peoples
gathered French support in the early 1790s. This was a high-
tide mark for the globalizing tendency of the French revolution, when 'Black Jacobins' like Jean-Baptiste Belley from
Haiti were for the first time able to add their voice to debates
on the abolition of slavery in the French national assembly.[72]
There were few limits to French universalising ambitions,
introducing a entirely new system of months, and proposing
decimal time units to replace hours, minutes and seconds – a
unique proposal to challenge the sexagesimal time system
handed down in the West since Babylonian times. The world's
first international scientific committee reviewed all existing
efforts to measure the globe, including the 1735 egg versus
apple expeditions, and found them all wanting.

In a complex blend of national pride and global benevo-
lence, astronomers Pierre Méchain and Jean-Baptiste Delambre were instructed in 1792 to remeasure the meridian, one
working south from Dunkirk and the other working north
from Barcelona. Their adventures through the revolutionary
turmoil of France – accused of espionage, arrested for debt,
burying errors, almost guillotined – read like an over-the-top
historical novel.[73] Amazingly, Delambre and Méchain survived their adventures and reported back to the committee in
1799. The metre became definitive, immortalized as the *Mètre
des Archives* in solid platinum.

The global metre may have been unalloyed, but it was not a

complete success, even in France. Napoleon, initially a fan, soon restored the familiar *ancien régime* Parisian measures when he saw how unpopular the new metric system was proving to be with ordinary people. Later in the nineteenth century came the realization that the meridian would always vary slightly because the earth is imperfectly round, invalidating the idea of an immutable metre 'taken from nature'. So the 1889 International Prototype Metre was not based on any earth measurement – as its inventors had intended – but was simply a copy of the 1799 platinum bar. The new version, along with 40 copies, remained the international measurement standard until 1960, when the metre was redefined by the distance travelled by light in a given amount of time. It was only in 1986 that the final link between measures and the globe was severed: Co-ordinated Universal Time (UTC) based on atomic measurement was introduced to replace Greenwich Mean Time, based on the earth's rotation.

Francophile diplomat, inventor and polymath Benjamin Franklin (1706–90) was among the earliest advocates outside France of the decimal *systéme internationale*. The majority of countries did in due course adopt the metre, and it is now the global system used in science, technology and, increasingly, commerce. But both the United States and Britain have steadily strengthened their political and cultural opposition to the French contribution. This resistance is trumpeted today by both globalization advocates ('see, it's not *that* insidious') and anti-globalization campaigners ('see, resistance *is* possible'). Ireland, recently named the second most globalized country in the world by *Foreign Policy* magazine, changed all its road distance signs and traffic speed limits over to kilometres in 2004.

The first of France's attempts to decide on behalf of all peoples the figure of the globe had ended in an own goal. Its second contribution, the metre, was largely a success. The third act in the story of France's mission to dictate the shape of the planet was ignominious defeat. Successful navigation needs a 'prime meridian' to start counting from. The equator midway between the poles is the obvious starting position for latitude, but there is no such natural meridian for longitude. Over the years Rome, Copenhagen, Jerusalem, Saint Petersburg, Pisa, the Bering Straits, Philadelphia and others had all been put forward as possibilities. By the nineteenth century, however, the choice had been whittled down to just three serious candidates: Greenwich, Paris – and the little island of El Hierro, far west into the Atlantic Ocean.

It was Ptolemy who was responsible for this wild card, at the far west of the known Roman world. In the 1550s, Mercator had used El Hierro as his prime meridian, and by 1634, Louis XIII of France decreed that the island should be the prime meridian. The argument ran that the island was uniquely well placed because no other lands fell on this meridian. More importantly for the French, it divided the Old World from the New. There was a also military consideration for Louis and Richelieu's favouring of the Canaries meridian – it would help clearly demarcate a free-fire zone where hostilities would be possible against fellow-Catholic Spain.

The British had backed a number of locations, including the Great Pyramid at Giza, but by the mid nineteenth century Greenwich had emerged as their prime meridian of choice. Given Britain's dominant role in maritime commerce, three-quarters of the charts in use around the world worked from Greenwich, as did the widely used nautical almanac. Aside from these practical considerations, the British mistrusted France's candidacy of El Hierro. The island was thought to be a 'stalking horse' exactly 20 degrees west of Paris. Many charts originating in France had a common grid with Paris degrees at the top and El Hierro degrees offset by 20 at the bottom. The fact that El Hierro was eventually found to be 20° 23′ 9″ west of Paris did nothing to blunt the suspicion that the French were being disingenuous or at best bloody-minded in their support for a neutral, universal meridian.

The choice of prime meridian was not just of symbolic importance. It was essential for agreeing standard international time. Until the mid-nineteenth century, travel had been so slow that it didn't much matter that every town operated its own time zone: there were up to 300 official local time zones in the USA alone. But the proliferation of railways and steamships meant that differing times became a nuisance for travellers and a menace for railway and shipping companies operating busy timetables. Trains running on different times frequently collided; ports didn't know when to expect ships. British railway companies began promoting standard time based on Greenwich in the 1840s; in 1852 Greenwich began telegraphing time signals. In the USA, the 'Standard Railway Time System' introduced by the railway barons in 1883 was also based on Greenwich.[74]

Despite or perhaps because of intense political and commercial rivalry between the Great Powers, the period 1865–1914 saw an unparalleled formation of worldwide organizations. Starting with the International Geodetic Association in 1864 and International Telegraph Union in 1865, over thirty international organizations were set up before the First World War, governing infrastructure, industrial standards, intellectual property, labour, agriculture, public order, human rights, health, education and research.[75] Some of these organizations were highly bureaucratic, others more like modern non-governmental organizations (NGOs). In this hive of activity, a notable absence was any body to reach international agreement on a prime meridian, urgently needed to ease global navigation and commerce.

So the British were receptive to an initiative by US President Chester A. Arthur (1829–86). In 1884, the dandy ex-lawyer and customs controller Arthur convened the International Meridian Conference in Washington DC. Arthur may be remembered more for the creation of the US civil service and his banning of Chinese immigration, but the meridian meeting was remarkable: one of the first global conferences, not just in its intentions (as the French metrification initiative had been), but in its representation (41 delegates from 25 countries), and in its impacts (agreeing a prime meridian and universal day).[76]

There was only one sticking point among the delegates: where was the official meridian to be? In Washington, the choice came down to a week-long battle between the French and British delegations, with the latter supported by the USA and more vociferously by Sir Sandford Fleming, the Scottish-born Canadian railway engineer who was a leading advocate of single standard time. The British and French delegates were not diplomats and lawyers, as they would be today and had been at Tordesillas, but distinguished astronomers. Jules Janssen, for the French, was a bushy-bearded, disabled ballooning enthusiast who had co-discovered the gas helium and invented a prototype movie camera. John Couch Adams, for Britain, was the diminutive co-discoverer of Neptune who had turned down a knighthood and was famous in Cambridge for his ability to work out complex formulae in his head.

Despite the international flavour of the conference, it was Janssen and Adams who politely but forcefully dominated the meridian debate. Noble global intentions, commercial pragmatism and petty nationalism waxed and waned. Then it was time to vote. A resolution proposing to fix the meridian at Greenwich was finally passed 22 in favour with only San Domingo (now the Dominican Republic) voting against.

France abstained, as did Brazil, but both later accepted the Greenwich meridian, if grudgingly.[77]

Curiously, the International Date Line – the jagged line running from pole to pole roughly opposite the Prime Meridian – was not fixed at the conference, and is one of few things today that is not covered by an international treaty. As the French might say, 'it works in practice, but unfortunately it doesn't work in theory'. A *de facto* line emerged from the Washington conference but countries near the line have always been free to decide their own positions. For some countries, this was an important decision.

Take the Philippines, which by the mid nineteenth century had been steadily losing its commercial and cultural connections with Latin America and Spain. The country was becoming more Asian in its orientation – except that because of the date line it was a whole day out from China. In 1844, governor general Narciso Claveria made the momentous decision that Monday, 30 December 1844 would be immediately followed by Wednesday, 1 January 1845. We can only wonder if the New Year's Eve celebrations in the Philippines that year were better than usual or a complete flop. But the move to share the same day as most of Asia was symbolic of an emerging worldview that turned its back on the links first dictated by the Treaties of Tordesillas and Zaragoza over 300 years before.

In 1867 the USA bought Alaska for what was widely considered the exorbitant sum of $7.2 million (about $90 million in today's money[78]). The move from the Russian calendar to US time-keeping required a change of not just one but twelve days. The most recent change to the International Date Line came in 1995, when the government of Kiribati – the string of 33 Pacific islands which gained independence in 1979 – finally got fed up with east and west being split between two days. President Teburoro Tito an-

nounced that the country would shift westwards into the same
time zone so that all 85,000 residents could share the same
day. Some people suspected that the move had less to do with
streamlining administration and commerce, and more to do
with a heavily stage-managed attempt to win tourist dollars by
becoming the first islands to see in the new millennium.

These quirks aside, the 1884 Washington conference stands,
literally, as a global landmark. The geopolitics of drawing lines
around the globe began in Tordesillas, a closed-door deal
between the powerful. In contrast, the Washington conference
was one of the earliest instances of the world's nations gathering
and voting, one nation one vote, on a strategic global issue. In
the nineteenth century, geography became the indispensible tool
of state control, for the British, French and other modernizing
nations like the USA and Japan.[79] Administrators made maps
and took censuses of their imperial possessions in minute detail.
Winning the Greenwhich meridian was a jewel in the crown for
the British Empire, now larger than the Mongol empire and truly
global. Symbolically, the most detailed map of the Indian sub-
continent in the eighteenth century had been by French cartographer J.B.B. d'Anville (1752), but this was replaced by the
mammoth British undertaking known as the Trigonometrical
Survey of India (1818–40).[80] Imperial and commercial concerns
and a pragmatic Anglo-Saxon world-view had prevailed over
the universalizing French approach. This set the tone for future
global deals, and opened the way for a new era of globe-trotting.

Globe-trotting:
the age of lightning travel

Jules Verne's book *Around the World in Eighty Days* appeared a decade before the meridian contest reached its climax.

Verne has been translated into 148 languages; he is the most translated author after Walt Disney Productions, the Bible and Agatha Christie.[81] Despite his global success, his biggest disappointment was not to have been elected to the elite *Académie Française*. His deranged nephew even shot him in the leg in a misguided effort to draw attention to this slight, but it is hardly surprising that the French establishment, smarting from its failure in Washington, was wary of an author who proclaimed 'that members of the English-speaking race make excellent heroes, especially where a story of adventure, or scientific pioneering work, is about to be described.' Verne 'thoroughly admire[d] the pluck and go-ahead qualities of the nation which have planted the Union Jack on so great a portion of the earth's surface.' To make matters worse, he actually made the Greenwich meridian central to the *dénouement* of his most famous book.[82]

However much the *Académie Française* may have disapproved of Phileas Fogg and his English pluck, getting round the world in less than 80 days was a (fictitious) achievement that captivated audiences worldwide. The only snag for budding globe-trotters was the cost: Verne reckoned the 1872 trip would have cost Fogg over £1 million in today's money.[83] By 1889, the cost was tumbling. In that year, an American journalist known by the pen-name 'Nellie Bly' set off on a highly-publicized attempt to beat Fogg's time. Elizabeth Jane Cochrane (1864–1922) was a feisty pioneer in investigative journalism and travelled unchaperoned with a small travel bag and £200 in gold (equivalent to about £13,500 today). She took hardly any US dollars because she was unsure if any other countries would accept them. The trip was a gimmick to increase sales of the Pulitzer-owned *New York World* and half a million readers wrote to the *World* guessing how long the trip would take.

Cochrane met Jules Verne *en route*, and returned to New York in January 1890, having travelled round the world in 72 days and six hours. She had beaten Phileas Fogg by nearly a week. At the age of 25, Cochrane became an instant celebrity, the 'American girl who had been the first to make a record of a flying trip around the world' as she described herself. Cochrane was a gift to the Madison Avenue admen. There were Nellie Bly trade cards, a board game called 'Around the World with Nellie Bly', the music hall song 'Globe Trotting Nellie Bly', and a book.[84] Yet the notable aspect of Nellie Bly's trip was that it was utterly uneventful, even bland. The world had changed in the 100 years since Captain William Bligh made his epic 4,000-mile voyage in an open boat after the mutiny on the *Bounty*. 'THE STAGE-COACH DAYS ARE ENDED,' screamed the *New York World* headlines. 'THE NEW AGE OF LIGHTNING TRAVEL BEGUN.'

Joseph Pulitzer may have thought he was exaggerating: in 1890, the Wright Brothers were still dreaming of opening a cycle repair shop in Dayton, Ohio. But by 1919, the first international air service was running between Paris and Brussels on a sustained commerical basis. Shipping company Cunard introduced the first around-the-world cruise on the *Laconia* in 1922: leaving from New York, the four-month cruise carried 2,200 passengers and called at 22 ports.[85] This was quicker and certainly more comfortable than the first around-the-world flight, made in 1924 by a team of US Army Air Service pilots. Their feat took 175 days, twice as long as Phileas Fogg and Nellie Bly. In that same year, Imperial Airways inaugurated a daily Croydon–Paris service and regular flights to Guernsey, Brussels, Ostend, Cologne, Basle and Zurich. The airline carried 11,395 wealthy passengers in its first year.

Global air travel remained a dicey business in the 1920s. In 1927, Imperial opened a service between Cairo and Basra. To aid navigation in the desert, the company arranged to have a furrow ploughed in the sand for several hundred miles. Passengers on Imperial routes actually had to take the train between Paris and Brindisi. In 1931, the first airmail service from London to Australia was introduced – it took almost a month. In the late 1920s the fastest round-the-world flight was 21 days, made not by aeroplane by the Graf Zeppelin inflatable.

It was in the mid-1930s that aeroplanes began to come into their own for global travel. American pilot Wiley Post made the first solo around-the-world flight in 1933, taking under eight days. Passengers could fly the whole way from England to Australia by 1935, followed over the next few years by weekly services to Nigeria, Hong Kong, South Africa and an Ireland–Newfoundland route from 1937. In 1936, the return fare London–Brisbane, booked in advance, was £288 – around £12,000 in today's money.[86]

World War Two forced major advances in aeroplane technology, notably the jet engine. In 1949 a US Air Force team flew round the world in under four days by jet and, in 1954, the Boeing company introduced the 707, the first commercial passenger jet. This opened air travel up to middle class passengers. Travelling the globe was no longer the preserve of adventurers, conquerors and diplomats. Only in the last 100 years has travelling round the world become fast, safe, ordinary – a fact that had crucial implications for the global migrations we examine in Chapter 5. In 1995, an Air France Concorde flew round the world in 31 hours – 850 times faster than Del Cano's voyage and 55 times faster than Nellie Bly's. You can't do it any faster – unless you go into space.

Get into orbit

'When I orbited the Earth in a spaceship, I saw for the first time how beautiful our planet is. Mankind, let us preserve and increase this beauty, and not destroy it!'
                                        Yuri Gagarin, 1961[87]

'Don't say that he's hypocritical, Say rather that he's apolitical. "Once the rockets are up, who cares where they come down? That's not my department," says Wernher von Braun.'
                                        Tom Lehrer, *That Was The Year That Was*, 1965

In the mid-1950s, the United States was basking in the glow of military victory in the Second World War and its self-proclaimed scientific and economic leadership. Nowhere was this complacency more in evidence than in the confident announcement that the USA would launch a satellite to orbit the earth in 1958. The organization of this advanced goal was poorly coordinated and marked by rivalry, inadequate funding and missed deadlines. The most advanced satellite project, Vanguard, was plagued with delays and technical difficulties. A second research team was led by brilliant German rocket scientist and former Nazi Wernher von Braun, who had been secretly scooped up by the US – together with his papers, rocket parts and key colleagues – at the end of the Second World War.

The Americans didn't realize that the Soviet Union had also gathered up Nazi rocket staff and blueprints, and little was known about the progress they were making on long-range missiles. Imagine the shock among guests gathered at a cocktail party on 4 October 1957 at the Soviet Embassy in

Washington DC, when they heard US official Lloyd Berkner call out for quiet. 'I've just been informed by the *New York Times* that a Russian satellite is in orbit at an elevation of nine hundred kilometres.' The ballroom fell silent. 'I wish to congratulate our Soviet colleagues,' added Berkner graciously, 'on their achievement.'[88]

This satellite was the small aluminium sphere *Sputnik* – Russian for 'fellow traveller'. It orbited the earth 1,400 times over three months, emitting a notorious 'beep-beep' radio signal every few seconds that was picked up by radio hams around the world. It was visible quite clearly with good binoculars. Sergei Korolev – the chief Soviet engineer of Sputnik – chose a sphere as much for its aesthetic qualities as for any technical consideration. He had a strong sense that he was making global history and would explode with anger if technicians failed to polish the Sputnik sufficiently – even the back-up. 'This ball will be exhibited in museums!' he shouted.

Sputnik, polished to an intense sheen, opened a space race every bit as aggressive as the fifteenth- and sixteenth-century contest between Spain and Portugal or France and Britain's battle to demarcate the globe in the eighteenth and nineteenth century. Until the launch, neither Soviet leader Khrushchev nor US President Eisenhower had been remotely interested in space. Eisenhower's nonchalance lost him significant political capital and the administration had to react rapidly to widespread public fear of overhead Soviet menace. The Sputnik crisis spurred a whole chain of knee-jerk responses in the USA.

Among these were the 1958 creation of NASA with its mission to win the Space Race by getting a man on the moon, massive increases in science and high-tech military funding; the Polaris nuclear missile programme; an overhaul of maths teaching; and the development of project management systems later adopted by big business. Two other Sputnik spin-offs turned out to have huge significance for globalization. The first was communications satellites; the second was the internet.

From a shambles in 1957, the revitalized US space programme managed to launch a tiny satellite weighing just 1.5 kilos in March 1958, immediately derided by Khrushchev as 'a grapefruit'.[89] During the 1960 US presidential campaign between John Kennedy and Richard Nixon, both used the space race to prove their Cold Warrior credentials. 'We are in a strategic space race with the Russians', asserted Kennedy, 'and we have been losing. The first man-made satellite to orbit the earth was named Sputnik. The first living creature in space was Laika . . . If a man orbits earth this year his name will be Ivan . . . If the Soviets control space they can control earth, as in past centuries the nation that controlled the seas dominated the continents . . . [W]e cannot run second in this vital race. To insure peace and freedom, we must be first.' Nixon insisted defensively that 'the United States is not losing the space race or any other race with the Soviet Union.'[90] Nixon lost.

On an ordinary spring morning in the fields around Engels, a small town on the banks of the river Volga as it heads down to the Caspian Sea, at five minutes to eleven, a mother and daughter looked up from their work to see a human figure in bright orange overalls and white helmet descending slowly from the skies. 'Don't be afraid,' this strange apparition called out as they edged fearfully away. 'I am a Soviet like you, who has descended from space'. 'And', he added a trifle self-importantly, 'I must find a telephone to call Moscow!'[91] Kennedy was wrong about the name. On 12 April 1961, Yuri Gagarin became the first person to orbit the earth.

Most of the Soviet scientists behind the project were given false names and job descriptions, and shielded carefully from publicity. Gagarin became an instant worldwide celebrity – the 'Starman'. He was self-confident enough to have a blazing, drunken and very public row with Khrushchev later that year. Few Russians were brave – or foolhardy – enough to stand up to the aggressive Soviet premier. Even Kennedy sat meekly through one of Khrushchev's gloating dinner-table tirades when they met in Vienna in June 1961.[92]

Starman's feat – to the minds of admirers in the early 1960s – eclipsed the achievements of Ferdinand Magellan, Francis Drake, Nellie Bly, Joshua Slocum, Wiley Post and other celebrated circumnavigators. He even sidelined Laika the dog, the unlucky Muscovite mongrel that had earlier orbited the earth a little bit faster, done it five or six times, and given her life into the bargain.[93] Gagarin's subsequent careers – both aeronautical and political – never lived up to his 108-minute journey around the planet aboard Vostok 1. Gagarin's orbit over the Straits of Magellan flipped the world. Previous demarcation lines, agreed at Tordesillas and Washington, had run north–south. Now the lines everyone was tracking on the globe were curvy space orbits. The ensuing space race utterly changed the way people thought about the world and created the technologies that run modern globalization.

For Kennedy, the urge to beat the Soviet Union in the space race became a geopolitical obsession and defining moment in the Cold War. 'Everything we do ought to really be tied in to getting on to the moon ahead of the Russians,' Kennedy told the head of NASA in 1962. Kennedy and vice president Lyndon Johnson claimed the cost of getting a man on the moon – US $40 billion – would reap dividends for the economy. But Kennedy didn't really believe it. What he correctly feared was that Europe and the developing world would make a value judgement that the Soviet Union was ahead of the USA in science and technology. For Kennedy, the space race was a mission to convince the globe that capitalism was superior to communism. 'Otherwise we shouldn't be spending that kind of money, because I'm not interested in space.'[94] Khrushchev too had been dismissive of space, but immediately saw the propaganda value of the Soviet lead.

Before Kennedy's assassination, the two leaders talked of a joint moon programme, but neither would have been prepared to sacrifice the prize of being first among equal superpowers. The space race became an inextricable combination of semi-friendly technical rivalry and highly dangerous Cold War posturing, from Cuban Missile Crisis to moon landings, and from joint space laboratories to strategic arms limitation treaties.[95] The pace only began to slacken once Neil Armstrong became the first person to walk on the moon in 1969. With the famous 1975 handshake between Aleksei Leonov and Tom Stafford over the French town of Metz, the race was effectively over, though competition continued under a military aegis.[96]

Over this period, communications satellites had proliferated. Just a year after Sputnik, a satellite carrying a tape recorder was used to send a Christmas greeting to the world from President Eisenhower. In 1962, Telstar was launched as the first direct relay communications satellite – a commercial partnership between AT&T, Bell, NASA and the British and French post offices. Through the 1960s and 1970s, satellites gradually superseded fixed cables for long-distance telephone calls as well as entertainment. Costs came down and media empires grew up.

One contested spin-off of the space race was the opening up to civilian use in 1995 of the Global Positioning System (GPS). This network of 24 satellites, begun in 1978, had been strictly for US military use. Only in 2000 did then US President Bill Clinton turn off 'Selective Availability' – the deliberate scrambling of the civilian signal that made it less accurate than the military version. GPS is now beginning to find everyday applications, like a $200 wristwatch that allows parents to locate their errant children, marketed by Californian company Wherify. 'Now you can have peace of mind 24 hours a day,' promises Wherify, 'while your child is the high tech envy of the neighbourhood!'

Americans see GPS as a US gift to the globe, as London saw the Greenwich meridian and the French the metre. Not everyone sees it that way. European Union (EU) countries are wary of the US military's ability to override the system at will. The EU has commenced a rival, resolutely civilian Galileo positioning system, scheduled for completion in 2008. The EU is actively canvassing countries like Israel, China and Brazil to join. Given $300–400 million a year maintenance costs for each GPS system, the global space race is clearly not over yet.

A second spin-off from the US space programme originated at the Pentagon's Defense Advanced Research Projects Agency (ARPA). In 1967, defence contractors working at four different universities built a computer network project called ARPANET to help them discuss complex research projects. The first message to test the network in 1969 was to be the word 'login'. 'We succeeded in transmitting the "l" and the "o"', recollects Leonard Kleinrock, 'and then the system crashed! Hence, the first message on the internet was "lo"! We were able to do the full login about an hour later.'[97] This clunky system became the internet, with email emerging in 1972 and the world-wide-web 20 years later in 1992. By 2005, there were over eight billion web pages, including guides to the towns of Tordesillas, Sèvres (home of the prototype metre), and the London Borough of Greenwich.

Knowing the globe

'No amount of travel in detached portions of the world enables one to contemplate the world and the human race as a whole. One must traverse the ball round and round to arrive at a broad, liberal, correct estimate of humanity – its work, its aims, its destiny.'

Andrew Carnegie, *Round the World* (1884)

Samuel Johnson (1709–1784) was unconvinced of the benefits of geographical education, especially for girls. 'You teach your daughters the diameters of the planets', he warned the English intelligentsia, 'and wonder when you are done that they do not delight in your company.' As usual, Johnson was out of step with his countrymen. In 1851, huge crowds flocked to a 20 metre-high Great Globe erected in Leicester Square by James Wyld (1812–1887). Wyld, a Member of Parliament and distinguished geographer, provided a geographic spectacle that outlasted the Great Exhibition by nine years. Visitors entered Wyld's Globe and climbed a series of staircases to see all around them the outlines of the world, an experience which *Punch* magazine described as 'a geographical globule, which the mind can take in at one swallow'.

Billionaire industrialist and philanthropist Andrew Carnegie (1835–1919) refuted the idea that the globe could be so easily swallowed. But he was a firm advocate of globe-trotting as a path to enlightenment. This chapter has emphasized the strategic importance of getting a 'correct estimate' of the globe. Exploration and demarcation led to dramatic pulses of planet-shrinking over the last 500 years. This knowledge and power made the difference between accidental imperialism and deliberate globalization. But planet-shrinking – by circumnaviga-

tors, scientists, intellectuals, conquerors and diplomats alike –
did not unite the globe. Instead it created powerful fault-lines,
a tectonic clash between universalizing tendencies and patriotic and personal self-interest.

On two occasions, 1494 and 1884, the leading empires of
the day actually drew physical lines around the globe to
cement their global grasp. On the third occasion, in 1957,
the line was an orbit traced over an earth split ideologically in
half by the Cold War. A geological fault-line caused the
December 2004 *tsunami*. It highlighted our global interconnections, but also a surprising ignorance of what Herman
Melville called 'the watery part of the world'. Where was
Aceh? Who did the Sentinel Islands belong to? Knowing the
globe, for the planet-shrinkers of this chapter, was a key
intellectual and strategic asset. It was the foundation of global
intent. Do we still have it?

When *National Geographic* magazine recently tested the
geographical knowledge of young people aged 18–24 in nine
countries, they discovered that only a quarter of young British
people and one in ten young Americans could even find
Indonesia on an outline map of Asia and the Middle East.[98]
Six out of seven young Americans could not find Iraq or Iran
on the map, although over a third knew that the island used on
the television show *Survivor* was in the South Pacific. As
Carnegie could have told the researchers, there is a clear
connection between geographical knowledge and travel. As
the chart overleaf shows, there are big differences in the global
outlook of young people from different countries.

Today, young Swedes are among the best-informed globe-
trotters: the vast majority travel internationally and know their
way around a world map. Young Germans, Italians and French
also have a fairly global outlook, with Canadians lagging some

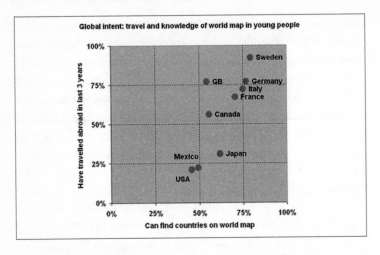

Global intent: travel and knowledge of world map in young people

way behind. Young Britons travel as much as other Europeans, but are less sure where they are going. In contrast, young Japanese people don't travel much, but know where they are not going.

Bringing up the rear are young Americans. Only a fifth of US youth have travelled abroad in the last three years, and their knowledge of global geography is significantly worse than that of young people in the other countries surveyed. One in ten young Americans couldn't even find the USA on a world map. They have a highly inflated view of the size of the US population, with a third believing there are one to two billion Americans. 'It gives the sense that there is this Americentric thing going on,' said John Fahey, President and CEO of the National Geographic Society, a mentality 'that we are big and powerful and have all these people in our country.'[99]

The Great Wall of China was a different sort of global demarcation, a signal that a big and powerful nation had turned its back on the world. We often hear that the Great Wall of China is the only human-made object that can be seen from space. Not so, according to NASA. There are 'many,

many human-made objects that can be seen from space . . . including buildings, mines, irrigated croplands, salt evaporation ponds, jetties and landfills along coasts, and yes, roads.' But the Great Wall isn't one of them – it is quite narrow and doesn't show up well because it is made of local stone. Even Chinese astronaut Yang Liwei admitted he couldn't see it.[100]

When China retreated behind the Wall, it gave up an opportunity for global dominance. Planet-shrinking passed to Spain and Portugal. Later, England and France jostled for the right to divide the globe. In the mid twentieth century, it was the USA and Russia who fought this battle. Today's geographical ignorance was unthinkable – the powerful were those who best knew the globe. Is the USA erecting an intellectual great wall, or has the importance of knowing the globe finally waned with the advent of GPS-enabled wristwatches and mobile phones? While explorers and power-brokers fought to draw north–south lines around the globe, traders were creating a new global meridian – one that ran east–west and was based not on treaties or space but on commodity supply-chains. US corporations now dominate these global supply-chains, even if Americans can't trace them on the globe. The next chapter looks at the emergence of this global trade meridian.

4

GOODS: THE GLOBALIZATION OF LUXURY

Some like it hot

'If a London merchant . . . can buy at Canton, for half an ounce of silver, a commodity which he can afterwards sell at London for an ounce, he gains a hundred percent. by the bargain.'
Adam Smith, *Wealth of Nations*, 1776

Don't ask a Scottish or German economist to explain the English passion for spicy food. As far as we know Adam Smith was not among the novelty-seekers and returning East India Company employees who sought out an Indian curry in late eighteenth-century London. He died 20 years before the Hindostanee Coffee House at 34 George Street, London was opened by retired Bengal Army officer Din Muhammad in 1810. And Karl Marx had long been consigned to Highgate Cemetery when the Veeraswamy restaurant opened its doors off Regent's Street in 1927. How could they have predicted that chicken tikka masala would become an everyday dinner dish in Britain?

Smith and Marx thought long and hard about commodities, but saw them as plain, everyday goods like a bag of flour, a wooden table, a bundle of linen, a barrel of wine, a pound's weight of four thousand pins. Most commodities started off – and remain to this day – dull, bulky and traded over short distances. But local trade in everyday goods could never have led to globalization. Global trade was created by merchants scouring the globe for exotic luxuries, to quench M. de Vogüé's thirst for colours and ideas from the East and the West. Feeding our growing appetite for luxury gave early corporations profits well in excess of Adam Smith's modest 100 per cent.

In 2004, the international trade in commodities was worth US $9 trillion. Shared equally, that would amount to $1,500 of traded goods for every man, woman and child on the planet. In 1913, $1,500 was what a notional world citizen *earned* in a year. Today, it's only what they *trade*. The Dutch were considered a unique hive of traders when they exported a fifth of their economic production back in 1870. Now, over a fifth of all the economic activity in the world is goods going from one country to another. How did it happen?

The trade in luxury stretches back into antiquity, but the pace quickened when ruthless state-chartered trading companies used their geographical knowledge, naval and military might, sophisticated management, and market manipulation to ship exotic produce from the four corners of the earth to Europe and then the United States. Venice (c.1250–1450), the British East India Company (1600–1874), H.J. Heinz (founded 1860s) and Vestey (f.1897) were pioneers of successive waves of global trade. US corporations like Wal-Mart (f.1962) and Dell (f.1985) are the modern pioneers, democratizing luxury.

Corporations shipped the goods, but it was our lust for the exotic that supplied the demand. Mass consumerism was identified a thousand years ago in China, and in Europe it appeared *before* the industrial revolution. Marx observed that we take even the most trivial commodity and turn it into a fetish. What he missed was the other side of the story: how our hunt for the exotic turns luxury into bland commodity. When the sixteenth-century Spanish conquistadores arrived in Veracruz in Mexico, they could not believe the heady aroma the local Totonac people derived from their orchids. Today, the once-prized spice is 'plain vanilla', a bog-standard commodity made in the lab or shipped in bulk from Madagascar.

Historians of a whole range of goods, from cod and coffee, guns and porcelain, to vanilla pods and the iPod, have charted the slippery slope from exotic luxury to banal commodity. There are now hundreds of histories of luxury goods 'that changed the world'. In the process, without any one producer, corporation or consumer really wanting it, they became utterly ubiquitous.[101] This chapter takes as its guide a classic everyday luxury: spice. For both advocates and critics of globalization, the story of spice is *the* story of global trade.[102] The development of the global spice trade is a colourful story of far-flung islands, fabulous profits, ruthless battles to corner the market, bizarre fashions and fiery cuisine. Almost every spice now has its own history – though the musty root galangal awaits rescue from oblivion.[103]

Spices shaped global trade and still act as a guide to where it might be going. So this chapter focuses in on spices. The global impact of sugar and rubber on human labour are addressed in Chapter Five, while gold and oil are central characters of Chapter Six on money. Many other goods have influenced global trade, from stimulants like coffee, cocoa and opium and textiles like silk and cotton to the down-to-earth potato and modern branded goods like trainers and mobile phones. The benefit of focusing here on a single traded good is that it shows patterns within the complex ebbs and flows of globalization.

The global spice trade started with a chaotic scramble by

Europeans to secure long-distance trade routes to meet soaring demand (roughly 1350–1600). There followed a period of concentration as the trade was monopolized by a few large corporations who despite their brutal efforts failed to prevent prices collapsing (c.1600–1790s). From the beginning of the early modern period, bio-pirates smuggled spices from their original environments for transplantation around the world, and fast-moving entrepreneurs innovated in an apparently saturated global market (c.1800–1900s). In the mid twentieth century, spices entered another phase of intense concentration in the hands of a few multinational corporations. Recently, there are signs that a new phase of fragmentation is beginning, led by the 'Fair Trade' movement and the desire of sated consumers to rediscover the exotic. The story of spices shows that globalization, far from being inexorable, is jerky and unpredictable. The current dominance of global corporations is not the culmination of a historical process. The invisible hand has no favourites.

Medieval massala

'The history of commerce is that of the communication of people. Their numerous defeats, and the flux and reflux of populations and devastations, here form the most extraordinary events.'

Montesquieu, 1689–1755

'A commodity appears, at first sight, a very trivial thing, and easily understood. Its analysis shows that it is, in reality, a very queer thing.'

Karl Marx, *Capital*, 1867

In 1390, King Richard II of England commissioned a recipe book, the *Forme of Cury*. A forerunner of Hugh Fearnley-

Whittingstall's *River Cottage Meat Book*, it describes hundreds of meat dishes, requiring a wide range of spices. Spices had been traded over long distances for over four thousand years. They were highly prized by Middle East civilization: Sheba brought spices to Solomon and Cleopatra seduced Caesar with spicy concoctions. Pepper was measured on the same scales as gold dust in Roman times. When Alaric seized Rome in 410, 5,000 pounds of pepper were a significant part of his booty. And when the cosmopolitan Abbasid Calilph Harun al-Rashid sent Charlemagne a gift from Baghdad in 802, it included perfume, balsam, silks, brass candlesticks, slaves, ivory chess pieces, a huge tent, an ingenious water clock, and, in case that failed to impress, an elephant.

A European ruler had never seen such luxury. Beginning with the First Crusade (1095–99), many more Europeans had the opportunity to experience Eastern luxuries for themselves, in between the fighting. Oriental spices were far more alluring than native Mediterranean spices like fennel, saffron and cumin. By the early fifteenth century, the European demand for spice was becoming what Marx called commodity fetishism. The demand for spices is understandable – as flavour enhancers for old and salted meat, as medicines against plague, for embalming fluids, as aphrodisiacs, to flaunt wealth at meat-rich banquets. Even so, we still struggle to understand the sheer obsession of medieval Europeans with spices. Fernand Braudel described it as a 'mania for spices'.

In medieval times spices were amongst the most highly prized of all luxury goods, affordable only by the European nobility.[104] 'A small sackful was enough to set a man up for life,' writes Giles Morton of the sixteenth-century nutmeg trade in England, 'buying him a gabled dwelling in Holborn and a servant to attend to his needs.' Dock-workers had their pockets sewn up to prevent pilfering; sailors carried small sacks of peppercorns instead of cash on long voyages. Spices were dangerous, a temptation, even an addiction.

To feed the habit, more and more people began to pore over the globe, searching for opportunity. Student Richard Hakluyt was transfixed by the shape of the world. He noted the relative positions and sizes of the continents, each with 'their special commodities, & particular wants, which by the benefit of traffike and entercourse of merchants, are plentifully supplied.'[105] In the end, Hakluyt chose tobacco not spices and actively promoted settlements in Virginia. But many of the planet-shrinkers of the previous chapters were obsessed with spices as much as faith and gold. Columbus was devastated by his failure to find oriental black pepper and became the first European advocate of the chilli pepper. Bullion and silk gave a powerful impetus for the development of global intent, but few commodities were as special as spices – the words have the same Latin root – and few demands as strong in the late sixteenth century as the lust for spices.

The effort to ensure a plentiful supply caused bloody conflict as one European power after another sought to establish monopolies over the produce of India's Malabar coast (pepper, ginger), Sri Lanka (cinnamon), a handful of remote spice-producing Indonesian islands (nutmeg, mace, cloves), and China (medicinal rhubarb). By the late fourteenth century, Venice had established a near-monopoly on the spices of the Indian Ocean that filtered through Alexandria and Beirut into Europe. The Venetians used their privileged geographical position and the naval innovations outlined in Chapter Two to make fabulous profits.

In the fifteenth century, it took two days' wages for a skilled carpenter to buy a pound of pepper in Europe. But if prices remained this high, there was only room for a limited number of lucky traders. The Venetian spice trade turned over roughly

US $15–30 million a year in today's money. With high profit margins, such sums were enough to bankroll palatial living and eye-catching banquets. When 'luxury fever' strikes, it rapidly draws in people at all levels of income.[106] As demand for spices increased down the social hierarchy, profits could be spread more widely even as prices fell. Other Europeans started looking for ways to get a piece of the action, initially within Europe and then focusing on the sources of supply in the eastern Indian Ocean. 'Whoever is lord of Malacca', realized traveller Tomé Pires in the early sixteenth century, 'has his hand on the throat of Venice.'

It was the Portuguese who took Malacca, gateway to the Spice Islands, and throttled the Venetians. Their advantage became even greater after the capture of Constantinople by the Ottomans in 1453 weakened Venetian supply-chains. As we saw, a single boatload of cloves and cinnamon covered the costs of Magellan's three-year circumnavigation. But it doesn't always pay to be the first into a new market. Despite their naval prowess, foothold in Malacca, and ruthless treatment of Asian producers and traders, the Portuguese struggled to assert control. The East Indies 'are a warren of all evil, and have no one good thing but the clove,' wrote Joaõ de Barros in 1543. 'Since it is a thing that God has made, we can call it good; but in so far as it is the material cause of our people going there, it is an apple of all discord. And one could curse it more than gold itself.'[107]

The main Portuguese curse was the Dutch. The Dutch navy, bankrolled by Amsterdam financial innovations, soon ousted the Portuguese from Malacca. As demand for spices continued to rise, a number of Northern Europeans set up new joint-stock companies with state-granted monopolies to exploit the trade. The English East India Company was chartered by Queen Elizabeth in 1600; the Dutch *Vereenigde Oostindische*

Compagnie (or VOC) in 1602; and the French *Compagnie des Indes Orientales* in 1664. These companies, alongside a dozen others with geographical monopolies, were the first recognizable multinational corporations, issuing shares and dividend payments and establishing techniques to manage far-flung employees outnumbering those at head office.

The economic historian Carlo Cipolla wrote an essay in the late 1980s in which he pinpointed the cause of a host of medieval events – including the Crusades, the Hundred Years War and the Renaissance – on the aphrodisiac properties of black pepper.[108] Although Cipolla's essay was a parody, the history of the 'spice race' abounds in anecdote: the King of Portugal lured into a price-fixing scam by a German company; or Queen Elizabeth I getting her fingers burned with a hoard of pepper pirated from a Spanish treasure galleon.

The companies didn't necessarily share the same commercial or territorial ambitions, so in theory Dutch, English and French interests in the Indies could have coexisted peacefully. In practice, these companies had 'imperial genes', and their monopolies were soon irreconcilable.[109] The North Europeans were initially overawed by the opulence of Indian Ocean trading empires; unlike the Spanish they did not debate whether indigenous people were fully human or born slaves. But the European treatment of spice producers – and each other – was brutal in any case. European domestic hostilities frequently spilt over into the East Indies, beginning with conflicts between the Dutch and Portuguese after Portugal was annexed by Spain in 1580.

The Dutch finally evicted the Portuguese from Malacca in 1641, aided and abetted by the rival Sultan of Johore. In 1658 they gained control of the cinnamon trade in Sri Lanka and by 1663 they had established trading rights in the pepper ports along the Malabar Coast of western India. The Dutch worked ruthlessly to keep spice prices high, massacring thousands of islanders, concentrating local production, sterilizing seeds and burning surplus spices in Amsterdam. 'No lover is as jealous of his mistress as the Dutch are of their trade in spices,' remarked a French observer in 1697.[110] The main problem they faced was near-continuous warfare with the English. In 1667, the Dutch agreed at Breda that England could keep the recently captured island in the Americas called Manhattan so long as they could hang on to the nutmeg-producing island of Run.

Consumption of spices in Europe grew fast in this period. Dutch imports of pepper more than doubled from 2,000 tonnes a year in 1600 to 5,000 tonnes in 1680, equivalent to about roughly 60 grams for every person in Europe.[111] At this point, the VOC was the largest corporation in the world, with 50,000 staff, 30,000 soldiers and 200 ships on its books. It employed a bigger proportion of the world's population than today's three largest car-makers combined, and paid its shareholders a handsome annual dividend of 40 per cent. But there were clouds on the horizon. Vibrant lower-price spice markets were developing in London and elsewhere in competition with Amsterdam. Although tensions between the spice-trading neighbours eased in the 1688 Glorious Revolution, when William of Orange ascended the English throne, the Dutch fumbled the transition from luxury market to everyday commodity.

The Anglo-Dutch era of peaceful world trade could not last when the French began to stretch their global muscles. One English journalist described the French as 'the universal Cormorant, that would, if possible, swallow up the whole globe itself.'[112] Territorial disputes soon erupted in America, Europe and India, culminating in the Seven Years War (1756–63). In terms of its multiple combatants and theatres, this was the first truly global war. It disrupted spice supply-chains. In the end, the British emerged in the stronger position, free of European hindrance to exert territorial dominion in India and commercial domination over China.

As spices became more widely available, they began to lose their attraction to the European nobility. Over-spiced banquets became unfashionable in France as early as the 1650s where a simpler cuisine emerged, making use of a range of new ingredients. This was coupled with a Puritan-led backlash in Britain and America against the sensuality of spices. The medicinal properties of some spices were also being challenged. This didn't mean the working-class market for spices fell, but when luxuries become commodities, prices plummet. In 1500, a skilled labourer had needed over two days' wages to buy a pound of pepper. By 1750, the price had halved.[113]

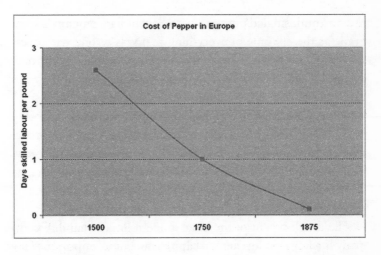

How could the Indies companies maintain profits? They had already screwed down producer prices to subsistence levels, but administrative costs were rising and sea transport remained stubbornly slow. The Dutch VOC attempted to diversify into more glamorous products: in 1620, over 80 per cent of its trade by value was in spices. By the late eighteenth century, textiles, tea and coffee made up over half its business. For the English East India Company, textiles had always been more important than spices, and by the 1750s, pepper made up just five per cent of its business. The spice trade had become a 'stack 'em high, sell 'em cheap' business.

Botanical outsourcing

'The discovery and disclosure of botanical knowledge did not have an overtly economic purpose, but botany and business were not exactly disconnected.'
Henry Hobhouse, *Seeds of Wealth*, 2003

Adam Smith singled out the Dutch East India Company's spice trade as the epitome of everything that was wrong with over-powerful, state-backed monopolistic corporations. By the time Marx's *Capital* appeared in English translation 110 years later, these charted companies were a thing of the past. A new type of company emerged in Britain and the USA to take their place, using the latest technologies, governance procedures and management theories to cater to – and create – new markets. The period from the 1780s to 1890s saw the change from state-sanctioned opium peddling to Heinz baked beans; from the merchant-adventurer to the robber baron.

The development of the large modern limited liability company is a key development in capitalism, but its importance for globalization can be overstated.[114] In fact, the new British and US corporations traded almost exclusively in local goods – steel, frozen meat – and fixed infrastructure – the telegraph and railway. The railroad and telegraph system, according to Alfred Chandler, 'provided the fast, regular, and dependable transportation and communication so essential to high-volume production and distribution.'[115] Industrialization laid the foundations for later phases of globalization, but it was primarily for local consumption at this stage.

In 1498, the legend goes, Vasco da Gama asked the ruler of Calicut whether he might take a pepper stalk with him for replanting closer to home. 'You can take our pepper', the Zamorin complacently replied, 'but you will never be able to take our rains.' Kerala's twin monsoons were thought to be essential to a high-quality crop. The Europeans, desperate to recover their profits, *did* take pepper plants: to Sri Lanka, Cambodia and Indonesia in the eighteenth century, and Malaya in the nineteenth century. The first crucial development in global trade was not the rise of the modern corporation but this upheaval in the sources of supply. Today it would be called outsourcing. At the time it was called botany.

Global transplantations changed the spice trade from a long-distance monopolistic trade with falling profits into a global trade based on multiple suppliers, low profit margins and cut-throat competition. Ginger was the first global migrant spice, introduced to Mexico and then Jamaica early in the sixteenth century by the Spanish. But the globalization of spices really got underway with the one-armed French adventurer Pierre Poivre (1719–1786). 'The possession of spice which is the basis of Dutch power in the Indies was grounded on the ignorance and cowardice of the other trading nations of Europe,' wrote Poivre. 'One had only to know this and be daring enough to share with them this never-failing source of wealth which they possess in one corner of the globe.'

After several attempts, Poivre managed to smuggle cloves and nutmeg away from Dutch control across the Indian Ocean to the French islands of Mauritius and Réunion, where the first crops were produced in 1776. There followed a rapid spate of

scientific expeditions in which exploration and botanical pro-
specting went hand in hand. English botanists, naval officers,
politicians and traders like Joseph Banks, Thomas Stamford
Raffles, John Bell and Hans Sloane became highly successful
commercial 'bio-pirates'. Spices dispersed rapidly around the
world, finding new homes as good as their original ones.
Turmeric was successfully grown in Jamaica in 1783. By
1818, cloves had reached Zanzibar.

The bio-piracy went both ways. In 1841, Mexican vanilla
was pollinated in Réunion by ex-slave Edmond Albius. Two
years later, nutmeg arrived from Asia in Grenada. The capsi-
cum or chilli pepper, Columbus' consolation prize, steadily
migrated eastwards to Europe and then across the Indian
Ocean. Paprika and saffron also became multinational travellers. This globalization of spice sources was echoed by numerous other commodities. France and Britain smuggled rubber
away from Brazil for plantations in Malaya and elsewhere;
American cocoa was established in West Africa; and Japan,
emerging from a long period of isolationism, usurped Italian
and Chinese pre-eminence in silk between 1830 and 1930.[116]

The state-chartered trading corporations were criticized by
the public for their government backing, yet they became
unpopular with government because they increasingly failed
to make enough money and drained too many domestic
resources. Politicians were continually trying to increase the
quantity of home exports the companies used to trade for
Asian products, even setting targets when charters were renewed. Although the companies generally paid good divi-
dends, their employees began to operate as entrepreneurs
on the side. Elihu Yale (1648/9–1721), a modest clerk for
the East India Company in Madras, returned to Boston with a
fortune made from dealing in gems and spices. His gift of
books and textiles to Connecticut College raised so much

money that it was renamed Yale College in his honour. In England, returning company officials like Thomas Pitt were often so wealthy from insider trading they were known as 'nabobs' – a name conveying envy and insult in equal parts.

By the time *The Economist* magazine was founded in 1843 to advocate free trade, state-granted monopolies had fallen from favour, and were struggling to keep up with the proliferation of global sources of supply. The French *Compagnie des Indes* was the first to go, abolished in 1769 both from economic dogma and poor financial results. Shortly after, the Dutch VOC ran into financial difficulties and rapidly unravelled (1799–1805). The British East India Company, although more diversified, was also in trouble. Virtually bankrupt in the early 1770s, it was also beset by a string of corporate scandals. It was blamed for exacerbating the disastrous Bengal famine, and forced to pay a heavy fine for the false imprisonment of Armenian merchant rivals.

In 1788 came a concerted effort to impeach director Warren Hastings, based on the novel principle of global corporate responsibility. 'The laws of morality are the same everywhere', argued Anglo-Irish parliamentary firebrand Edmund Burke (1729–97), leading the high-minded prosecution. 'There is no action which would pass for an act of extortion, of peculation, of bribery, and oppression in England, that is not an act of extortion, of peculation, of bribery, and oppression in Europe, Asia, Africa and the world over.'[117]

Although the prosecution failed, the company lost its lucrative monopoly with China in 1834. Fifteen years later, the Navigation Acts requiring goods to enter British ports in British ships were repealed. The company was by now a hybrid – part 'service' company, part state organ. Its core business was collecting taxes and administration rather than commodity arbitrage. Harshly criticized for its role in sparking the

1857–8 rebellion in India, by 1874 it was out of business altogether.

In the end the Company fell more because it lost the debate on free trade than due to poor financial performance or corporate irresponsibility. 'Free trade' originated with a coterie of eighteenth-century French economists – Anne Robert Jacques Turgot, François Quesnay and Dupont de Nemours (whose son founded the chemical company) – who actively sought government appointments to promote their free trade ideas. This group was highly cosmopolitan: Turgot's best-known work, *Réflexions sur la formation et la distribution des richesses* (1766) was written for two young Chinese students. Another member was Jacques Claude Marie Vincent, Marquis de Gournay (1712–1759), a widely travelled merchant who had studied the East India Company. His favourite motto was *laissez-faire, laissez passer*. Adam Smith acknowledged the importance of this French thinking on his theories.

In Britain, the debate focused in on local trade problems. In 1815, grain imports into Britain were taxed under the Corn Laws. Following Adam Smith's lead, 'free trade' economists like David Ricardo attacked such tariffs as an ineffective but costly subsidy to wealthy landowners – and in effect a stealth tax on manufacturers. The debate became acute when potato blight devastated the Irish crop in 1845. The potato was another botanical migrant that arrived in Ireland in the 1650s, became the staple crop by the 1780s, but in 1846 it suffered a destructive fungus. British Prime Minister Robert Peel argued that reduced grain prices could help stave off famine in Ireland. Free trade proponents argued with an almost religious fervour, and after fierce debate the tariffs were repealed, ushering in a fifty-year period where Britain enforced its global vision of free trade – the Pax Britannica – by gunboat if necessary. The tariff reform helped British manufacturers – but did nothing to alleviate the Irish famine, which killed an estimated 700,000–800,000 people and forced another two million to emigrate in the coming decades. Nor were the virtues of free trade applied evenly across the Empire – strenuous efforts were made to dismantle the Indian textile industry, for example.

One important consequence of the victory of the laissez-faire movement was a huge rise in domestic investment. In England, the amount of capital raised for railway building increased a thousand-fold between 1825 and 1849.[118] With the passage of the Joint Stock Companies Act in 1856, companies no longer needed to be chartered by the state; they were free to incorporate by simple registration. In the US, similar legislation soon followed, state by state. With limited liability, shareholders could invest more safely, and the additional investment fuelled the Industrial Revolution. But at this stage, large companies were mainly domestic, with few global ambitions. In global businesses like the spice trade, it was not new corporations but individual entrepreneurs who now seized their opportunity to cut out the ailing state-chartered middlemen, in Europe and in the newly independent American states.

In 1797, the schooner *Rajah*, captain Jonathan Carnes, berthed in New York with 75 tons of what he described as 'wrinkled blackberries' aboard. Carnes made a 700 per cent profit on his cargo, which was actually black pepper, shipped directly from Sumatra. Using faster ships and direct sourcing, Salem, Massachusetts became for 50 years the centre of a revitalized pepper trade, with monthly sailings giving a major impetus to a burgeoning maritime industry. In its heyday, Salem taxes contributed five per cent of the US federal budget – mainly from pepper. A similar low-cost business model operated in Europe. Dozens of small spice enterprises now sprang up, such as Silvo (1833), Schwartz (1841), Durkee (1850), Tone Brothers

(1873), Schilling (1881) and McCormick (1889). Spice traders soon got into tea and other luxuries that were fast being commoditized. These businesses, far from being modern limited liability companies, were family concerns little different from the spice-selling apothecaries of medieval days.

Everyday luxury: the rise of mass consumption

'*We were frugal, while we were only masters of one city; now we consume the riches of the whole globe, and employ both the masters and their slaves in our service.*'

Tiberius (42BC–AD37)

'*I need not tell you the many good effects this must produce, when business & amusement can be made to go hand in hand.*'

Josiah Wedgwood (1730–92)

The rise of large companies in the second half of the nineteenth century is widely seen as a key development in globalization. The power of these corporations challenges the pre-eminence of the nation-state. The claim is supported by the longevity of multi-national companies that first appeared at that time. The foundation of General Electric, the world's ninth largest corporation in 2005, coincided with the first appearance of the term 'global' in 1892. Fifty US companies on today's *Fortune 500* list are over 150 years old, including such household names as J.P. Morgan Chase & Co. (formerly the Manhattan Company, 1799); Du Pont (1802); Altria (formerly Philip Morris, 1847); The *New York Times* (1851); and Levi Strauss (1853).[119]

The focus on corporations obscures an important point in the history of global trade, however. The global consumer predates the modern corporation, just as the 'industrious revolution' took place well before the industrial revolution. From as early as 1650, European households experienced an explosion in demand for everyday luxuries from east and west – tulips, jewels, porcelain, silks, artworks and coffee as well as spices. In the eighteenth century, the best pashmina shawls from Kashmir changed hands for the cost of a house, leading to a copycat industry in Paisley, Scotland. Nor was the early development of global consumerism an exclusively European phenomenon.[120]

In China, the consumption of everyday luxuries was a recurrent feature of the Tang, Sung and Ming dynasties, led by urban female trend-setters. The Chinese authorities on occasion attempted to punish what they considered to be 'conspicuous consumption'. The term was only coined by US economist Thorstein Veblen in 1899, but as Veblen pointed out, the phenomenon was far from novel. Samurai warriors set similar fashion standards in Japan. In the mid eighteenth century, South Indian weavers had a higher standard of living than their counterparts in Britain, with a propensity to amass gold jewellery. Luxury fever, despite the best efforts of elites, could not be contained.[121]

Consumerism penetrated class barriers most in Europe. By the late seventeenth century, growing numbers of households in the Netherlands, Germany, France and Southern England became industrious as never before. This meant hard work, time-keeping, hygiene – and packages of global commodities. 'You see, Madame,' the Abbé Baudeau in 1776 lectured an anonymous consumer, 'in a simple breakfast, united before your eyes and in your hands the productions of all climates and of the two hemispheres.' Baudeau listed crockery from China, coffee from Arabia, sugar from America grown by Africans, a silver coffeepot from Potosí and table linen from Riga woven by the Dutch – not to forget French bread and cream.

Long before the rise of the modern corporation, astute entrepreneurs responded to the voracious appetites of the new consumers. In the mid eighteenth century, English potter Josiah Wedgwood developed a range of novel techniques to sell his affordable luxury porcelain to both royalty and middle-class markets – for example using 'sale or return' gimmicks. Patrons included Empress Catherine II of Russia, who ordered 952 pieces of porcelain in 1774. He introduced the first money-back guarantee and opened luxurious showrooms in London in 1768 to attract shoppers. 'What woke Wedgwood up in a cold sweat', writes Nancy Koehn of Harvard Business School, 'is the same thing that would wake the modern entrepreneur' like Michael Dell – the unfulfilled demand of the everyday consumer.

Shopping for the exotic became a leisure activity in its own right. One of the first recognizably modern shopping environments appeared on the Nevsky Prospect in St Petersburg. In the 1830s, this wide, well-lit street offered a dazzling array of foreign goods to window-shoppers. Contemporary lithographs show that over half the shop signs were bilingual or exclusively French, English or German. 'Displayed along with foreign goods . . . were foreign styles, foreign men and women, all the forbidden allure of the world outside,' writes Marshall Burman.[122]

Through the 1850s and 1860s, Baron Haussmann drove a network of expansive *boulevards* through the medieval heart of Paris under orders from Napoleon III. Part of the motivation for straight streets was riot control, but this major urban remodelling also created the ability to 'shop till you drop'. With the new boulevards came the modern department store, pioneered by the Boucicaut family between 1838 and 1852. Their *Bon Marché* on Rue de Sèvres in Paris was the largest emporium in the world, offering global wares, fixed prices, 'advertorials' in fashion journals and promotional events. The global appetite predated M. de Vogüé.

By the 1860s, Irish linen-trader Alexander Stewart was earning $1 million a year from his eight-storey department store on Broadway, New York. Rival stores – Macy's, Altman, Lord & Taylor – proliferated and the entire section between 9th and 23rd Streets was soon known as Ladies' Mile. Britain was quick to catch on to these changes in shopping habits. It was Yorkshireman William Whiteley's ambition to sell 'everything from a pin to an elephant'. His eponymous store employing 6,000 staff opened in 1885. It was so vast it had a golf course on its roof. Adolf Hitler later earmarked it as his London headquarters and ordered the Luftwaffe not to bomb it.[123] Global consumerism and the new shopping habits were not just European and US phenomena: by the turn of the twentieth century, there was a department store – *Paris en America* – in Belém at the mouth of the Amazon. Not just the luxuries but the building itself were imported from Europe.

Critics of globalization blame the corporation for mass-consumerism. But it was only in the late 19th century that the corporation finally began to respond to the already powerful demands of global consumers.

The benevolent butcher

> 'It is not from the benevolence of the butcher, the brewer, or the baker that we expect our dinner, but from their regard to their own interest.'

> Adam Smith, 1776

Fifty years ago, America's ten largest corporations included General Motors, Standard Oil, General Electric, US Steel and AT&T – pioneers of the modern corporation.[124] From the 1860s, key improvements in business management and finance were allied to major technological innovations – the steam-ship, railroad, telegraph – and helped to create the giant corporation familiar today. Daniel McCallam, general super-intendent of the Erie Railroad, is widely credited as being the first modern management theorist. Western Union built a monopoly as ruthlessly as the Dutch East Indies Company. Inventions of commercial importance included the light bulb, the typewriter, the fountain pen, the air brake, the Kodak camera, the movie projector, the phonograph, and the zipper.

All this helped built the power of domestic industry, but the most important development in trans-continental trade was refrigeration.[125] Refrigeration was to the nineteenth-century butcher what spices had been in the sixteenth century – a gift for extending shelf life and making meat an everyday luxury. As with many pivotal inventions, there is little agreement about who actually invented refrigeration. Several US inven-tors were at work on domestic refrigerators from the early 1800s, but by the mid nineteenth century James Harrison in Australia seemed to be in the lead on refrigerated transport – until his effort to get chilled beef to England aboard the sailing ship *Norfolk* in the early 1870s ended in malodorous failure. Raoul Pictet in Switzerland also had a promising technology, but his machinery ended up freezing the first artificial ice rink in London. Frenchman Ferdinand Carré succeeded in instal-ling a commercial system aboard the first refrigerated ship *Paraguay*, which began shipping beef from Argentina to France in 1877.

On *Fortune* magazine's 1955 top ten list was the Great Atlantic and Pacific Tea Company (A&P), which started life in 1859 as a tea, coffee and spice mail-order firm selling at a premium out of Vesey Street in New York. Alongside it were two meat-packing companies founded by a butcher and a ditch-digger: Gus Swift and Philip Armour. In the late nineteenth century, these two entrepreneurs simultaneously spotted the potential to slash the transport costs of Midwest beef if railroad cars could be refrigerated. Swift did it first, halving prices for East Coast consumers. Swift's management style was dominant: he convinced his staff to put their entire life savings into the company when financial markets balked during the panic of 1893.[126]

The meat-packing industry made beef an everyday luxury, but there was nothing benevolent about these butchers. Chicago became the world's largest concentration of industrial capital, mass production and human misery. The stockyards attracted visitors as various as Charles Dickens and actress Sarah Bernhardt. 'Once having seen them', wrote Rudyard Kipling, 'you will never forget the sight.' Philip Armour, himself a workaholic, fiercely resisted any efforts to improve hygiene and labour standards in Packingtown, despite the adverse publicity of Upton Sinclair's exposé *The Jungle* (1906).[127] McDonald's is positively benign compared to the nineteenth-century meat-packing firms.

While Swift and Armour believed the secret to mass markets was screwing down prices by squeezing suppliers and workers, another entrepreneur thought the exact opposite. Henry John Heinz started selling jars of horseradish sauce made to his mother's recipe to the discerning housewives of Pittsburgh in the early 1860s. He believed overworked US housewives would pay *more* for high-quality, time-saving produce. Urbanization was leading to the disappearance of household vegetable gardens, and housewives needed help in the kitchen. And the American diet, a legacy of the Puritan suspicion of spice, had become bland. For Heinz, the future of spices was not as individual commodities, but as ingredients in branded foodstuffs.

Heinz was right. His product range was soon far greater

than the '57 Varieties' slogan, but he kept it because he liked the look of the numbers. Heinz benefited from innovations in refrigeration, transport and packaging; invested in employee welfare; and he did something unthinkable to Phil Armour. He lobbied for higher federal standards on food quality.[128] Heinz made his first sales trip to London's Fortnum & Mason in 1886. He clearly had global ambition. 'Mountains and oceans do not furnish any impassable barrier to the extension of trade,' he confided to his diary. 'Our market is the world.' But this was wishful thinking. Heinz's global operation outside the USA in 1905 amounted to an office near the Tower of London and a factory in Peckham.[129] Geo. Hormel of Austin, Minnesota also saw the potential, opening a luncheon-meat operation in 1891. The added ingredients of Hormel Spiced Ham (renamed Spam in the 1930s) were not so much spices but salt, water, sugar and sodium nitrite.

Compared to Chicago's stockyards, London's Smithfield market – dating back to the tenth century – was chaotic. Slaughtering a quarter of a million cattle and a million and a half sheep each year, it was notoriously dirty and crowded by the mid nineteenth century. When the Corporation of London eventually bowed to public pressure and built new and more spacious premises in 1868, it laid the market out with 162 identically sized stalls. But the stuffy gentlemanly capitalists of the City of London didn't see Liverpool butcher Derek Vestey coming.

The Vestey dynasty was Britain's answer to Swift, Armour, Heinz and Hormel. The US population had more than doubled to 98 million between 1870 and 1913. This huge domestic market gave a major boost to the development of strong corporations – and kept them busy. The Vesteys had their eyes on a bigger market still; the British Empire. By 1895 the firm was importing eggs from China and beef from Brazil to

London's first cold store. The company supplied canned 'bully beef' to troops around the world in the First World War. Ginger did little to improve the taste, but bully beef made William Vestey a fortune and earned him a knighthood.

In 1923, Vestey married his US stenographer Evelene Brodstone. Brodstone became the world's highest-paid female executive, credited with global trouble-shooting on five continents. Vestey's was a vertically-integrated company, controlling huge livestock estates in Latin America, South Africa and Australia, operating its own shipping line, running London cold stores and a chain of butchers' shops, as well as reexporting canned meat and powdered eggs across the British Empire.[130] This family-owned business became the first large-scale global corporation, and the Vesteys Britain's wealthiest family.[131]

The benefits of empire were reflected in the British economy as a whole. When Britain repealed the Corn Laws and Navigation Acts, it embraced free trade on behalf of its empire, and lent hard on France, Germany, China, Persia, the Ottoman Empire, Africa and Latin America to lower trade tariffs. The value of British trade increased tenfold between 1820 and 1870.[132] In the period of the Meridian conference, a quarter of *all* international trade was British – truly a lion's share. World trade continued to grow between 1870 and 1913, and Britain still dominated. British exports tripled over this period, most of them to an empire now in excess of 410 million people. Despite the free trade rhetoric, British imperial administrators discriminated in favour of home products, from heavy machinery and textiles to tinned beef and Camp Coffee.

Rapid industrialization and increasing productivity in Germany, France, Mexico, Japan and the USA started to nibble into the UK's share of global trade. By 1913, eight per cent of

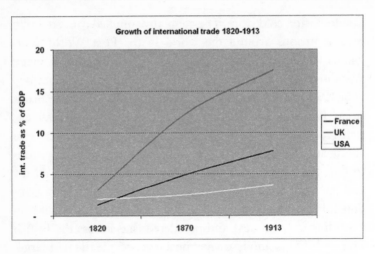

all economic activity in the world was exported merchandise, up from five per cent in 1870. But despite the dreams of Heinz and Hormel, the US economy remained overwhelmingly domestic, and in France, nine out of ten workers produced for the home market. On the eve of the First World War, Britain was still the dominant trading nation, controlling nearly a fifth of all international trade. One in five British workers was producing for export.

'Life offered, at a low cost and with the least trouble, conveniences, comforts and amenities beyond the compass of the richest and most powerful monarchs of other ages,' wrote English economist John Maynard Keynes triumphantly of this pre-war period of everyday luxury. 'The inhabitant of London could order by telephone, sipping his morning tea in bed, the various products of the whole earth, in such quantity as he might see fit, and reasonably expect their early delivery upon his doorstep.'[133]

Reasonable or not, these expectations were shattered in 1914. The Vesteys may have had a Great War, but world trade stagnated from 1913 to 1950. World war was followed by the Great Depression, when tariff barriers were re-erected in many countries, then by the Second World War. World trade, totalling $17 billion in 1913, had limped up to $24 billion by 1929, but was back to $21 billion in 1950. German, Japanese and British traders were especially hit hard. Not so the Americans.

The 'golden age' of global trade

'In the future there will be two kinds of corporations; those that go global, and those that go bankrupt.'
C. Michael Armstrong, CEO, AT&T

'Nothing you have ever experienced,' the down-on-his-luck commodity trader played by Dan Aykroyd warns Eddie Murphy's panhandler-made-good as they enter the New York Commodity Exchange in the 1983 film *Trading Places*, 'will prepare you for the unlimited carnage you are about to witness.' In the real-life carnage of 1939–45, it was Britain and the USA that traded places. The USA had become the world's largest economy as far back as 1871, and this sleeping giant of the world economy awoke in the Second World War. By the late 1940s, the USA edged past Britain to become the predominant power in world trade. In spite of all the challenges of the Sputnik era, it would hold on to this position.

America's dramatic overtaking of Britain in world trade would have come as no surprise to Willoughby M. McCormick, selling root beer door to door in Baltimore in 1889. In the late nineteenth century, the spice trade had become a collection of family enterprises looking for ways to shorten global supply-chains and still feed the everyday hunger for the exotic. The teenage McCormick's motto was 'Make The Best –

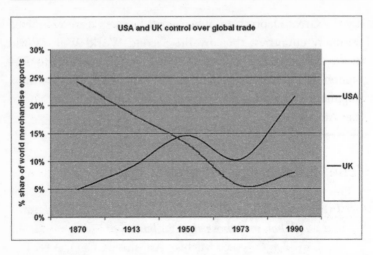

Someone Will Buy It.' He soon made enough money to buy out a local spice trader and by 1900 that 'Someone' did not have to be American: McCormick had a sales office in New York and was exporting spices to four continents. In 1905 the company got into tea and was an early promoter of the tea bag. It floated on the stock market in 1926, weathered the Great Depression and emerged in the 1930s and 1940s as a company admired for its management, packaging innovations and ability to sterilize spices. It was a philanthropic corporation – but with global ambition. Many other US businesses also quietly improved productivity in the 1920s and 1930s. In the 1940s the war effort mobilized US logistics on a global scale – Spam fed the Soviet army and jeeps moved it around. US corporations began to look beyond the domestic market in earnest.

After 1945, McCormick went on a spending spree, buying out first its US and then English, French and Dutch competitors. By the 1970s it had operations and joint ventures in dozens of countries, and a gross profit margin of around 40 per cent.[134] This Sparks, Maryland company had become a spice trader in the best traditions of Venice, Amsterdam and

Salem. It would be stretching the point to claim that the Sputnik Contraction had a direct impact on the spice trade, but the massive US investments in technology – both military and civilian – accelerated the nation's global reach. Domination of world trade no longer relied on imperial preference. Multinational corporations would create their own empires based on global supply-chains and aggressive marketing.

Trading economies of all sorts benefited from the period of unparalleled growth between 1950 and 1973. Western Europe gradually recovered and started to trade again. Exports from Africa and Latin America grew four or five per cent each year. Trading from both the Soviet Union and Asia grew at almost ten per cent a year – the fastest rate yet seen. 'The world economy grew very much faster from 1950 to 1973 than it had ever done before,' according to Angus Maddison, the leading statistician of economic history. 'It was a golden age of unparalleled prosperity.'

By the mid-1960s, the proportion of world production traded internationally had surpassed the previous high of 1929 and before long a tenth of all economic activity was traded across borders. In the following chapters we will examine the key contributions of labour, finance and culture in fuelling this astonishing period of global contraction. From the mid-1950s, the corporation developed a global appetite, epitomized by Sony's portable transistor radio. The first McDonald's restaurant opened in Canada in 1967. In 1971, Coca-Cola decided it would like to teach the world to sing.

Despite the oil crisis of 1973, world trade grew at a more modest five per cent a year right through to the end of the twentieth century. In only one year did the quantity of goods in world trade actually fall: 2001, exacerbated by the destruction of the World Trade Center. Some pundits saw this as the end of

the Golden Age, but the latest figures from the World Trade
Organization show that trade is accelerating. In 2004, global
trade topped $11 trillion, up nine per cent from the previous
year, and double the level of 1973. The 2004 growth rate of
exports in the Asian region was almost 15 per cent. In China,
exporting is not the cream on the cake of domestic growth – it
is the economy's *raison d'être*, and trade grew a staggering 20
per cent in 2004.[135] Today, one in five people around the
world is producing merchandise for export, many of them
working for 64,000 multinational corporations. Never have so
many luxuries been traded around the world.

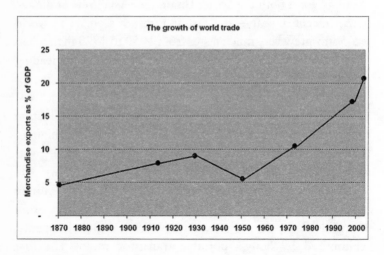

McCormick is a barracuda to its suppliers and customers, but
a minnow in the world trade pond. The company's sales in
2003 totalled US$2.7 billion – nowhere near high enough to
get into *Fortune* magazine's annual 'beauty parade' called the
Global 500 (Masco, the US kitchen and bathroom company
ranked number 500 in 2004, had sales of $12.5 billion).
McCormick may be the leading member of the oligopoly that
controls the global spice trade, but that trade is worth $8.5

billion – just 0.1 per cent of global merchandise in 2004. Today, the world's largest corporation Wal-Mart employs 1,700,000 people. Proportionately, it is twice as big as the Dutch VOC at its peak, and is growing 10 per cent a year.

Wal-Mart is headquartered in remote Bentonville, Arkansas. In 2005, the Chinese electrical company Haier briefly pondered whether to buy US manufacturer Maytag, makers of the sacred Hoover brand. This flexing of Chinese corporate muscle caused patriotic shock in the USA. Haier is based in the port of Qingdao, in the north-east Chinese province of Shandong, previously barely known in the West as the home of a brewery founded by German colonialists in 1903. Wal-Mart and Haier both lie on the same line of latitude 36 degrees north of the equator. This is the new global meridian, and it is dictated not by nations or astronauts but by multinational supply-chains.

The 'platinum age' of global supply-chains

We are now in a platinum age of international trade, led by the supply-chains of giant corporations, that makes the contractions of the 1880s and 1950s seem like tickles. Is this a good thing? Economists from Turgot and Adam Smith right through to Milton Friedman, Joseph Stiglitz and Amartya Sen today have asserted that trade increases growth, bringing wealth to both the exporter and especially the importer. 'A rising tide lifts all ships'; 'wealth trickles down'. Just look at Amsterdam in the 1650s, Paris in the 1850s, London in the 1880s, Bentonville in the 1960s, Bangalore in 2005 – or look at Burma and North Korea – if you don't think global trade is the answer, say globalization advocates.

On the 500th anniversary of the global spice trade, two academics from Berkeley and Harvard wrote a paper entitled 'Does Trade Cause Growth?'[136] There is hardly a more pressing question in a world where 1.1 billion people cannot afford even the cheapest everyday luxury because they live below the global poverty line of one dollar a day. After detailed statistical analysis of hundreds of countries, Jeffrey Frankel and David Romer announced their results: openness to international trade *is* good for growth. The results were widely publicized and gave a new sense of urgency to the recently founded World Trade Organization (WTO).

A few months later, riot police were battling anti-globalization protesters on the streets of Seattle, host to the annual meeting of the WTO. The WTO claimed it was trying to reduce barriers to trade (such as agricultural subsidies in rich nations) so that poorer nations can enjoy the wealth that trade brings. The protesters said the organization was in the pocket of global multinationals, trying to suck profits and intellectual property out of developing nations. They couldn't both be right.

Both were wrong. There turned out to be little convincing statistical evidence that opening up to trade causes economic growth. It depends on what sort and size of trader you are, who your neighbours are, when you do it, and how you do it. Religion, language and geography are defining factors, but the benefits also depend on what sorts of policies are put in place to encourage trade. Contrast the cautious, state-managed opening up of the Korean economy in the 1970s to the madcap 1990s liberalization in Russia. Contrast the prosperous USA, where average tariffs on imports were just 7.4 per cent in 2000, to even wealthier Norway, with tariffs of 32 per cent. Opening up to world trade is not a universal panacea. Countries have many options to manage their integration into global trade, despite the strictures of the WTO. And in the end, it is not countries that actually trade with each other – it is firms and households.[137]

After Seattle, it transpired that the scale of global trade had been exaggerated. Half the countries of the world don't trade with each other at all. Of the 200,000 commodities that make up world trade statistics, many are bulky goods like bags of cement that mainly get used at home, sometimes get moved between neighbours but are easy to produce or too heavy to be worth trading across continents. Only the smallest islands these days don't have a cement factory within a few hours' truck ride.

Network of world trade, 2003 (billion dollars)

	Total exports	Exports within own region	Exports outside own region	% of exports outside region
North America	997	404	593	59%
Latin America	378	59	319	84%
Western Europe	3,145	2,130	1,015	32%
C./E. Europe/Baltic States/CIS	401	98	303	75%
Africa	173	18	155	90%
Middle East	299	22	277	93%
Asia	1,901	949	952	50%
Totals	**7,294**	**3,680**	**3,614**	**50%**

How much international trade is actually global, in the sense we have defined it? Buried in the appendices of the WTO's annual trade statistics reports is a complicated table called the 'network of world merchandise trade by region'.[138] When the numbers are deciphered, they show that half of all international trade takes place within the same region or continent.

According to my calculations in the table above, the Middle East and Africa are most engaged in global trade, with 90 per cent or more of their exports going elsewhere. Latin America is also doing quite a lot of inter-regional trade, though most of it only going as far as North America. The former communist countries export three-quarters of their trade outside the region, but again most of it only goes as far as Western Europe. North America's trade is over half global; Asia's is half local. Europe, far and away the biggest exporter, is mainly a local trader. Nor is it necessarily the case that the proportion of trade that is global is actually increasing. 'People talk about the "global economy",' says Michael Milken, former junk bond king and jailbird and now chairman of a research institute, 'but it's really a market of regional economies – some strong, some less so.'[139]

The antagonists of the Battle in Seattle – economists, policy-makers and campaigners – all exaggerated the global scale of trade. Ordinary people were more realistic. In 2003, the Pew Research Center (a trust founded by Sun Oil Company founder Joseph Pew in 1948) asked 38,000 people in 44 countries what they thought about growing international trade and business ties. In 31 countries, a majority saw increased international trade happening round them, but in countries as varied as France, Bangladesh, Venezuela, Ivory Coast and Bulgaria, half or more of people said they *didn't* see any increase in international trade. When asked if they were for or against trade, on average 12 per cent of respondents around the world said that global trade was actually *bad* for their family, while another nine per cent weren't sure or didn't want to say. These critics and sceptics, in rich and poor countries alike, equate to one in five of the world's population.

Many people don't know what to make of global trade. Global corporations like McDonald's, Wal-Mart and Microsoft provide the everyday luxuries we love to hate. Nearly 50 million people a day in 120 countries eat at McDonald's. Over 140 million people shop in Wal-Mart stores every week. Half a billion people use Microsoft Windows. But labour unions, smaller competitors, non-governmental organizations – and governments – are at permanent loggerheads against them. Corporate CEOs are the new 'nabobs', admired and loathed in equal measure. Half of the biggest economies in the world are now multinational corporations, we are told, and they are incapable of acting responsibly because of their obligation to make profits for their shareholders. But businesses have to go global to survive, say management gurus. Corporations are the most efficient way of meeting consumers' needs, say economists. Multinationals could halve poverty and battle AIDS if there was less red tape, claim CEOs. The trade debate has become as rhetorical as the 1550 Valladolid debate on the status of the Native American, or the 1788 oratory to impeach Warren Hastings.

Today, around ten per cent of the world's total economic activity enters global trade. This may be a lower figure than many people expect: more Tasmanian Devil than stampeding elephant. On the other hand, this trade amounts to around $1 trillion, and much of it is in the hands of the so-called global corporations.

The global corporation: fact or fiction?

In 1983, economist Theodore Levitt wrote an influential paper called 'The Globalization of Markets' for the *Harvard Business Review*. He suggested that with the homogenization of world tastes, global companies should sell standardized products using standardized marketing all around the world. Was Levitt right? Are corporations getting bigger and more global? The question is surprisingly difficult to answer. 'Multinationals are everywhere', Grazia Ietto-Gillies at London's South

Bank University told me, 'except in economic theories and economics departments.'

Disquiet about the scale and power of trading companies has existed since the days of the Venetian spice monopoly. There were already around 500 multinational corporations in the year 1600, and that number doubled by 1700. The state-chartered East Indies companies were not just more powerful than governments – they *were* governments. Yet when they fell from favour and ran into debt, governments rapidly abolished them.

By the mid nineteenth century, there were some 2,500 companies with operations in more than one country, and 3,000 on the eve of the Great War. US President Ulysses Grant (1822–85) suffered from big business corruption in his administration and referred to the rent-seeking habitués of the Willard Hotel in Washington DC as 'those damned lobbyists'. The 1890 Sherman Antitrust Act led to investigations of 'big sugar' and 'big steel'. Under Presidents Theodore Roosevelt and William Howard Taft, 'trust-busting' made headway, with action against the American Tobacco Company and Standard Oil Trust. Sentiments against Standard Oil were whipped up by the first anti-corporate book: *The History of the Standard Oil Company* (1904) by 'muckraking' journalist Ida Tarbell, as influential as Las Casas' sixteenth-century exposé of Spanish brutality in Latin America and Adam Smith's peroration of the East Indies companies. Corporate-taming legislation enjoyed a brief revival in the 1930s, challenging the dominance of large retailers like A&P.

In the golden age of trade from the 1950s, many companies looked abroad, and there were 18,500 multinationals by the late 1980s. These companies enjoyed widespread public and government support (although the AT&T group was dismantled in 1982–84). *Global Inc.* – a recent anti-global coffee-table book if that's not a contradiction in terms – opens with a stunning graph plotting the historical growth of multi-nationals on one axis against the growth of countries on a second axis. In the mid-1980s, transnational corporations (TNCs) appear to suddenly outstrip countries.[140] A new period of tension arose in the 1990s, when over 30,000 new transnationals were formed. In the middle of the decade came the Year of the Sweatshop, when anti-corporate critics alleged abuses by multinationals in Nigeria, Colombia, Indonesia, and at home.

After a string of corporate scandals in the US and Europe (Enron, WorldCom, Parmalat), the desire to challenge the basis of corporate power – which has been sporadic in history – seems to be returning. New York Attorney General Eliot Spitzer has been cast as a modern-day Edmund Burke or Ida Tarbell. The long-running and inconclusive cases by the US Department of Justice and European Union against Microsoft (1998–2004) were efforts to make anti-monopoly regulation stick, and such regulations now exist in half the countries of the world. Today, there are over 63,834 transnational corporations. Their 866,000 foreign affiliates employ 53 million people – equivalent to the entire workforce of Central America and the Caribbean.[141] The historical tension between state, corporation, consumer and citizen is resurfacing, but in a global context. Have corporations becomes too powerful?

In 2000, the US-based Institute for Policy Studies (IPS) claimed that half of the world's top 100 economies were multinational corporations.[142] The finding immediately became a hot potato in the globalization debate. 'By now, we've all heard the statistics,' wrote Naomi Klein in *No Logo*, 'how corporations like Shell and Wal-Mart bask in budgets bigger than the gross domestic product of most nations.' But the IPS was criticized for comparing gross domestic product with sales, making companies look bigger than they really were. 'The impression gained by the anti-globalist rhetoric is that corporations are now typically bigger than the typical country in the world', according to Paul de Grauwe and Filip Camerman, 'and this is manifestly incorrect.' In his book *Open World*, Philippe Legrain accused Naomi Klein – not the IPS – of 'a schoolgirl error' or – worse – deliberate dishonesty.[143]

In an effort to clear the air, I have corrected the error.[144] Four companies – Wal-Mart, BP, Royal Dutch/Shell and Exxon rank among the world's top 50 economies. A list of Global 100 economies includes 37 corporations in it, as the table shows. If we take the top 150 economies, 79 are companies. On that basis, it is true that over half of the world's largest economies are indeed companies.

The Global 100: countries and corporations (in italics)

Rank	Global 100	Income (US$bn)	Rank	Global 100	Income (US$bn)
1	United States	11667.5	51	Romania	73.2
2	Japan	4623.4	52	Nigeria	72.1
3	Germany	2714.4	53	Peru	68.4
4	United Kingdom	2140.9	54	Ukraine	65.1
5	France	2002.6	55	*General Motors*	63.5
6	Italy	1672.3	56	*Daimler Chrysler*	58.0
7	China	1649.3	57	Bangladesh	56.8
8	Spain	991.4	58	*Toyota Motor*	56.6
9	Canada	979.8	59	*Ford Motor*	56.5
10	India	691.9	60	*General Electric*	50.1
11	Korea, Rep.	679.7	61	*Total*	50.1
12	Mexico	676.5	62	Morocco	50.1
13	Australia	631.3	63	*Chevron Texaco*	48.5
14	Brazil	604.9	64	Vietnam	45.2
15	Russian Fed	582.4	65	Slovak Republic	41.1
16	Netherlands	577.3	66	Kazakhstan	40.7
17	Switzerland	359.5	67	*ConocoPhillips*	39.9
18	Belgium	349.8	68	*AXA*	39.9
19	Sweden	346.4	69	*Allianz*	39.0
20	Turkey	302.0	70	*Volkswagen*	36.3
21	Austria	290.1	71	*Citigroup*	35.5

22	Indonesia	257.6	72	*ING Group*	34.7
23	Norway	250.2	73	Croatia	34.2
24	Denmark	243.0	74	*NTT*	33.0
25	Poland	241.8	75	Slovenia	32.2
26	South Africa	212.8	76	*AIG*	32.1
27	Greece	203.4	77	*IBM*	31.6
28	Finland	186.6	78	Luxembourg	31.1
29	Ireland	183.6	79	Ecuador	30.3
30	Portugal	168.3	80	*Siemens*	30.0
31	Thailand	163.5	81	*Carrefour*	29.6
32	Hong Kong, China	163.0	82	Tunisia	28.2
33	Iran, Islamic Rep.	162.7	83	*Hitachi*	27.5
34	Argentina	151.5	84	Guatemala	27.5
35	Malaysia	117.8	85	*Ass. Generali*	27.3
36	Venezuela, RB	109.3	86	*Matsushita E I*	26.6
37	Czech Republic	107.0	87	*McKesson*	26.4
38	Singapore	106.8	88	*Honda Motor*	26.4
39	Hungary	99.7	89	*Hewlett-Packard*	26.2
40	New Zealand	99.7	90	*Nissan Motor*	26.2
41	Colombia	97.4	91	*Fortis*	24.8
42	Pakistan	96.1	92	*Sinopec*	24.6
43	*Wal-Mart Stores*	94.5	93	*Berkshire Hath.*	24.4
44	Chile	94.1	94	*ENI*	24.3
45	*BP*	93.5	95	Bulgaria	24.1
46	*Exxon Mobil*	88.8	96	Serbia & Mont	24.0
47	*Royal Dutch/Shell*	88.1	97	*Home Depot*	24.0
48	Philippines	86.4	98	*Aviva*	24.0
49	Algeria	84.6	99	*HSBC Holdings*	23.8
50	Egypt, Arab Rep.	75.1	100	*Deutsche Telekom*	23.6

Source: World Bank, Fortune & author calculations

In the mid-2000s, both companies and countries are growing fast, and it is difficult to judge whether and when Wal-Mart will overtake Pakistan; or if the major oil companies will outstrip Chile. Advocates of free trade say that the size comparison is fatuous anyway because countries still have the power to regulate corporations – and because the top 30 countries earn far more than the biggest corporations. Critics point out that corporate lobbyists outnumber legislators 30 to one in Washington DC and Brussels. Corporations today have more staff, more money and more access to international decision-makers like the WTO in Geneva than many countries.[145] The integrity of the nation-state as the organizing principle of the modern world order must be compromised when every single one of the *Fortune* top 100 global companies earns more than Trinidad and Tobago, the country with the world's median gross national income. These companies are now unquestionably big players on the world scene, in the sense that Venezuela and Nigeria are. But how global are they?

Corporations like to make global claims: 'solutions for a small planet'; 'world leader in luxury'; 'refreshes people across the globe'; 'kyosei with the people of the world'; 'Our passion is to put a YUM on our customer's faces all over the world'.[146] But the standard definition of 'transnational' is very weak: if Bolivian brewery Cervecería La Paceña takes a 10 per cent stake in a Paraguayan bottle-maker, it would technically be defined as a transnational corporation (TNC).[147] There are more TNCs headquartered in Denmark than in the USA, UK and Japan combined. Many of the world's 64,000 multinationals are small companies doing a little bit of business with their neighbours.

A better guide to whether companies are global or not is the UN's 'transnationality index' – the average ratio of foreign to total sales, assets and employees.[148] Coca-Cola – one of the world's most recognized brands – is highly transnational. General Electric, founded in the same year as the word 'global', is steadily transforming from a predominantly US-based corporation into overseas markets. Conversely, McDonald's, despite having restaurants in 120 countries, remains stubbornly fixed to its North American heritage. On average, according to the UN, companies have become steadily more transnational over the last decade. In 1993, over half (53 per cent) of the operations of the most international 100 companies were in their home country. By 2002, after the global contraction of the 1990s, well over half of their operations (57 per cent) were abroad. In the early 1990s, only ten of these large companies had three-quarters of their operations abroad. A decade later, the number had doubled to twenty.

Some researchers propose a more sophisticated approach, measuring *how many* other countries the TNCs have spread into. Alan Rugman at Indiana University has pored over the annual reports of the world's 500 largest companies, and come up with a still more rigorous definition of a 'global company'. Global means sales of 20 per cent or more in all of the three main economic regions (Europe, the Americas, Asia), but less than 50 per cent in any one region. His conclusion is that only nine of the top 500 corporations are truly global. Companies like McDonald's, Nike and Wal-Mart, favourite targets for anti-globalization protesters, are strong in one or at most two regions. Global companies like Coca Cola, Louis Vuitton and Philips, Rugman told me, 'are so few as to render the concept of "globalization" meaningless.'

These global companies come from a range of sectors, but they are all purveyors of the exotic – sometimes a daily indulgence like a coke, sometimes a less frequent luxury. But all, like the spice traders of the nineteenth century, are facing the challenge of keeping their products desirably distinct at a time of falling costs and rising demand. Rugman challenges Theodore Levitt and a generation of globalization gurus, by claiming big businesses will become *less* global in future. More and more companies in the Global 500 are providing services not goods, he believes, and these businesses tend to be more regional in their ambitions and capabilities.

Rugman's methodology and conclusions will be disputed by both sides.[149] For example, many service companies are developing global ambition, and some global manufacturers, like IBM, are moving into services. The internet will accelerate these trends. The classic example of a local service business that cannot go global is hairdressing. But parts of even this business (like taking bookings) could be outsourced. Many large corporations, like Wal-Mart, already have global supply-chains and if their current business is mainly in North America and Europe, they are growing fast in Asia.

What do we learn from these studies? In the last decade, big corporations have got bigger, and many are as big as countries. Their international reach is growing, based on global supply-chains, although few are yet truly global corporations in terms of their sales. But it is misleading to equate big with global, and neither necessarily equals American. Proportionate to their economy, France and Britain are home to many more giant TNCs than the USA. French retailer Carrefour and Dutch store Ahold are more global than the giant Wal-Mart; and BP is more global than ExxonMobil.[150] Today Brazil, China, India, Mexico and Thailand are all home to Global 500 corporations. Cemex of Mexico is more transnational than Sony.

Neither their size, nor their global reach, nor their home base alone explains the controversy that multinational corporations arouse. Law professor Joel Bakan, reviewing the historical development of the legal form of the corporation, concluded that it is a legal institution with inherent patholo-gical tendencies. In contrast, John Micklethwait and Adrian Wooldridge's history of the company refutes the silent corpo-rate takeover thesis. After an admittedly 'irresponsible youth', they argue, the limited-liability joint-stock company came of age to become a positive force worldwide.[151]

The history of global trade illustrates how this debate became polarized. Global trade is about both extent and intent. Global minnows like Elihu Yale or McCormick have attracted less criticism than ambitious sharks like the Dutch

VOC or Wal-Mart. From the mid-1990s, as in the 1780s and 1890s, arose a pervasive feeling that corporations were 'over-large *and* over here, there and everywhere'. In a sense, they were doing their job too well – bringing luxury too easily within reach. In the early 1960s, McDonald's introduced signs in all its restaurants announcing over one billion hamburgers sold. By the mid-1990s, it had to replace the signs because it had passed 99 billion – there was no room left on the signs.

Consumers still wanted the sights and colours of the globe, but they were prepared to bite the hand that was feeding them, because global trade was failing to deliver. Corporations were serving up banality instead of exoticism, and were seen to be cutting corners – both ethical and environmental – in the process. This is why the scrutiny of global supply-chains, beginning in 1995, focused on ubiquitous branded goods such as petrol, trainers and hamburgers, rather than any of the other 200,000 goods in international trade, such as antiques (World Customs Union six-digit code number 970600), insulin (300331), or accessories for dolls (650291).

The Vestey family experienced this change acutely. It became considered unpatriotic for its vigorous efforts to minimize income tax payments. It is probably the only family to have faced land disputes on three continents: challenged in Australia by Gurindji aboriginals (1966–75); by local crofters around the 40,000-acre Assynt estate in the Scottish Highlands in 2004; and in Venezuela in 2005 as part of President Hugo Chavez's land reform programme. The company become embroiled in the anti-globalization movement when Tim Vestey was called as a witness in the 'McLibel' trial about whether the company had supplied beef from Brazil to McDonald's in 1980s (it had). In the late 1990s, several members of the younger generation of Vesteys became vociferous vegetarians and high-profile anti-globalization protesters. 'If you're on the work treadmill', noted self-proclaimed 'eco-toff' and Vestey heiress Julia Stevenson, 'who has time to read *The Ecologist?*'[152]

But managing global supply-chains proved to be a major challenge – beyond the power (and appetite) of many individual governments and too risky and complex for many companies. Closing loopholes in corporate governance systems and accounting standards was necessary but not sufficient. So from the late 1990s, the United Nations and other international institutions cautiously introduced partnerships, norms, codes of conduct, compacts and voluntary initiatives, involving labour unions and non-governmental groups as well as businesses, to promote responsibility and accountability in global trade. The jury is out on whether corporate social responsibility can deliver.

Many people mistrust giant corporations and appear to feel more comfortable with much smaller organizations. But don't the large traders have the expertise, resources and duty to tackle problems in global trade? In the early 2000s, the oil industry was central to implementing a transparency initiative encouraging oil-rich governments to tell their populations how much money is paid for drilling concessions. When Nike, after years of work investigating sweatshops, announced the results of its factory inspections in 2005, few consumers applauded the effort – or criticized the slow progress in improving labour conditions. Nike's share price, let alone the price of trainers, did not flicker.

The coming global contraction – perhaps only a decade away – is unlikely to see a wholesale reform of the corporate legal framework, as some critics demand. Anti-corporate campaigners are more sophisticated in detecting corporate abuses than they are in offering plausible alternatives. But the current plethora of voluntary initiatives will surely give way to major innovations in how relations between states, corporations and citizens are governed at the global level. Global trade will feel the impacts.

The spread of universal expectations for high labour standards may reduce some of the comparative advantage behind long supply-claims. As we will see in the next chapter, this has happened in the past. As developing countries expand economically, in a context where trade is growing faster that the overall world economy, they will start to eat into Western purchasing power, reducing the east–west trade gradient still further. Regional trade will grow at the expense of global. Some goods in global trade – green beans from Kenya to Kensington – will simply become 'unaffordable luxuries' when traders or consumers are forced to pay the full environmental costs of air freight and local pollution. Crucially, global consumers continuously reassert their demand for the exotic. They have little loyalty to traders, as Totonac vanilla producers and William Whiteley discovered. The search for new sources of global inspiration has something implacable, almost cannibalistic about it.

Some likely developments of the coming contraction can already be discerned in the spice trade. This is now a plain vanilla business, but its recent history may still provide insights into the future patterns of global trade.

Spice of life

In January 2004, hundreds of spice traders from thirty countries converged on Hyderabad, the capital of Andhra Pradesh. This Indian state makes a plausible claim to have the world's fieriest cuisine – as measured in the internationally agreed measurement of spiciness, the Scoville Unit.[153] In the late 1990s I spent several weeks working in the village of Mulkanoor with very small rural banks. Dishes like *til ki* – a delicious, searingly hot chutney of sesame seeds, tamarind and hot green peppers – were served for lunch, dinner and breakfast.

So Hyderabad was an appropriate venue to host the 8th World Spice Congress. Delegates deserved a spicy breakfast before tackling tricky issues like improving the market for small cardamom seeds, banning the use of carcinogenic 'Sudan' red dyes, and reducing the destructive 'race to the bottom' between producing nations fighting to supply a handful of global buyers in the face of wildly fluctuating but generally downward prices. Two developments discussed at the congress look set to throw the spice trade into another period of global upheaval. The first is the use of communication technology by producers; the second is a revitalization of consumers' appetite for the exotic.

A small group of companies – McCormick, Man, Tone Bros – runs the world spice supply-chain, and governments have always been powerless in the face of an oligopoly.[154] In the 1980s, inspired by OPEC's oil cartel, Indonesia placed strict quotas on nutmeg production in an effort to push up prices reminiscent of the Dutch East India Company. The initiative unravelled because the Indonesians could not secure the participation of Grenada, and because of the age-old problem of rampant smuggling.[155] But if governments have less power, mobile phones and the internet are removing information asymmetries and providing new export niches in the spice market, to the benefit of producers and small traders. 'There just aren't so many secrets any more,' according to one Rotterdam spice trader. 'The farmers in Vietnam are walking around with mobile phones. They know the market price as soon as I do.'[156]

Today, the USA consumes a fifth of all traded spices, but

Singapore, Japan, Germany and France are all significant importers. The spice trade is global: in 2003, India spent as much on spice imports as the UK did; and Saudi Arabia as much as Spain.[157] Madagascar has edged ahead of traditional producers like China, India and Indonesia, while Brazil, Guatemala and Vietnam are also increasing their exports rapidly. For the nimble entrepreneur, this period of flux offers opportunities that may be missed by the big traders, as in the 1500s when Portuguese mariners broke the Venetian monopoly or the 1750s when Salem merchants stole a march on European companies. With modern technologies, arbitrage can be an attractive business for small operators with good market intelligence.

India still devotes 24,000 square kilometres to spice growing, an area larger than the whole state of Vermont or the farmland of Denmark, and produces two and a half million tonnes of spices a year. It has dozens of vibrant spice markets and consumes 90 per cent of production. Its exports – over US $400 million a year – are not to be sneezed at. In 2003, the spice trade came full circle when India started to earn more from exporting chilli peppers than its own black pepper. The Spices Board of India, working with local producer groups, is promoting exports with a strong focus on quality, backed by an 'Indian Spice' label. This is astute, because the market for local produce is growing faster than the market for inauthentic global brands.[158]

The reputation of Roquefort cheese and Murano glass date back to medieval times, and in the early twentieth century, French winemakers developed their system of *Appellation d'Origine Controllée* (AOC), in part for quality control but also to fight foreign competition. Italian consortia for Parmesan cheese (1934) and Parma ham (1963) followed suit. European place of origin labels now cover 100 products from

Modena balsamic vinegar in Italy and Meissen porcelain in Germany to Swiss watches, Czech Pilsener beer, Scotch whisky and Irish Waterford crystal. A recent survey found that 40 per cent of European consumers were willing to pay 10 per cent more for local labelled products.[159]

Outside Europe, strong local labels include Cape wines; Florida oranges; Darjeeling tea; Blue Mountain coffee; Bukhara carpets; Havana cigars; and Mexican Mezcal. Basmati rice exports are worth some US$600 million to India and Pakistan. In all, the world market for locally-labelled goods now amounts to $100–150 billion.[160] Indian pepper and authentic spices from elsewhere will benefit from this trend. As a gauge that the trend is genuine, McCormick has recently started labelling premium peppers with country of origin.

In mid-2005, Christian Aid blamed free trade for the suicides of 4,000 farmers in the Indian state of Andhra Pradesh over a five-year period, trapped with ever increasing debts and lower market prices.[161] Local-origin labels cannot alone deliver enough of a premium to avoid this tragic spiral of falling commodity costs. But many consumers now demand that exotic produce must include decent wages for producers.

In 1927, the Federación Nacional de Cafeteros de Colombia (Colombian Coffee-Growers Federation) was founded to support small coffee producers, and over time developed a financial buffer to support them when the world market price fell. This is the essence of the movement called 'fair trade'. In the post-war period, Christian activists in the USA and Northern Europe began to educate consumers about fair trade. In 1946, Mennonite Edna Ruth Byler imported handicrafts from Puerto Rico to the USA, followed by products made by Palestinians and Haitians. In the early 1970s, the initiative moved out of her basement, and in the mid-1990s was renamed *Ten Thousand Villages*.

During the 1960s, other organizations became involved in fair trade: Oxfam in the UK and Fair Trade Organisatie in the Netherlands launched trading subsidiaries. In 1979, Richard Adams set up Traidcraft – the first public limited company with an explicit mission to pay over the going rate for its supplies. In the 1980s, 'solidarity coffee' from small producer cooperatives in countries such as Nicaragua and Guatemala began to be served at progressive gatherings (it was often left undrunk). Higher quality fair-trade labelled coffee was launched in the Netherlands in 1986–1988 under the Max Havelaar mark, sourced from Mexico.

Fair-trade coffee sold well, and has enjoyed double-digit growth rates in the Netherlands, UK and USA. Many more consumers say they will buy fair-traded commodities. Fair-trade organizations are trying to understand how to get them to put their money where their mouths are. Mainstream traders, after dismissing fair trade as a fad for years, suddenly noticed the market growing out of a niche and rushed to get in on the act in 2004.

South Indian cooperatives began developing fair-trade labels for black pepper in 2003.[162] India is also leading a counter-attack to protect intellectual property. In a reprise of the eighteenth-century phase of bio-piracy, in the 1980s botanical prospectors shifted their attention to rainforests and other remote areas, looking for plants with medicinal properties – especially the elusive 'cure for cancer'. Indigenous people were powerless to protect their knowledge of the medicinal properties of plants. Two Indian expatriates based at the University of Mississippi Medical Centre, Jackson secured a patent for turmeric, even though it had been used as a medicine in India for thousands of years. In 1995, after widespread protests about bio-piracy, the patent was overturned. This landmark victory, according to Indian scientist Vandana Shiva, opens the way for peasants in developing countries to reclaim control over many natural commodities that are being pirated by corporations and academics.[163]

Indian spice growers are learning from the history of global trade. 'Ningalkku njangalude mazhakkalam edukkam, pakshe njangalude chedikale edukkan kazhiyilla', a Keralan farmer today would reply if asked for pepper seedlings by a bedraggled and avaricious mariner. '*You are welcome to our monsoons. But you may never take our plants.*'

5

MUSCLE: PLANET ON THE MOVE

'The discovery of America, and that of a passage to the East Indies by the Cape of Good Hope, are the two greatest and most important events recorded in the history of mankind . . . By uniting, in some measure, the most distant parts of the world, by enabling them to relieve one another's wants, to increase one another's enjoyments, and to encourage one another's industry, their general tendency would seem to be beneficial. To the natives, however . . . all the commercial benefits which can have resulted from those events have been sunk and lost in the dreadful misfortunes which they have occasioned.'

Adam Smith, *Wealth of Nations*, 1776

An Indian helicopter pilot trying to reach the remote Sentinel Islands after the 2004 *tsunami* came under attack – from bows and arrows. The photograph of this unbalanced military confrontation made newspaper front pages, light relief as the death toll from the Indian Ocean tidal waves mounted into the hundreds of thousands. The Sentinelese, now a few hundred individuals, have long been fiercely protective of their privacy. Marco Polo reported that they were 'very cruel, and kill and eat every foreigner whom they can lay their hands upon.' How this news got back to him remains a mystery.[164]

The flying arrow is a recurrent symbol of anti-globalization. In 1895, lone circumnavigator Joshua Slocum heard the swish of an arrow pass his ear as he was sailing close to the coast of Tierra del Fuego aboard his yacht *Spray*. A second arrow 'struck the mainmast, where it stuck fast, vibrating from the shock,' wrote Slocum of this typical 'Fuegian autograph'. Suspecting hostile Fuegians onshore, he reached for his 'dear old rifle'. Three Fuegians emerged from hiding and scarpered over the hills. Their weaponry was little changed from their ancestors, who arrived 10,000 years earlier, and no match for Slocum's Martini-Henry, the Swiss-Scottish rifle that became the imperial weapon of choice. Slocum, unlike the real-life riverboat sharpshooters who inspired Conrad's *Heart of Darkness*, tells us he was not shooting to kill. Perhaps he was just a bad shot.

As Magellan, Cook and many other planet-shrinkers discovered at the cost of their lives, many native peoples wanted only to be left alone and would use cudgels, axes – even the archetypal vat of boiling water – to defend their isolation from the rest of the world. So far, we have discussed globalization as a mental, exploratory and commercial process – imagining the globe, charting it and trading round it. This chapter turns to the experience of people on the move, as hunters, lovers, explorers, warriors, refugees, workers, tourists, and as commodities in their own right. While a few peoples, like the Sentinelese, have maintained their distance, globalization has transplanted huge numbers of people. Sometimes mobility was motivated by an innocent quest for the exotic; too often it was driven by a callous consumerism ready to exchange human lives for the novelty of the day.

The sheer scale of these waves of muscle defies the imagination, and their impacts make for sobering reading. For while mass-migrations have provided welcome escape and new opportunity, they have unleashed decimation, exploitation and disease on an unprecedented scale.

Early migrations – from Swindon to Sweden (100,000BC–AD1500)

The first global migrations began millions of years ago when small groups of modern humans began to spread from the 'crowded' savannas of East Africa. Early migrants often moved very slowly – just a few kilometres on average each year. One motivation was that in each generation, a handful of explorers would feel the need for fresh hunting and fresh marriage partners, and move several days walk from the older members of their clan. At times, migrants used boats instead of feet, and went much greater distances. Few of these earliest migrants left traces: one theory suggests that the entire human species is descended from a single woman – the so-called African Eve – who lived about 143,000 years ago. Her offspring numbered 50,000 people by 100,000 years ago – the same as the residents of Swindon today.

Could such small numbers have run out of space in Africa? Whether they were pushed out by population pressure, linguistic variation and tribal clashes; obsessed with technologies like the sailing boat; or driven by a deep psychological compulsion to journey and find new space, the result was that between 100,000 and 60,000 years ago, the first African emigrants began arriving in the Middle East and Asia. By 55,000 years ago humans made it all the way to Australia.[165]

In Europe, modern humans coexisted with the Neanderthals

for a few thousand years (43,000–40,000 years ago), but the latter soon disappeared entirely. A similar process occurred on the island of Flores, where discoveries made in 2004 suggest that a third and much smaller human species died out 18,000 years ago.[166] By 13,000 years ago, migrants had crossed the Bering Strait to Alaska and begun the steady southwards peopling of the Americas. By ten thousand years ago the descendents of these migrants had reached the southern tip of the Americas. Such was the ingenuity (or desperation) of early migrants that very few habitable areas remained unpopulated – like the Indian Ocean islands of Mauritius and Madagascar and remote Pacific islands like Hawaii and New Zealand. But by 13,000 years ago, most of the globe had reached 'the starting line'.[167]

Most of the hospitable globe was inhabited, but not densely. The world population had only inched up from Swindon to Sweden, about five to ten million people. Nor had migrants maintained close contact with each other. But this changed between 10,000 and 6,000 years ago, when the first societies in the Middle East moved from hunting and gathering based on stone-age technologies to farming the first crops and domesticated animals, and living in villages. From this point until the time of Pythagoras and Aristotle, humans were at their most divergent, with tens of thousands of clans, tribes and languages, and a process of genetic isolation that created discernible differences in appearance. Thanks to crop-growing and village life, the inhabitants of the world known to Ptolemy numbered 225 million – more numerous and more diverse than today's inhabitants of Zaire, Vietnam and Turkey.

Two thousand years ago, Europeans outnumbered stay-at-home Africans for the first time, by 25 million to 17 million. There were another seven or so million people spread throughout the Americas – and a lesser number in Australia and elsewhere. A third of the world's population lived in India, and another quarter in China. The Romans thought all roads led to Rome, but three in every four people lived in Asia, and the Asians had a higher standard of living, too. China was industrially far in advance, mass-producing iron at levels not reached in the West for hundreds of years.

The world population grew little from the time of Ptolemy to the ninth-century Baghdad world map to the first global contraction of the 1490s. But if the overall population was static, individuals were increasingly mobile, trading in multi-cultural bazaars like Bantam, plying the long-distance Indian Ocean maritime trade, and running overland caravans across the Sahara and along the Silk Road, which operated along its full length from 100 BC. Intrepid travellers like William of Rubruck (c.1220–93), Marco Polo (1254–1324) and Ibn Battuta (1304–68) – and no doubt many explorers coming from east to west whose names and exploits have been lost – started to reconnect the disparate populations in Europe, North Africa and Asia.

Growing and increasingly interconnected populations became vulnerable to the destructive forces of warfare, famine and plague. The period 1200–1350 saw violence of unprecedented scale and violence between the nomadic Mongols and sedentary peoples of Persia and China, drawing in peoples from Hungary in the west to Korea in the east. Starvation was the frequent companion of the bloodshed in China. Famine also appeared on a continental scale in Europe, a result of climatic changes known as the Little Ice Age (1315–22), causing widespread crop failures. In 1337 France and England became embroiled in vicious provincial fighting (which was to continue sporadically for 116 years).

War and famine left city-dwellers, farmers and soldiers in no fit state to resist the plague that originated in central Asia and took root in China in the early 1330s. The Black Death spread west along both commercial and military routes, to Constantinople, Kaffa and Sicily (1347), through the Mediterranean countries (1348), reaching Mecca, Germany, Scandinavia and the British Isles in 1349 and from Russia to Yemen by 1351. The plague spread so fast because inter-regional migration was reaching new heights. In Europe, the pre-plague population of some 80 million was reduced in two years to 50 million. The European mortality over these years is estimated as being one-third to one half; similar proportions probably apply to the Middle East, Asia and North Africa.

The overall impacts are complex. The Black Death increased serfdom, spread fatalism and limited international trade, but it also strengthened the hand of surviving peasants, increased labour mobility and made economies more reliant on money. The impacts varied regionally, but in human terms the European and Asian worlds in the 1350s were much smaller than they had been a few years before. Perhaps the experience of plague lay behind the medieval quest for luxury. One spice in particular, sugar, generated one of the darkest episodes in global mobility. Out of sweetness came forth slavery.

One tonne per life: sugar and slaves

> 'Sugar, which does not smell and which has the magical power to make almost anything superficially palatable, has indeed united the world's taste more than anything else. It is the culinary expression of democracy.'
>
> Theodore Zeldin, 1999[168]

By 1500, the world population had recovered from the catastrophic losses of the Black Death and other plagues to reach nearly 440 million people. Two-thirds of the world's people remained in Asia, while the African population was catching up with Europe. But for those with global intent, the populous planet suffered from labour shortages, and slavery became the solution.

Slavery had been widespread in Greek and Roman times, and had continued in Africa, Europe, the Middle East and Asia through to the tenth century. The victims were as likely to be Spaniards or Poles as Africans or Arabs.[169] In medieval Europe, Christian norms made enslaving other Christians morally unacceptable; serfdom was considered a pragmatic solution to labour shortages. During the first global contraction, however, the traditional distaste for enslaving one's own subjects crumbled. Columbus was comfortable with slavery – his home port of Genoa was a major receiving point for slaves from the Black Sea. But when he asked the Spanish crown for permission to enslave some Caribbean natives, he was refused. When he ignored these orders and shipped slaves back to Spain in 1495, he was required to return and release them. But early colonists found an alternative to slavery: the infamous *encomienda* system of forced labour in exchange for religious instruction. By 1550, the merits of slavery were being widely promoted. Slavery would lead to religious conversion – an argument used to secure Papal blessing – while providing household servants, sex partners, miners, galley-rowers. Most of all, slaves would cater to the European sweet tooth.

Popular for thousands of years among Asian elites, sugar gradually migrated westwards to the Levant and Egypt. European crusaders developed a taste for sugar in the Holy Land, and its cultivation spread to Cyprus, Morocco, Andalusia, Sicily and the Algarve. The Portuguese took sugar to the recently settled islands of Madeira, the Canaries, Cape Verde and São Tomé. Apart from their hotter and wetter climate, these Atlantic islands enjoyed a crucial advantage over the Mediterranean for growing sugar – they were close to Africa and away from prying eyes. Europeans rapidly discovered that sugar is back-breaking work. But if the Portuguese were going to use slaves, they wanted it out of sight and out of mind. The Atlantic islands were far enough away; Brazil even further. Between 1450 and 1600 the Portuguese shipped 175,000 slaves from West Africa, transforming what had been a series of regional slave markets into a transatlantic trade where the tickets were one-way.

The French pharmacist Nostradamus made one uncharacteristically clear prediction: there was a great future for sugar (*Traité des Confitures*, 1557). When the Doge of Venice entertained Henri III of France to dinner in 1572, every single item of the dinner service – cutlery, glasses, plates, chandeliers, the works – was confected from sugar. Within decades it was transformed from dazzling novelty into everyday commodity. Sweetened coffee and cocoa became the breakfast beverages that fuelled industrious European households and coffee-shops provided the focal points for early stockbrokers.

By the late eighteenth century, the population of Western Europe was around 100 million and getting richer. To cope with spiralling demand for sugar, the Spanish, English and French set up plantations in their Caribbean and Indian Ocean colonies – St Domingo, Jamaica and Mauritius – while the Portuguese expanded sugar plantations in Brazil. In 1700, world sugar production was around 60,000 tonnes, and by 1787 it reached 300,000 tonnes. 'Sugar, rum, and tobacco, are commodities which are nowhere necessaries of life,' noted Adam Smith sourly, but 'are become objects of almost universal consumption.'

The growth of the sugar trade democratized luxury, but with it came a dangerous tolerance for brutality in production.

The Dutch spice traders had been considered ruthless, but the scale and ethics of sugar and tobacco plantations were at a different level. At least 11 million Africans were shipped to the Americas as slaves from 1500 – greater than the combined populations of Portugal, Spain and Britain at the time. The impact of this unparalleled human transplantation was to shift the world's centre of gravity irrevocably, with the French and British Caribbean receiving at least 3.8 million slaves, Brazil 3.6 million, Spanish America 1.5 million and North America another 400,000.[170] The surviving slaves made a huge contribution to the economic vitality and social diversity of the New World.

Every tonne of sugar consumed in Europe came at the cost of one slave's life.[171] In the eighteenth century, Britain's maritime and commercial supremacy saw it become the leading slave nation, responsible for shipping over three million Africans to the Americas. The story of the abolition of slavery is often told as one of British moral leadership after what Niall Ferguson has called an 'astonishing volte-face' in the late eighteenth century.[172] Led by the Clapham Sect of abolitionists and a nationwide mass-movement against slavery, the trade was abolished by parliament in 1807, followed by the abolition of slavery altogether (1833). The British started shipping slaves back to West Africa and setting them free. After an abrupt switch in the national psyche, the British Empire became a progressive global force.

This account is unsatisfactory for a number of reasons. The achievements of English Methodist and parliamentarian William Wilberforce (1759–1833) and fellow abolitionists are real enough. The Royal Navy captured hundreds of slave ships run by many other nations. But the idea of a rapid and profound change in national ethics is misleading. The reality is that most Europeans, North and South Americans only gradually and grudgingly accepted that slavery would have to be abolished. 'Slavery,' noted Edmund Burke, 'is a weed that grows on every soil.'

In the sixteenth century the English had criticized Spain for its enslavement of native Americans, and slave-owning had never become widespread within England. By the late eighteenth century, slavery was under fire again on both pragmatic and moral grounds. Adam Smith decried the 'dreadful misfortunes' that befell the native peoples of the Americas and East Indies as a result of growing links with Europe. Though he omitted Africa, like Turgot he disapproved of slavery, mainly because he believed it was inefficient. His fellow-Scot William Murray, Lord Mansfield, judging the case of an escaped slave in 1772, found slavery 'so odious, that nothing can be suffered to support it but positive law'. In Enlightenment Europe and the Americas, there was growing repugnance to slavery based on principles of natural rights which had been slowly developing after the pioneering work of Dominican friars in Spain described in the last chapter.

Wilberforce first raised the issue of slavery in parliament in 1789, and in 1791 his first bill to make slave-trading illegal was roundly defeated; in 1805 it was blocked in the House of Lords. Slavery had already been banned in Haiti and France before the 1807 British abolition of the trade. The British tolerated the existence of slave owning for a whole generation after banning the trade. Nearly two million more Africans were shipped to the Americas *after* the British abolition, suggesting the naval effort to stamp out the trade was far from comprehensive; a substantial part of the Royal Navy was on other duties like defending imports of opium into China. When a second movement for total abolition gathered steam in the early 1830s, plantation owners demanded – and received – compensation of £1.3 billion in today's money from tax payers

for the loss of their slaves. The Bishop of Exeter received
£12,700 for his 665 slaves, equivalent to £1,270 per slave.[173]
The move against slavery was slow and halting, as much
driven by economics as morals.

The issue was equally murky elsewhere. From the 1820s the
USA was literally split in two over the issue of abolition, down
the demarcation line drawn up in the 1760s by English
geographers Mason and Dixon. In France, planters convinced
Napoleon to overturn the abolition and slavery returned until
1848. It continued unabated in Cuba and Brazil until the late
1880s, despite the enormous economic leverage that Britain
and France could have exercised to stamp it out. Little was
done to improve work conditions on the plantations after
abolition, and sugar production in 1894 was actually two and
a half times higher than it had been in 1787.

If Europeans had genuinely switched against slaving, would
they so quickly have devised the barbaric system of 'indentured labour' to replace it? Using account books instead of
manacles, indenture trapped millions of Asian 'coolies' in debt-
slavery from which they could not escape. As we will see, the
reliance on cheap sugar – as well as other plantation commodities like tobacco, cotton, tea, rubber, cocoa and coffee –
created an ethical callousness on the part of consumers towards distant producers that continued long after the abolition
of slavery.[174]

The great migration (1820–1900)

In 1820, the world population was one billion. By the eve of
the Great War in 1913, it stood at 1.8 billion. Over 100 years,
100 million people – African, Asian, European, American –
migrated to all corners of the planet. It was an unparalleled

experience directly affecting one person in ten around the globe. Never before had there been such an exchange of goods, culture, religion and genes. Historians tend to capitalize this period as 'The Great Migration' not just because of its scale but because of its supposedly universal benefits. But there were many losers from global migration.

When Pedro Alvares Cabral was dispatched to India in early 1500, he took with him from Portugal a force of 1,200 men. The Chinese fleets that roamed the oceans in the early fifteenth century had up to 30,000 people aboard. In the first global contraction, people with global intent moved across the world in thousands, but most intended to return home. In the early modern period, millions of Africans were permanently uprooted, and hundreds of thousands of Europeans ventured to the new colonies – where life expectancy was short but financial rewards were great for the survivors.

In the seventeenth century, 700,000 English people emigrated, mainly to North America and the Caribbean, with 50,000 more each decade through the whole eighteenth century. Over a million Germans and Swiss went to North America and the West Indies between 1689 and 1815. When French colonial boosters proposed a utopian settlement at Kourou in Guyana in 1763, 17,000 would-be emigrants rapidly assembled at Atlantic ports. Of the 13,000 who set sail, 9,000 died in Guyana.[175]

But the nineteenth century saw a one-way global migration that dwarfed all previous movements of people. Over 25 million Europeans migrated, especially after steamships slashed the cost of a one-way third-class berth. The main destination was the United States, but they also left for Argentina, Brazil, Australia, New Zealand and many other destinations across the entire globe. Many migrants were those on the economic periphery, looking for better opportunities. In

1820, the USA already had a slightly higher average standard of living than most European countries, and by 1870, the US had become even more alluring for all except Dutch, Belgian and British workers.

Emigrants were pushed as much as pulled. As European states became more powerful and sensitive to the risk of revolution, they actively created a stream of political migrants. Many were indentured labourers or convicts, while others were religious or political refugees, especially after the failed rebellions and desperate famine of 1848–51. It was in this period that the passport, previously a privilege granted by the Persian court, the Indian village headman and the odd European monarch, began to be used by paranoid states as a way of controlling the movements of subversives. 'The creation of the modern passport system', writes John Torpey, 'signaled the dawn of a new era in human affairs, in which individual states and the international state system as a whole successfully monopolized the legitimate authority to permit movement within and across their jurisdictions.'[176] Until 1858, British passports had been issued only in French, the diplomatic language, but after this point, a British passport – in English and French – could no longer be issued to foreigners. The passport became for the first time a proof of national identity.

The UK was the largest source of European migrants, exporting around two million people per decade from 1870 to the 1920s. Almost half of the 12 million UK emigrants from 1820–1913 were Irish, fleeing the effects of famine from the mid-century. Millions more were impoverished Scottish and Welsh. The Italians and Germans also migrated in large numbers. The *rate* of emigration was highest in countries like Sweden: one in a hundred people left every year. Sparsely populated France was a rare European recipient of migrants in this period.

Despite the migration, periodic wars and disastrous cholera epidemics, the population in Europe continued to rise rapidly, doubling from 82 million in 1700 to 165 million by the rebellious year of 1848 and topping 230 million by the end of the century. For those who remained, another migration was also underway, from countryside to the burgeoning cities when industrialization gathered pace. In the early 1880s, 44 per cent of the British workforce was employed in industry; in Germany it was already over a third.[177] Urbanization and a declining agricultural workforce enabled or necessitated greater dependency on food imports, creating a further cycle of industrialization.

Despite growing incomes, work conditions were notoriously bad in the new cities. Liverpool sugar refiners were forced to recruit hundreds of Germans because locals would not accept suffocating conditions that were known to lead to early death. In London, Henry Mayhew, editor of the humorous magazine *Punch*, wrote four distinctly unfunny volumes about *London Labour and the London Poor* (1851–61). Mayhew exposed in lurid detail the extremes of poverty among an underclass of 30,000 street vendors, labourers, prostitutes and criminals in the Empire's capital. The London streets were at the centre of a global trade network, with thirty boys specializing in gutta-percha, and tea, sugar and spice stolen from the docks being 'things in excellent demand'.

'I can't make it out how it is,' one man told Mayhew, 'but I remember that I could go out and sell twelve bushel of fruit in a day, when sugar was dear, and now, when sugar's cheap, I can't sell three bushel on the same round. Perhaps we want thinning,' he added – an ominous echo of Thomas Malthus' *Essay on the Principle of Population* (1798). Efforts to tame the impacts of industrialization, like the 1833 Factory Act in Britain banning the employment of children under nine, and later legislation in France banning under-fives (1841), were part of the same cautious and contested reforming trend as the abolition of slavery. Sixty-hour weeks in harsh conditions remained the norm for older children and adults through the nineteenth century.

For those who could afford it, emigration to less industrialized lands was an attractive proposition. Despite the bucolic dreams of many immigrants, especially from Eastern Europe, they found themselves sucked into urban industries, notably Chicago's Packingtown and Pittsburgh's iron and steel foundries. Driven by poverty and politics as much as aspiration, European emigration nevertheless raised living standards all round.[178] From 1870 to 1913, average incomes in Western Europe almost doubled; in the receiving countries of North America, Australia, New Zealand and Latin America, incomes more than doubled.

Elsewhere, however, this period of migration was far from great. In Africa and Asia, the standard of living was stagnant. In terms of numbers, destinations and distances, the Asian global diaspora was the most dramatic. From 1834 to 1937, 30 million Indians dispersed right across the British Empire, from Australia and Malaysia to Mauritius and the Caribbean. Another 12 million migrants left China for South-East Asia, South Africa, Cuba and the USA. The motivations of these migrants are explained by the fact that incomes in India and China had fallen in real terms between 1700 and 1870.[179] The creation of railways and canals also relied on immigrant labour. The Suez Canal opened in 1869 at the cost of an estimated 125,000 Egyptian lives.[180] The global commodity trade pushed these countries backwards economically; the global trade in muscle pulled them apart socially. Some Asian indentured labourers managed to send money home, and some even returned home themselves. But for the most part, the Asian migration, like the European, was irreversible.

Few places were untouched by the migrations. One was Tierra del Fuego, where living standards were so primitive that a shocked Charles Darwin, visiting on the *Beagle* in 1832, began to devise a theory of evolving civilization. 'Whilst observing the barbarous inhabitants . . . it struck me that the possession of some property, a fixed abode, and the union of many families under a chief, were the indispensable requisites for civilisation. Such habits almost necessitate the cultivation of the ground', Darwin mused in *The Descent of Man and Selection in Relation to Sex* (1871), before concluding that 'The problem, however, of the first advance of savages towards civilisation is at present much too difficult to be solved.'

Darwin himself was vehemently against slavery, but his most troublesome legacy was 'Social Darwinism', developed by followers like Francis Galton. Although slavery had been largely abolished, the belief that human groups ('races') were evolving at different speeds – even in different directions – led to the renaissance of the concept of the savage. This had devastating consequences for Africa. From an already depleted population of some 70 million in 1800, five and a half million more Africans were enslaved in the nineteenth century, with 3.3 million going to the Americas. By 1870, Europeans outnumbered Africans two to one; were five times as wealthy; and were hundreds of times better armed. Slaving had weakened Africa's economies and societies, but it was only after the abolition of slavery that Europeans developed a strong racist superiority complex.

Coupled with rising strategic and commercial tensions, this led to the 'Scramble for Africa', the period from 1884 when Europeans raced each other to annex African territory at an astonishing rate. The Scramble was not just military, but commercial and religious, and was facilitated by European superiority in weaponry, transport and communications. By

1913, Britain had nearly 30 per cent of Africa's population under its control, France 15 per cent, Germany a tenth, and Belgium another seven per cent.[181]

The great migration brought precipitous declines in native populations. Indigenous peoples had already been devastated by the unintended result of introduced diseases (as in the 1520 smallpox epidemic in Mexico), or brutally harsh treatment (as in the seventeenth-century Bolivian silver mines). In Mexico the pre-conquest population of five to ten million was just 1.6 million in 1618.[182] In the future United States, the native population shrank from two million in 1500 to 750,000 in 1700 and just 325,000 in 1830.

In the late nineteenth century, however, colonization was accompanied by systematic attempts at extermination, as in Van Diemen's Land where the very last inhabitant died in 1876, or the 1904 German campaign against Herero herdsmen in Namibia. In the US, the native American population fell by half between 1850 and 1890 as land-hungry settlers and railroad builders lobbied government to restrict the survivors to reserves. There was also a marked hardening of attitudes in India after the Mutiny and Rebellion of 1857.

Just as Darwin's thoughts on savages heightened global conflicts, along came the penny-farthing. In 2004, *The Times* newspaper (founded 1788) organized a poll to identify the greatest British invention of the past 250 years. Among the shortlisted candidates were vaccination, electricity and the world-wide-web. But the result was an unexpected landslide victory vote for John Kemp Starley's Rover Safety Bicycle, invented in 1885.[183] The bike isn't mentioned in most books on globalization and world history: the indexes go straight from 'Bible' to 'Bin Laden'. Disdained by historians but much loved in the real world, the humble bicycle, as much as the steamship, refrigerated railroad and telegraph, was central to assimilating the population upheavals of the great migration. It was a bridge between the global contraction of the 1880s and modern globalization.

By the 1890s, Frank Bowden's Raleigh Company in Nottingham was churning out 30,000 bicycles a year. The proliferation of easy-to-ride bicycles like the Rover enabled workers to get to factories, farmers to markets, urban socialists to bond with each other, women to throw off their corsets. The bicycle facilitated the globe-trotting exploits of Phileas Fogg and created the oldest international sporting fixture: the *Tour de France* (1903). Bicycles also gave birth to industrial innovations like ball-bearings and many bike makers moved directly into cars (Rover, Morris, Skoda, Ford) and airplanes (the Wright brothers). Crucially, it ended the social isolation of remote communities, enabling an unprecedented degree of genetic mixing. In effect, says geneticist Steve Jones of University College London, the bike slowed the pace of natural selection.[184]

But for all its benefits, one innovation in bicycling comfort and safety – the pneumatic tyre invented by Dunlop in 1888 – relied on the most brutal abuse of human labour ever recorded: wild rubber tapping.

Red rubber: the cost of inner tubes and the pursuit of world peace

'The number of Indians killed either by starvation – often purposely brought about by the destruction of crops over whole districts or inflicted as a form of death penalty on individuals who failed to bring in their quota of rubber – or by deliberate murder by bullet, fire, beheading, or flogging to death, and accompanied by a variety of atrocious tor-

tures, during the course of these 12 years, in order to extort
these 4.000 tons of rubber, cannot have been less than
30,000, and possibly came to many more.'

Roger Casement (1864–1916)[185]

The global contraction of the 1880s and 90s was notable for
the dramatic rates of economic growth in Europe and the
Americas, enabled by unparalleled labour migration and the
surging demand for commodities. But this contraction also
saw the emergence of a liberal movement increasingly critical
of the violence and exploitation lying not far beneath the
surface of the late nineteenth-century global system. Facilitated
by telegraph and newspapers, eyewitness accounts of European battlefields, New York sweatshops and colonial plantations led to widespread calls for a more responsible model of
trade and diplomacy centred around new global institutions.

Novelists were among the first to reveal globalization's
grimy underbelly. Harriet Beecher Stowe's powerful indict-
ment of Southern slavery, *Uncle Tom's Cabin* (1852), helped
stir up Abolitionist sentiment in the US – sowing the seeds for
Civil War in the process. In 1860, Eduard Douwes Dekker, a
Dutch colonial official, wrote *Max Havelaar or the coffee
auctions of the Dutch Trading-Society*. Dekker's novel was an
exposé of the appalling work conditions suffered by Indonesian coffee farmers under the Dutch colonial system. The book
sold well in the Netherlands, was translated into 30 or more
languages, and strongly influenced the Dutch abandonment of
slavery in 1863.

The new breed of 'muck-raking' journalists – from Henry
Mayhew in London to Nellie Bly in New York – exposed
scandal after scandal, from mental patients in lunatic asylums
and Chinese coolies building the trans-continental railroads to
Polish immigrants in the Chicago meatpacking yards and the

1911 fire at New York's Triangle Shirtwaist Company factory, which killed 146 young, mainly female garment workers. Some of those making the fortunes began to see that piecemeal factory regulation was not a sufficient response to reforming society. The new philanthropists were often parochial: the Wills family endowed Bristol University with vast sums of tobacco cash and Quaker chocolate-maker Joseph Rowntree set up a model village for some of the 4,000 people he employed in York.

Other industrial 'barons' had more global vision; none more so than Alfred Nobel, the Swedish industrialist whose wealth was founded on dynamite. Nobel (1833–1896) blamed himself for the death of his brother in a factory explosion but it was apparently after reading a premature and critical obituary of himself that he decided to devote his last years to leaving a positive global legacy. In this spirit he endowed a prize for those working 'for fraternity between the nations, for the abolition or reduction of standing armies and for the holding and promotion of peace congresses'.

Businessmen like Jean Henri Dunant (1828–1910) seemed unlikely candidates for Nobel's Peace Prize. But by chance, Dunant witnessed a gory nine-hour battle at Solferino between the Austrian and Franco-Piedmontese armies in 1859. Over 5,000 troops were killed in the futile conflict, but it was the fate of the 30,000 wounded that most shocked Dunant. Many were bayoneted in cold blood or died for lack of medical attention. Dunant wrote a shocking account of the bloodbath, and in 1864 devised the International Red Cross and the Geneva Convention on the treatment of battlefield casualties. For his role in setting up this first non-governmental organization, Dunant won the first Nobel Peace Prize in 1901.

Railway and steel baron Andrew Carnegie (1835–1919), the second richest man in the world, became the most generous and global of all the millionaire philanthropists as a direct result of a trip round the world in 1884. 'We have seen so much of such misery before', he wrote, 'that I fear we begin to grow callous.' With a firm belief in education as the way to escape 'abject and repulsive misery', he endowed 3,000 libraries, not just in the USA, but around the world from the Caribbean to Fiji.

For some liberals, business philanthropy and non-governmental do-gooders were not enough to combat callousness and secure fraternity between nations – what was needed was a new system of global governance. The sixteenth-century Dominican ideas of international law were revived in the Enlightenment, notably by Montesquieu. His concept of the law of nations, published in 1748, was a 'civil law of the whole globe, in which sense every nation is a citizen'.[186] *The Spirit of the Laws* in turn influenced American constitutionalists like James Madison. In the early 1780s, Benjamin Franklin devoted some of his considerable energies to devizing a European 'system for perpetual peace' while living in the village of Passy near Paris. Immanuel Kant was writing on the same theme in the mid-1790s. However, the globalizing tendency of late eighteenth-century liberalism soon gave way to a pragmatic national focus in Europe, the United States and the new independent nations of Latin America.

The pacifist ideals developed by Franklin in Passy were dusted off by an upper-class French lawyer, economist and parliamentarian called, by coincidence, Frédéric Passy (1822–1912). Passy tirelessly touted his *Ligue internationale et permanente de la paix* as a way to combine the virtues of free trade and pacifism. This dream of international arbitration was deflated by the Franco-Prussian War (1870–71). But Passy soon formed a cross-channel alliance with working-class carpenter turned trade unionist Randal Cremer (1838–1908). Passy and Cremer set up the Interparliamentary Union in a bid to put pacifism and international arbitration firmly on the global agenda. Attracting dozens of parliamentarians from eight European countries and with growing links to the USA, the concept of using arbitration to resolve disputes began to gain traction – enough at least to win first Passy and then Cremer early Nobel Peace Prizes (1901–03), alongside Dunant.

Andrew Carnegie was one of their more influential converts, writing passionately about the Brotherhood of Man, and setting up an Endowment for International Peace. Thanks to rapid communication around the European empires, this liberal transatlantic movement influenced the development of early independence movements, notably the first Indian National Congress held in Bombay in 1885. Young Chinese nationalists exchanged ideas with Irish nationalists while exiled in London in the 1890s. Ho Chi Minh, the future North Vietnamese leader, became a communist in London while working as a pastry-cook under French chef Auguste Escoffier. Other European capitals also served as ideological melting-pots.

Developments in Africa also had a powerful impact on the emerging global movement. As part of the African carve-up agreed by European powers at the Berlin Conference in 1884–85, the Congo was being run as a private fiefdom by Belgian King Leopold II (1865–1909). In 1900, Liverpool shipping clerk Edmund Dene Morel noticed something fishy in the company books. Ships chartered by Leopold were leaving Belgium carrying only guns and dynamite, yet returning from the Congo laden with wild-tapped rubber and ivory. Suspicious about the terms of trade, Morel investigated further and soon discovered that Leopold was running a giant slave camp of rubber-tappers. Morel, turning journalist to publicize the outrage, called the article on the blood-soaked trade *Red Rubber*.

Local British consul Roger Casement was asked to investigate the allegations. Casement was a closet homosexual and an increasingly radical Irish nationalist. In his own mind, both experiences gave him an insight into the misfortunes of the Congolese. In his 1904 consular diary, Casement described 'the daily agony of an entire people' – whippings, mutilations, executions and starvation inflicted by a 'savage soldiery'. The British Government, knowing that the findings could not be effectively suppressed, reluctantly agreed to publish Casement's testimony.

The campaign by Morel and Casement caused outrage in liberal society, which had previously thought little about where the rubber for bicycle tyres was coming from. Joseph Conrad's *Heart of Darkness* (1902), Mark Twain's *King Leopold's Soliloquy* (1904) and Arthur Conan Doyle's *The Crime of the Congo* (1908) were part of the mounting uproar that eventually forced Leopold to surrender his private empire to Belgium in 1908. It was perhaps fortunate for the Congolese that their wild rubber trees were soon exhausted and the murderous trade closed down.[187]

Casement was transferred as consul-general to Brazil in 1908 – whether as reward or as punishment we don't know. Here he uncovered still more exploitation among rubber-tapping Indians in the Putumayo region of the Amazon. This time the oppression was at the hands of ruthless rubber baron Julio César Arana (1864–1952). Casement's shocking finding was that each tonne of rubber came at the cost of seven or eight human lives – far worse than the excesses of sugar slavery.

Casement's *Putumayo Report* was released in 1912. Coming as it did on top of several unofficial accusations, it again caused outrage – but also a moral dilemma. Arana was living in Biarritz; his Peruvian Amazon Company employed British managers and was registered in London. The rubber market was booming, with new demand for tyres from the motorcar. Rival plantations in Malaya were insufficient to meet demand.[188] Keynes perfectly expressed the moral position of many imperial consumers in the face of such exposés. For the privileged minority, the fruits of globalization had never been sweeter. They regarded the global regime as 'normal, certain, and permanent, except in the direction of further improvement, and any deviation from it as aberrant, scandalous, and avoidable.'[189] Norman Angell's book *The Great Illusion* (1909) portrayed a world so interconnected that war was no longer possible.

One in ten people were directly involved in the great migration. Far from creating a global melting pot, it polarized differences and created a rift between the savage and the civilized. Criticism of this new global regime was mounting – from socialist dreamers, billionaire philanthropists, outraged activists and nascent nationalists. From the 1880s, literary outrage gave way to efforts to build new systems of global governance, from peace conferences to international NGOs. A concrete manifestation of the backlash was the new Peace Palace funded by Andrew Carnegie and built in The Hague. The timing could hardly have been worse: the Palace opened in 1913. With the advent of world war, these tentative moves towards more responsible globalization were killed stone dead.[190]

The decimated globe (1914–50)

> '*One man's death is a tragedy; a million deaths is a statistic.*'
> Joseph Stalin (1879–1953)

> '*Who, after all, speaks today of the annihilation of the Armenians?*'
> Adolf Hitler (1889–1945)[191]

Few individuals have put more effort into the morbid task of understanding global destruction than Quaker weather fore-

caster Lewis Fry Richardson. Richardson spent his life measuring the magnitude of all deadly quarrels in the world from
1820 to 1950. If he could find out what caused quarrels,
maybe they could be stopped. Richardson's body count of 315
wars and thousands of smaller violent conflicts was finally
published as the *Statistics of Deadly Quarrels* in 1960. To his
intense frustration, he failed to find 'any trend towards more,
nor towards fewer, fatal quarrels.' He simply could not find
any statistically convincing cause for war. Neighbouring countries with different religions were often at each other's throats,
but overall, the outbreak of international conflict was unpredictable – even random.[192]

After 1914, the world's 1.8 billion people came under the
sway of a handful of men whose world-view was formed by the
contraction of the 1880s. The global forces unleashed by
Wilhelm II, Lenin, Hitler, Stalin, Hirohito and Mao utterly
changed the course of globalization in the twentieth century and
made it the most destructive in human history. Two world wars,
hundreds of international and domestic conflicts, the revival of
slave labour, genocide and repression – and the pandemic
diseases made possible by these conflicts – killed 200 million
people, more than one in eight of all people alive in 1900.[193]

If the nineteenth century saw global migration, the twentieth
century was the age of global decimation. Apart from the
hundreds of millions of individual tragedies, the cumulative
psychological burden reinforced a callous 'winner takes all'
view of global exchange and brushed aside all alternatives. The
period from 1914 to 1950 is often portrayed as a time of 'de-
globalization', where trends in trade, migration and foreign
investment went into reverse. This is an unconvincing attempt
to disassociate globalization with negative developments.
Although there was no outstanding planetary contraction in
these dark decades, they could only have happened in an

interconnected world. Trade did not grind to a halt in the period 1914–50, and nor did global migration. Globalization, far from being an innocent victim of this dark period, was at its very core.

The rogues' gallery of twentieth-century decimators includes assassins, kaisers, emperors, imperialists, general secretaries, and an American entrepreneur. Hiram Stevens Maxim (1840–1916) was born in Maine and migrated to England as a prolific inventor of light bulbs, mousetraps – and a self-loading machine-gun. Like most innovations, firepower had a long, multicultural and chancy gestation. The Chinese had invented gunpowder in the tenth century but failed to see its use in weapons. The Japanese developed significant innovations in gun-making but walked away from them because the Samurai saw guns as a cultural threat. In 1861, inventor Richard Gatling offered a multi-barrelled gun to US Federal troops, who turned it down because it was too heavy. It was Maxim's ingenuity, doggedness and passion that plunged destructive capacity to new depths.

The military establishment was initially dismissive of Maxim's machine gun, but after the Lakota and Cheyenne defeated Custer's 7th Cavalry at Little Bighorn (1876), became acutely aware of what could happen when natives had the same or better weaponry. Military tacticians woke up to the potential of the machine-gun after it was used in Matabeleland (1893–94) and the Sudan (1898). A single Maxim was found to have the destructive capability of 100 rifles, and only needed four or five troops to man it.[194] As Hillaire Belloc tastelessly quipped:

> *'Whatever happens, we have got*
> *The Maxim gun, and they have not.'*

In 1908, the German army adopted a modified Maxim, and the British army introduced their Vickers machine-gun in

1912. Within two years, the machine-gun was raising the destructiveness of warfare to a wholly new level.

Ever since the Punic Wars between Rome and Carthage, many conflicts have been fought on several continents and by multiple combatants. The bloodshed has frequently spread from the battlefield into civilian populations, too. The Thirty Years War (1618–48) destroyed a third of the German population. 'Whole cities, like Magdeburg, stood in ruins,' according to Norman Davies. 'Whole districts lay stripped of their inhabitants, their livestock, their supplies. Trade had virtually ceased. A whole generation of pillage, famine, disease, and social disruption had wreaked havoc.'[195] Winston Churchill called the Seven Years War (1756–63) the 'first world war'. The little-known War of the Triple Alliance between Paraguay, Uruguay, Argentina and Brazil (1865–70) was one of the most destructive on record.

The Great War and Second World War combined the global characteristics of earlier conflicts – vast geographical scope, multinational combatants, massive military and civilian mortality – but on a completely different scale. The causes of the twentieth-century world wars may have been a concatenation of parochial flashpoints, from the Balkan tensions which led to the assassination of Archduke Franz Ferdinand by Gavrilo Princip in June 1914 to Hitler's obsession with capturing the Škoda armaments factory in Plzeň, and the Japanese army's role in the 'terrorist attack' at Mukden that justified their incursion into Manchuria in 1931.

The sinking of the *Lusitania* in 1915 was part of no global game, but the belligerents of the world wars did have broader motives. Kaiser Wilhelm II was convinced that Germany had been short-changed in Africa. In the 1930s, Hitler expressed admiration for the British Empire, and the Japanese clearly wanted large chunks of that same empire for their Greater East

Asia Co-prosperity Sphere. In both cases, the geopolitics was perhaps more regional than global in focus; drawing the USA into war made little strategic sense. Despite Trotsky's calls for world revolution, Lenin and Stalin's vision for communism soon became regionally-focused.

If the causes were parochial, the conflicts threatened the global order. The British, French and Germans were forced into a global mobilization of men and resources. In both wars, troops came from and fought on more continents than ever before. The fighting was more destructive, too. The grisly parade of technologies that followed the Maxim included high explosives, trench warfare, land mines, strategic aerial bombing, poison gas, tanks, submarine torpedoes, extermination camps, slave labour and the atomic bomb.

One unintended catastrophe could only have happened because of the global upheaval: the 'Spanish Flu' pandemic at the end of the Great War, which killed more people from more countries than died in combat in both world wars. Despite its name, its origins were global, appearing in its deadly form in Brest, Freetown and Boston simultaneously in August 1918. In six months, the virus had killed 25–50 million people worldwide, including 500,000 in the USA, 600,000 in Britain and France and as many as 17 million in India. The 'flu killed one in five of the population even in remote communities like Western Samoa. The island of Marajó in the mouth of the Amazon, opposite the rubber capital of Belém, appears to be the only place on the planet that was not affected.

Inextricably connected to the experience of world war was a new development called 'democide' – the mass murder of one's own people. Racially-motivated genocide, whose roots can be traced back to the colonial exterminations of the 1890s, was taken to new depths by the Nazi regime. Meanwhile, in Russia and China mass murder became an ideological weapon of such ferocity that we still have trouble coming to grips with it. In 1998, British comedian Michael Palin was filmed falling asleep in Mao's bed while reading the *Little Red Book* in his Pacific travel series *Full Circle*.[196] Not funny, objected the left-wing French academics who had just published the *Black Book of Communism* to coincide with the 80th anniversary of the Russian Revolution. The *Livre Noir* showed that communist regimes – from Lenin through to Pol Pot to Sendero Luminoso – had slaughtered 85–100 million of their own people. Mao alone was responsible for the deaths of 65 million Chinese.[197] Mass murder became a global phenomenon in the mid twentieth century and remains troublingly present into the twenty-first.

The period 1914–50 is described by neo-liberal historians as an aberration when globalization collapsed or went into reverse. It is better understood as a clash between two power-ful global forces. The first, arising from revulsion against the horror of war, was a 'never again' mentality which led to an unprecedented interest in new global institutions. At the same time, however, individuals and nations alike developed a 'beggar thy neighbour' psychology. This was occasionally manifested as isolationism, but more often in a hyper-aggres-sive form of global competitiveness. The tension between cooperative and competitive impulses lay at the heart of the global decimation.

Gertrude Stein self-indulgently called Paris-based American writers like Hemingway, Scott Fitzgerald and herself the 'Lost Generation'. Americans actually came off relatively lightly from the decades of global decimation, but the 1920s saw the emergence of a 'Win Generation' in every affected country, determined to make the most of every global opportunity, no matter what the impact on others.[198] From the vindictiveness of the Versailles Treaty in 1919 to the suppression of labour protest; from stock-market speculation and cultural hedonism of the 1920s to the anti-immigrant, tariff-raising policies of the 1930s, global exchanges took on a new edge of hostile competitiveness. In Britain, relations with the empire took on a grudging and exasperated tone, expressed in E.M. Forster's *A Passage to India* (1924). To many, the empire was more trouble than it was worth. In the US, over six million immigrants arrived from 1914–49, but in a sour context of anti-immigrant rhetoric and policies.

This global competitiveness clashed with a new movement for global institutions. The birth of the modern global system is usually credited to Churchill and Roosevelt, who in the early 1940s began developing joint ideas for a series of world bodies that Roosevelt liked to call the 'United Nations'. But the roots of these ideas lay in nineteenth-century visions of international arbitration and strong civil society organizations like the International Red Cross, which received renewed support in the 1920s and 30s.

The most enduring of these inter-war global institutions is football's World Cup, first held in Uruguay in 1930. But there were dozens of high-minded global bodies, from the Permanent Court of International Justice and Disarmament Commission to the Health Organization and Permanent Central Opium Board. Some of these did little more than collect statistics on their assigned problem. Others chalked up notable successes, especially the three bodies specifically dealing with migrants and workers: the Commission for Refugees, the Slavery Commission and the International Labour Organization.

The centrepiece of the whole system was the League of Nations, dream child of British Foreign Secretary Edward Grey, South African premier Jan Smuts and US President Woodrow Wilson. 'For the first time in history,' said Wilson in September 1919, 'the counsels of mankind are to be drawn together and concerted for the purpose of defending the rights and improving the conditions of working people – men, women, and children – all over the world. Such a thing as that was never dreamed of before [and] there is no other way to do it than by a universal league of nations.'

Established with high hopes in 1920, the League of Nations worked on the principle that each of its member states would have one vote in the Assembly. 'One nation, one vote' had been used before, at the 1884 Meridian Conference for example, but remained a radical notion in the era of one-to-one deals and 'ententes' among powerful nations that led to the Great War. Most nations joined the League, which was to enforce its arbitrations through trade sanctions. However, the League had one arm tied behind its back from the outset. Wilson utterly failed to sell his global vision back home. The USA Senate defied the president and refused to join.[199]

History judges the League an abject failure, but in the mid-1920s it looked like a plausible global institution that had effectively resolved a number of tricky turf wars. The problem was, the late 1920s and early 1930s saw a positive eruption of new tensions. This was not just fallout from the Versailles settlement in Europe, but a global trend, with conflicts in Paraguay, Abyssinia, Spain and, most damagingly, Manchuria. Without a peacekeeping force or the participation of the US in economic sanctions, the League became increasingly ineffective. Membership started to dwindle, as first Costa Rica and Brazil and then in the 1930s Japan, Italy and Germany left. By 1935, global fatalism was overwhelming global idealism. More and more people, remembering Marshal Foch's gloomy prediction that the Treaty of Versailles was an 'armistice for twenty years', began to fear he had been right.

The Second World War is inseparable from the Holocaust – a horrific attempt at multinational genocide – and from Stalin's 'democide' of his own peoples. The war shifted huge quantities of people, material and money across continents. British and French imperial and colonial troops from Indochina, Madagascar, India, Australia, New Zealand, South Africa, Canada, Nigeria and elsewhere fought on three continents. Their experiences gave a powerful boost to demands for self-determination, as did the experience of African-American troops and women workers. The war spawned the atom bomb, moving global destructive capacity from decimation towards total obliteration.

Despite all the carnage, the world population reached two and a half billion in 1950. People were more spread between the continents than at any time before or since. With peace returning rapidly in many countries, the stage was set for still greater population growth, alongside a huge increase in the number of nations, a stronger international governance system and growing individual mobility. In the late 1940s, the US population passed 140 million, the same as its defeated enemies Germany and Japan combined. But the Soviet Union, despite its huge war losses and civilian 'purges', was even bigger, with 173 million people.[200] As a bruised Britain and France looked on, these two nations squared off, preparing to create a global institution – the United Nations – but also ready to split the globe in two.

Hyper-mobile planet (1950–2005)

> '*Apart from their other advantages and pleasure, travel and tourism I think serve a much wider human purpose which is becoming increasingly important as the world becomes more and more closely knit.*'
>
> Jawaharlal Nehru (1889–1964)[201]

The defining historical development of the last fifty years is the steady march of world population, from three billion in 1960 to four billion in 1975, up to five billion in 1988, and reaching six billion in the millennium year 2000. Today there are more than ten times as many people alive as there were in 1700. People became more mobile than ever before. Travel within nations increased greatly, thanks to the train, car and bicycle. There was also a remarkable growth of international mobility. In terms of proportions, the global migrations of the last 50 years may be smaller than the nineteenth-century great migration, but in absolute numbers, we live on a hyper-mobile planet.

In 1948, the General Assembly of the United Nations adopted the Universal Declaration of Human Rights, proclaiming freedom of movement. Progress towards that goal has been mixed, with a globe-trotting elite free to travel as never before while many others have been forced to migrate against their will. For the majority of the world's peoples, however, freedom of movement remains a hypothetical notion.

Holidaymakers are the newest form of global migrants. Vacationing has to some extent united the world. But migration causes new global divides, and refugees and slaves remain a stubborn legacy of previous global contractions. Hypermobility also facilitated the global spread of two destructive forces: terrorism and pandemic disease. The world's population will increase by a third again in the coming generations. Hyper-mobility will be constrained, however, by the rising cost of long-distance transport and also by the use of outsourcing using communications technologies.

Tourism has long roots, from Marco Polo through to the eighteenth-century Grand Tour taken by the English upper classes to Paris, across the Alps to Italy, and – for the occasional rebel like Lord Byron – all the way to Greece. In 1841, Thomas Cook organized his first 'tour' – taking 500 middle-class temperance campaigners all the way from Leicester to Loughborough. By 1872 he was offering a 222-day world tour. In the late 1870s, Karl Baedeker produced his first travel guide to Egypt, and Switzerland was receiving a million tourists a year, a fifth of them from the USA. As we saw in Chapter Three, the cost and time involved meant that global travel through to the 1930s remained the preserve of the novelty seekers and the super-rich – like Nellie Bly and Andrew Carnegie – or desperate migrants.

All of that changed after the Second World War, as a result of peace, rising affluence, and the Boeing 707. In 1950, there were 25 million international tourist trips, equivalent to one per cent of the world's population. Tourists grew by over ten per cent a year from 1950 to 1964, when there were over 100 million international holidaymakers. This was the age of lightning travel for middle-class tourists. Since then, numbers have continued to rise steadily, faster than population growth, except for a brief hiccup in the early 1980s and again in 2001. In 2004, according to the World Tourism Organization, there were some 760 million international trips. Allowing a fortnight on average for each trip, that makes 30 million people on holiday at any one time. No wonder Louis Vuitton is one of the ten most global companies.

Most people side with Nehru in interpreting growing international travel as a positive sign of globalization. Not many countries have gone as far as Kiribati and changed their time zone in a bid to attract more tourists, but tourism is the world's biggest business. It employs 212 million people worldwide and provides over eight per cent of global employment, according to the World Travel and Tourism Council. Tourism generates a staggering $4.7 trillion of income – nearly 11 per cent of global GDP.[202] By 2020, according to forecasts, there will be 1.5 billion tourist trips a year. How global is international travel? Most international travel remains the preserve of the rich, and as parochial as the eighteenth-century English Grand Tour. In 1950 Europe and the Americas received 95 per cent of all travellers.

The world is opening up – but slowly. In 2004, these were still the destinations for three-quarters of all travellers, and by 2020 two-thirds of travel will still be to Europe and the Americas.

One cliché in the globalization debate is that hardly any Americans have passports and are somehow introspective.[203] It's not true: in 2000, US travellers made an impressive 171 million foreign trips, up from 131 million in 1990. What *is* true, according to the Bureau of Transport Statistics, is that almost two-thirds of those trips were day trips to Canada and Mexico. Including overnight trips to North American neighbours and other trips to the rest of the Americas brings the total up to almost 90 per cent of total foreign travel. Most of the rest was to Western Europe. The number of US trips in 2000 to the wider world was less than five per cent of total foreign trips. Only two or three Americans out of every hundred travel outside their comfort zone of the Americas and Europe. However, the rate has doubled since 1990, and this gradual emergence of a broader world-view – limited though it may be – is reflected by the steady growth in the number of US passport applicants in recent years (see chart).

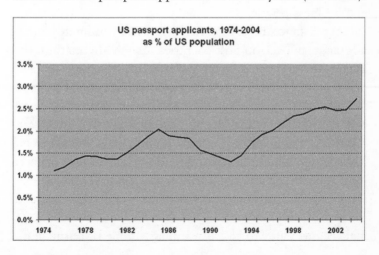

US passport applicants, 1974-2004
as % of US population

The British, who invented the Grand Tour, are not much more cosmopolitan. Four in ten British people never take a holiday, at home *or* abroad. According to the Office for National Statistics' *International Passenger Survey*, this proportion has remained constant since 1971. Of those that do travel, half go no further than France or Spain. Only 14 per cent of foreign holidays are to destinations outside Europe and the USA – and this proportion has actually fallen since 1971. Just five per cent of the British population makes a long-haul trip each year, probably little different from the proportion stationed around the world at the height of the Empire.

The German wanderlust, traced by late writer W. G. Sebald back to the experience of displacement caused by a million tonnes of Allied bombs, is expressed in Mediterranean travels,[204] while the French have been notoriously reluctant to leave their own country until recently. Despite Nehru's belief that travel could provide wider human purposes – cultural understanding and broadening the mind – global hyper-mobility remains the preserve of a limited Western elite of tourists and business people.

Long-distance travel from rich nations may be limited, but it has major impacts in host countries. As the aftermath of the 2004 tsunami showed, small countries had become dependent on even quite limited numbers of global travellers. Travel and tourism accounts for more than half the national income and employment in half a dozen Caribbean or Indian Ocean countries. In the British Virgin Islands, it is 95 per cent. The economic contributions are welcome; the broader impacts more mixed. Tourism can help revitalize cultural heritage, but also brings the privatization of shared assets like beaches, and social problems like prostitution. And air travel is becoming a major contributor to global warming – some favourite destinations like the Maldives will be hardest hit by rising sea levels and more frequent storms.

The rapid growth of tourism should not obscure the larger phenomenon of migrant workers. The mid nineteenth century may have been, proportionately, the great migration, but the last 50 years have seen the greatest ever stream of migrants leaving their native land in search of opportunities for work, education, reunification with family members, or to escape oppression. There were around 75 million international migrants in 1960 – around 2.5 percent of the world's population. By the year 2000, this number had climbed to 190 million people – approaching three people in every hundred around the world. 'We are living in an increasingly globalized world that can no longer depend on domestic labour markets alone.' noted Brunson McKinley, head of the International Organization for Migration in 2005. 'This is a reality that has to be managed.'

Managing migration became a serious challenge when more and more migrants concentrated on a short list of 30 countries. The United States remains the largest individual host of international migrants, with 35 million migrants in 2000. The major change from the pre-war period is that European countries, and especially Germany, France and the UK, have attracted more immigrants since 1960 than any other region. On the other hand, the highest proportion of migrants is found in the Gulf States – three-quarters of people in the United Arab Emirates are migrants.[205] Much of the apparent growth in migration after 1980 was due to the emergence of newly independent states after the collapse of the Soviet Union, which almost overnight created a large new group of migrants.

As Western Union well knows, remittances from migrant workers in rich countries amount to $100–200 billion a year and form a vital source of income in the home country. One estimate puts remittances at more than ten per cent of national income in countries like Albania, Bosnia and Herzegovina, Cape Verde, El Salvador, Jamaica, Jordan, Nicaragua, Samoa and Yemen. Migration is no longer a permanent decision and has become a two-way street – the US loses 200,000 migrants a year. When skilled workers return home, as many want to, the home country benefits from a so-called 'brain gain'. Nevertheless, many developing countries are increasingly opposed to emigration. A third of doctors practising in the UK were trained overseas, and this imposed a serious 'brain drain' on sub-Saharan Africa. In 2003 alone, Britain recruited over 11,000 healthcare workers from South Africa, Zimbabwe, Nigeria and Ghana. Adam Smith had no way of predicting the complications the 'invisible hand' could raise when the free-trade ethos permeated national healthcare and education labour markets.

Although modern migrant numbers are proportionately lower than they were in the nineteenth century, they have been accompanied by a rise in anti-immigrant sentiment, fuelled by xenophobia, and fears about culture, terrorism and jobs. Starting with the economic shocks of the 1970s, more and more states adopted measures to reduce immigration. In 1976, just six per cent of countries had such policies. By 2001 the number had rocketed to 40 per cent and will continue to rise. Visa restrictions are far more imbalanced than comparable restrictions on trade, such as import tariffs. In the USA, half of those asked in a recent survey saw immigrants as a problem, and this pattern is repeated in most countries. Only in Canada are a clear majority still in favour of immigration.[206]

Among the most desperate migrants are refugees: those who flee their countries from a well-founded fear of persecution. At the close of the Second World War, 65 million people were displaced in Europe alone, with tens of millions of Asians also

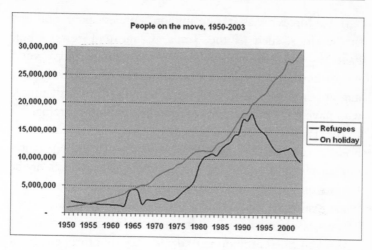

suffering upheaval.[207] In the early 1950s, there were still 1.5 to two million refugees, with a major new wave coming from Hungary. As decolonization and the widespread conflicts of the Cold War gathered pace in the 1960s and 1970s, refugee numbers rose, from Algeria and Rwanda, then Bangladesh and Uganda, finally from Indochina and Afghanistan.

Upheavals in Central America and the Horn of Africa swelled the total number to around 18 million refugees by the early 1990s. At this point, there were as many refugees as holidaymakers in the world (see chart). To the credit of refugee agencies, tens of millions of refugees were safely returned, while many others were resettled on the other side of the world. In the mid-1990s, holidaymakers pulled ahead, although crises in Rwanda, Bosnia, Kurdish Iraq and elsewhere meant that there were still ten million refugees worldwide in 2004. With today's dead, wounded and refugees increasingly the victims of ethnic, economic and ecological resource conflicts, rather than imperial or Cold War ideologies, the refugee will remain a feature of global mobility far into the future.[208] Other victims of the clash of global and national forces are some nine million 'stateless' people around the world – such as the Roma, Crimean Tartars, ethnic Eritreans and Bedouin – who live in a strange limbo world where they have no right to any nationality. Other involuntary migrants are the 20–25 million 'internally displaced' people who have fled conflict but not found neighbouring refuge.[209]

The 1948 UN Declaration on freedom of movement has been a mixed success, then. How have the new global institutions performed compared to their maligned predecessor the League of Nations in preventing conflict in the last 50 years? Some historians assert that the world is finally getting safer. The cause is not so much global peacekeeping institutions, let alone the US-led promotion of democracy, but through global trade. *New York Times* journalist Thomas Friedman developed Margaret Thatcher's dictum that democracies don't go to war into the 'Golden Arches Theory of Conflict Prevention': no two countries with a McDonald's had ever gone to war with each other. The NATO bombing of Serbia did little to dent the confidence in global supply-chains as the route to world peace. Appealing as the idea may be, the real danger of confrontation between China and Taiwan and the continuing crisis in the resource-rich Congo fit into Lewis Fry Richardson's equations. Global trade may not be a convincing cause of deadly quarrels, but nor is it a reliable guarantee of peace.

The Universal Declaration of Human Rights promoted mobility and it also prohibited slavery. In the 1960s, Saudi Arabia and other countries finally bowed to pressure and banned the institution. But there is a dark side to the story of post-war hyper-mobility. Thirty million women and children throughout Asia and the Pacific have been 'trafficked' over the past 30 years, in what the United Nations Children's Fund calls the 'largest slave trade in history'.[210] There are currently over 12 million forced labourers worldwide – and that is a conservative estimate, says the International Labour Organization (ILO). Half are children.[211] Slavery is not confined to stubborn pockets of pre-global practices in parts of Asia and West Africa, as many people believe. One in five forced labourers has been trafficked internationally, to provide economic or sexual services, and the ILO believes that there are at least 360,000 forced labourers in rich nations. 'Forced labour is a truly global problem', says Roger Plant of the ILO, 'present in all regions and types of economy.'[212]

From the ruinous terms of trade offered to West African cocoa farmers to the brick kilns of South Asia, from the soya estates of Brazil to the organized crime syndicates that traffic prostitutes and farm workers into Europe, forced labour is not a hangover from history but part and parcel of modern globalization. This shocking global trade is worth at least $32 billion a year. These statistics do not include hundreds of millions of children who work 'voluntarily' because their parents cannot earn a living wage. Labour abuse is still rampant in the production of commodities, and human muscle remains a flourishing if illicit trade commodity.

Two hundred years after slavery was first made illegal, and 100 years after the emergence of an international movement condemning labour abuse, there are more refugees, stateless people and slaves in the world than ever before. These linked problems affect as many people as lived in the United Kingdom when it abolished slave trading in 1807, or as lived in the United States of America as the Abolition movement got underway in the 1840s. Is there a psychological switch that will finally generate global revulsion against these extreme forms of involuntary mobility?

One clue lies in our response to the global spread of communicable diseases. From the Black Death to nineteenth-century cholera to the Spanish Flu, these pandemics have been a recurrent theme in the history of global migrations. Despite centuries of innovation in inoculation and vaccination, smallpox was still killing 1–2 million people a year in the mid-1950s when the Soviet Union called for an eradication campaign. The eradication of smallpox in 1979–80 was a triumph for health institutions. After concerted global action, the disease was finally stamped out. Many public health experts saw this victory as heralding a period when collective action could make major advances against global problems.

However, at the same time as the successful smallpox campaign, the AIDS virus moved across to humans from chimpanzees in West Africa. AIDS may have started through traditional local cultural practices – especially eating 'bush meat'. But its transcontinental spread through the 1960s and 1970s depended on small numbers of hyper-mobile travellers by air, land and sea. Today, 8,000 people die of AIDS and 14,000 are infected with HIV every day. Worldwide, over 40 million people now have HIV and half are women. Young adults are disproportionately affected, and 15 million children have been orphaned by AIDS.[213]

In the late 1980s and 1990s, widespread fear of the disease led to dramatic changes in behaviour among many Western homosexuals and intravenous drug-users. However, similar changes have not occurred in Sub-Saharan Africa. As a result, the region has taken the brunt of the disease, leading to catastrophic falls in life expectancy in countries like Swaziland and Uganda. Up to ten per cent of the continent's population could become infected in the next two decades on current trends. And the disease continues to spread in other regions.

'We are still moving into a globalisation of the AIDS epidemic,' according to the director of UNAIDS, Peter Piot. 'Think of Eastern Europe, Central America, Asia and maybe tomorrow, the Middle East as well.'[214] AIDS campaigners have struggled to find the switches that will make people defend their own lives. But they have also run up against a strand of isolationism that has deep roots in the global rift between the 'civilized' and the 'savage'. This was manifested in the obscene debate in pharmaceutical companies about the 'affordability' of fighting AIDS and providing low-cost anti-retroviral therapy for those infected with HIV. Some economists felt it necessary to undertake cost-benefit analyses of the fight against AIDS, hoping to prove that it is in the interests of rich nations and multinational corporations to strengthen the African economy, and thus world trade. Weighing up profit-able commodities – nutmeg, sugar, rubber or vaccines – against human lives is a recurrent theme in global history.

Two recent incidents illustrate our commitment to hyper-mobility. The first was the 2001 destruction of the World Trade Center. Terrorists have targeted global travel, particu-larly airplanes, for over 30 years. In 1976, Palestinians hi-jacked an Air France plane at Entebbe in Uganda. But the scale of the 9/11 atrocity led to an immediate change in interna-tional travel behaviour. In November 2002, the SARS virus appeared in Guandong in China. A handful of travellers then spread the disease to Hong Kong, Vietnam and Singapore. By July 2003, there had been 8,100 cases and 774 fatalities in 26 countries around the world, leading to paranoia and rapid changes in travel behaviour.[215] Within months, however, travel patterns were 'back to normal'. Global terror and global pandemics increase levels of fear and uncertainty, but are so far incapable of changing our deep-rooted desire for mobility and our ability to create hermetic ethical seals. 'We really only count the dead who come from our community,' observes philosopher John Ralston Saul.[216]

One development which will certainly unsettle that continuity: the global migration of jobs rather than people. In the previous chapter, we traced the origins of outsourcing – the transplantation of production to reduce costs – to the spice growers of the eighteenth century. Recently, outsourcing has been joined by 'offshoring' – the migration of white-collar jobs from rich nations to poorer ones with a well-educated work-force. Offshoring affects jobs in back-end processing, call centres, accounting, software, product design, telemarketing, procurement and research and consultancy services. With jobs migrating instead of workers, the global centre of gravity will shift eastwards.[217]

To date, offshoring has mainly been a phenomenon among English-speaking countries – common language is crucial at present – and the overall impact relatively modest. Around one million jobs had migrated eastwards, mainly from the USA and UK, by the end of 2005.[218] But trends in outsourcing and offshoring are growing fast, and will radically alter the rela-tionships between companies, workers and host economies. The migration of jobs is a major opportunity to cut corporate costs and reverse the brain drain in developing countries, but it makes tens of millions of service workers in the US and Europe vulnerable. For that reason it both fascinates and terrifies the rich world.

The planet, 100,000 years ago, was less populous than Swindon. The peak rate of migration was reached in the nineteenth century. In the face of job migration, closed borders and environmental limits to long-distance travel, the absolute numbers of people on the move may actually start to decline in the early twenty-first century. How big will the globe end up? There are three key dates in the study of global population trends. In the fertile decade 1963–72, the world population was growing at its fastest rate, over two per cent a year. The global baby boomers numbered 650 million people – more than the entire world population in 1700. In the year 1989, 87 million people came into the world – more than the entire population of the two Germanys that were poised to reunite. This was the biggest annual addition to the world population ever recorded. Since then, the growth rate and total numbers of new additions have fallen a little. The latest forecasts are that world population will reach its peak of nine billion in the year 2075, and will then stay at around that level.[219] The global population increased *ten times* in the last three hundred years. Growing by half again over the next 70 years sounds manageable by comparison. But the recurrent issue of how to share out the riches of the world – both its natural wealth and money – will have to be resolved. In the next chapter, we turn to money, the oil of trade and juice of globalization.

6

JUICE: MONEY, OIL AND THE GLOBAL CASINO

'Money is none of the wheels of trade. It is the oil which renders the motion of the wheels more smooth and easy'.
David Hume (1711–1776)[220]

Every day the world's foreign exchange dealers trade $2 trillion worth of currency. This is also the market value of all the gold ever mined.[221] Scottish Enlightenment thinker David Hume would have seen a connection between the two facts. Today, there is none. So far, the history of globalization has been presented as the story of exotic goods – spices, sugar, rubber, labour, travel, the very concept of the globe – that became cheap and mundane. In this chapter, the process is thrown into reverse.

Gold and silver backed the first currencies, but the quantity of precious metal in circulation could not keep up with investment needs. States increasingly set up strong central banks to issue paper currencies based on trust. To meet the need for global investment an international Gold Standard gradually emerged from the 1860s. Yet alongside the search for stability, the eighteenth and nineteenth centuries witnessed a continuous stream of speculative bubbles, which came to a head in the late 1920s.

Mistrust of international speculators influenced the construction of a new international financial system put in place in 1948. By the 1970s, global gambling again jeopardized the link between global currency and gold. The US dollar became the world's reserve currency, and financial markets were cut loose from national regulation. Money became a global commodity in its own right. Speculation and mounting debt fuelled binges of global investment.

Money was no longer the oil of commerce; oil became money. Unlike gold, oil had been plentiful until the 1970s. But with the perception of scarcity, it increased in price and increasingly underwrote international finance, including loans to poor nations. These soon became un-repayable. Global financial flows became the most contested area of the globalization debate. Financial historians are more sharply divided today than ever about whether money markets are an effective vehicle for investment or a recurrent manifestation of irrational exuberance.

All the time, the biggest debt of all was building up in the atmosphere in the form of carbon dioxide. As evidence for the greenhouse effect became undeniable, oil-dependent economies entered into the biggest financial gamble in history. The clash of currencies in the twenty-first century will not be between the dollar, euro and yuan, but the battle to unpeg economic growth from the 'carbon standard'.

From barter and cowries to sovereigns and dollars

'In 5,000 years there have been only four times that we have changed the way we pay. There was barter to coinage; coins to paper; paper to checks; and then cards.'
David Evans and Richard Schmalensee, 2005[222]

Economists, historians and philosophers have all struggled to understand money as a global force. Through history, money has struggled to find a balance between competing demands. It must be rare enough to build trust and store value; but common enough to enable widespread exchange. Money is the juice of globalization, in two senses: oiling the wheels of commerce and acting as a gambling bet. It is the manifestation of our 'frozen desires', and those desires are now global.[223] But money has been frequently and deliberately used to *limit* global exchanges, as a clog in the wheels of trade.

The earliest currencies to replace barter were locally rare or valuable commodities. Cowrie shells, ivory, livestock, grain, feathers, nails, tools and textiles were all used to pay for brides, blood money, religious taxes and ostentatious ceremonies, as much as for trade. Bartering and multifarious currencies hampered long-distance trade, involving additional transport costs, uncertain quantities, risks on quality and costly delays. What traders needed was a medium of exchange that would serve as a store of value and a unit of account too. Gold and silver were the first monies to find wide acceptance in all three functions. These precious metals were the first juice of globalization, long used in antiquity.

The first clear attempts to sabotage long-distance exchanges can be traced to ninth-century BC Sparta, when war-veteran turned lawgiver Lycurgus banned precious metals and replaced them with low-value iron coins specifically to discourage foreign trade and build local self-reliance. An extreme case was the Pacific islanders of Yap, who used carved stone coins. These were good as a store of value but had some limitations as a medium of exchange – the higher denominations were so heavy that it took twenty men to move them.

The first recognizable coins appeared in Lydia, straddling the Mediterranean and Asian trade routes, in c. 635BC. Lydia's King Croesus (ruled 561–546 BC) is credited with introducing the first bimetallic currency[224], at around the time that Pythagoras was formulating his theory of the spherical globe. According to Herodotus, one of the first uses of the coins was for that archetypal local trade, prostitution. But the Lydians became renowned long-distance traders, in sharp contrast to the isolationist Spartans.

Greek and Macedonian coinage was the first to spread widely, into Persia and across Asia Minor with the conquests of Alexander the Great (r. 336–323 BC). Alexander was as much central banker as warlord, grappling with the twin problems of scarcity and abundance by trying to enforce a one to ten equivalence between gold and silver. The Romans in turn needed vast quantities of coinage to pay imperial troops and this led to the first experiences of debased coinage, rapid inflation and conflicts between bankers and rulers. Despite continuous doubts about its quality, Roman coinage was widely distributed across the known world.

In the Arab trading world, the Caliph Abd al-Malik (r. 685–705) standardized the traditional gold dinar and silver dirham, which served as the regional currencies until at least 1200. In China, a shortage of precious metal and a reluctance to risk carrying it on long journeys coincided with the invention of paper and printing to give birth to the first paper currencies under Emperor Hien Tsung (r. 806–820). Despite periodic experiences of hyper-inflation, paper money was in wide circulation across Asia as a result of the Mongol conquests. 'In this city of Kanbalu is the mint of the grand Khan, who may truly be said to possess the secret of the alchemists, as he has the art of producing paper money,' wrote Marco Polo in 1304.

'The coinage of this paper money is authenticated with as much form and ceremony as if it were actually pure gold or silver . . . and the art of counterfeiting is punished as a capital offence. When thus coined in large quantities, this paper currency is circulated in every part of the grand Khan's dominions, nor does any person, at the peril of his life, refuse to accept it in payment . . . All his subjects receive it without hesitation, because, wherever their business may call them, they can dispose of it again in the purchase of merchandise they may have occasion for . . . With it, in short, every article may be procured . . . All his majesty's armies are paid with this currency, which is to them of the same value as if it were gold or silver. Upon these grounds, it may certainly be affirmed that the grand Khan has a more extensive command of treasure than any other sovereign in the universe.'[225]

In Europe, at a more modest scale, the Anglo-Saxons and continental counterparts kept a close eye on the minting of coins from the eighth century on. By early medieval times, the growth of trade and need to raise taxes for the logistics of major state projects like the Crusades led to renewed efforts to improve the regional acceptability of local metal-based currencies. The Knights Templar pioneered the development of international credit facilities. In 1156 we find an early example of a foreign exchange contract, when two brothers borrowed Genoese pounds and agreed to repay a bank's agents in Constantinople a month later with an appropriate sum of bezants that included handling fees and disguised interest.

The thirteenth century saw the use of money spread into the rural economy across Europe, with the introduction of low denomination coins to pay daily wages for peasants and soldiers.[226] One result was a widening gap between rich and poor, city and country. Landowners, now paid in cash not in crops, could move off the land and build new bases of power in urban palaces. Spicy banquets soon became a symbol of the conspicuous consumption this move enabled.

A major stumbling block in international finance was the Islamic and Catholic objection to usury (or at least to excessive interest rates). Jewish financiers openly and Christians clandestinely found ways around this. Theories of finance were the subject of intense debate amongst the Franciscan and Dominican orders, which in this sense can be seen as prototype international think-tanks. By the turn of the fifteenth century, Florentine traders argued against the injunction on usury on both theological and pragmatic grounds. The Protestant Reformation further weakened it, and by the mid-sixteenth century interest rates were routinely advertised.

Another innovation crucial to international finance was the system of double entry bookkeeping, long-known and widely-publicized from 1494. By the early seventeenth century, advances in finance and accounting enabled a radical departure from traditional partnership models relying on undependable royal backing. International trade was rapidly subsumed into new joint-stock companies, notably those exploiting the East Indies.

Financiers in this period came to expect annual returns of ten per cent from lending money; far more for a riskier venture. These gains were far in excess of the level of background economic growth. So alongside banking and accounting techniques came a culture of international financial speculation, initially among specialized Italian and German bankers like the Medici and Fuggers, then in the wider group of 'gentlemanly capitalists' centred in Antwerp, Amsterdam and London.[227] The expectation of high returns was justified because banking was a risky business. Transport was prone to accident and delay. Rulers reserved the right to coerce or confiscate money in times of need. 'Some [banking houses] lasted one generation, two generations,' says management guru Peter Drucker. 'Then they miscalculated, misspeculated, and ended bankrupt. Individuals made enormous fortunes. But the industry never made a penny.'[228]

Banking was also having teething problems elsewhere. In the fourteenth century, Persia, Japan and India experimented unsuccessfully with paper money. The Chinese paper banking experiment ended abruptly in 1455 when confidence in the regime collapsed. The Ming restoration of silver currency would provide an important boost to Chinese exports around the globe, so long as enough silver could be found to pay for them. Other parts of the world never abandoned commodity currencies in the first place. The cowrie shell, originating from the Maldives, was still in widespread use in Africa. This and other local currencies were later supplemented by manillas – chunky pieces of jewellery made of copper or bronze, increasingly imported from Portugal. In North America, carefully carved clamshells called wampum were common currency. Early European colonists in the Americas often joined the local commodity currency or created new ones, such as tobacco. The Mayans traded cocoa beans, the Aztecs exchanged feathers. The Incas thrived with no discernible currency at all.

From the 1490s, Portuguese incursions into Africa and Spanish conquests in the Americas saw increasing quantities of pillaged, extorted and then mined gold and silver arriving in Europe. In a couple of years, Columbus coerced gold from

Caribbean natives that had taken thousands of years to amass, and he was disappointed with the proceeds. In the sixteenth century, the Iberians shipped 150 tonnes of gold and 7,500 tonnes of silver from the Americas. Francis Drake purloined so much bullion from the Spaniards between 1577 and 1580 that Keynes described his loot as 'the fountain and origin of British Foreign Investment'.

Despite these depradations, enough bullion made it back to Spain to first underwrite and then undermine the empire. In 1545 a vast deposit of silver was discovered at Potosí in modern-day Bolivia. In the seventeenth century, new extraction technologies coupled with brutal labour exploitation saw the exports of silver to Europe rise to 25,000 tonnes. In the eighteenth century, exports nearly 40,000 tonnes. Contemporary observers reflected on the fact that the Spanish failed to invest their riches in economic development. 'The money produced by the mines will necessarily go abroad to pay for imports,' observed Irish banker Richard Cantillon. 'This will gradually impoverish the State and render it in some sort dependent on the Foreigner, to whom it is obliged to send money every year as it is drawn from the Mines.'[229] Much of the silver migrated to China, whose exports were so highly prized that it attracted hundreds of tonnes of silver a year, from the Americas via Manila, and then from new silver mines opening in Japan. Payments for India's exports came in gold, often hoarded in the form of family jewellery.[230]

In the seventeenth century, a few London goldsmiths turned their expertise in handling foreign coinage to advantage by taking deposits and issuing promissory notes in exchange. Civil servant and diarist Samuel Pepys (1633–1703) sent his father a goldsmith's note for £600 in 1668. This system of paper money was slow to supplant coin, nor did goldsmiths' safes rapidly replace time-honoured ways of storing money. During the panicky period in 1667 when Londoners thought a Dutch invasion of the capital was imminent, Pepys carried around, in a specially made money belt, the modern equivalent of £33,000 in gold. He shouted at his father and refused to speak to let alone sleep with his wife because he was so unhappy with the slapdash way they had buried a further large stash of gold coins and paper notes in their back garden – in full sight of Pepys' nosy neighbours.[231]

In the event, the Dutch did not invade, Pepys recovered his buried gold and made peace with his wife and father. By the 1690s, England had a national bank, and with it the vital concept of a national debt. Although the Bank of England was founded later than banks in Amsterdam, Delft, Nuremburg, Barcelona and Sweden, it was London's financiers, according to widely-travelled scientist, entrepreneur and pioneer economic statistician Sir William Petty (1623–87), who were in a strong position to become the linchpins of global finance. But to do so, they would need a global currency.

By the mid seventeenth century, silver and gold had become truly global commodity currencies. The central role that Europe played in the global flows of bullion gave the region a decisive advantage in international finance. A recurrent problem was that the increasing supply of bullion was out of step with growing population. The amount of money in circulation in Europe was well in excess of the value of the actual coinage. Gold and silver remained rare, but they were seldom equally rare at the same time or in the same place. As a result, the exchange rate of the two metals fluctuated constantly. The joint-stock trading companies could find few European manufactures that Asians would accept in exchange for spices, textiles and porcelain. As a result, and despite strenuous government efforts to stop it, silver continuously migrated to the east. The line between useful arbitrage and destructive speculation was a fine one, and most countries found themselves powerless to retain their preferred metal.

There were 68 grams of gold for every person on the planet in 1500. Despite the pillage of the Americas, that share had fallen to 52 grams by 1700. Balancing scarce gold against silver was a headache for Isaac Newton, Master of England's Royal Mint from 1699 to 1727. Despite careful calculations, he failed to correctly rebalance the relative prices of the two metals. Speculators found they could make about 1.4 per cent profit on silver in Amsterdam, and over the next 50 years silver steadily disappeared to the continent. As a result of Newton's poor maths, Britain stumbled into creating the gold standard.

Gold and bubbles (1719–1929)

'There is on Earth just so much gold, so many things, so many men, so many desires'

Davanzati, 1588[232]

'Gresham's Law, properly understood, can be a powerful tool in the hands of historians for the study of monetary history. The catchy phrase, "bad money drives out good," is not a correct statement of Gresham's Law nor is it a correct empirical assertion. Throughout history, the opposite has been the case. The laws of competition and efficiency ensure that "good money drives out bad." The great international currencies – shekels, darics, drachmas, staters, solidi, dinars, ducats, deniers, livres, pounds, dollars – have always been "good" not "bad" money.'

Robert Mundell, 1998[233]

The silver mine in the Bohemian village of Joachimsthal produced coins of outstanding quality. The coins were pushed
aggressively by the local Fugger bank, which had won a con-
cession on the mines in return for loans to the emperor. From the
sixteenth century, the Joachimsthaler style of coin caught on, and
the name *thaler* was later applied to Spanish pesos and Portuguese pieces of eight. Both were common currency in North
America, and in 1792 the Coinage Act established a single
legal tender in the USA, using the anglicized version of the
name, the dollar. But the dollar's position as a *de facto* global
currency was far in the future. Alexander the Great, the
Romans, and the Mongols had all created currencies that
were good in large parts of the known world. The City of
London developed ambitions for the first good global money.
But to do that, London's bankers would first have to survive a
speculative bubble of spectacular proportions.

When he needed to discuss marine insurance in the 1680s,
Samuel Pepys went straight to Edward Lloyd's coffee house,
where merchants, ship owners, and insurance brokers were the
exclusive clientele. By the early 1700s there were at least 500
coffee-shops in London, many known for their specialized
financial clientele. 'The coffee houses of late seventeenth- and
early eighteenth-century London could be viewed as an amal-
gam of open-plan office, internet café, post office, pub and
newspaper library,' writes Richard Dale.[234]

In London, coffee and money went together. At *La Procope*
in Paris, literature not finance was the talk of the day. When
the Dutch wanted to exchange news on the latest exotic tulip
varieties in 1634, they gathered in the less sober environment
of the tavern. To Scottish misanthrope Charles Mackay in
1841, the tulip mania was an 'extraordinary popular delu-
sion', epitomized by a drunken sailor accidentally eating a
bulb worth $10,000. The Dutch bubble in tulip futures (1634–

1637) has become a *cause célèbre* in the globalization debate. Because speculative bubbles challenge the notion of efficient markets and 'rational economic man', they have become a hot topic in economic history.

If stock markets are prone to manic-depressive behaviour, as Edward Chancellor and Charles Kindelberger have argued, then investment should be regulated.[235] In contrast, Peter Garber claims that the Dutch tulip futures market made economic sense. Garber, an economist at Deutsche Bank and Brown University, found little evidence of crazy speculation and concluded that there was a rational futures market, supplemented by 'a meaningless winter drinking game, played by a plague-ridden population that made use of the vibrant tulip market.'[236]

A similar phenomenon emerged eighty years after the tulip mania with the Mississippi scheme launched by charismatic Scotsman John Law in Paris, and in the South Sea scheme promoted simultaneously in London (1719–20). The 1710 South Sea Company was modelled on the East India Company, but its ostensible purpose – a trading monopoly with the islands of the South Seas and Spanish America – gradually became more ambitious: the buy-out of the entire national debt. After ten years of spectacular stock growth, news that the King of Spain was not entirely enthusiastic about the proposed monopoly combined with a new bout of plague to cause a major 'market correction'. The Bubble burst and shares fell by 90 per cent.

Irrational or not, the South Sea Bubble led to a major knee-jerk reaction. A company director was shot by an angry shareholder. A member of parliament demanded that the remaining directors be sewn up in sacks with snakes and their filthy lucre and drowned. In 1720, corporations were made illegal as was selling stocks without legal authority. The

Bubble Act remained in force for 105 years.[237] Some historians misleadingly treat the eighteenth-century speculative bubbles much as they do the slave trade, as temporary aberrations on the way to the nineteenth-century golden age of benign globalization.

As the incomplete list in the table below shows, speculative bubbles have been part and parcel of financial developments over the past 400 years. Sevententh- and eighteenth-century bubbles may have been relatively harmless entertainment designed to fleece wealthy 'gulls'. From the mid-nineteenth century, with the rise of global currencies and joint-stock companies, the impacts became both more serious and more global.

Selected stock market and other bubbles[238]

Country	Holding	Years
Holy Roman Empire	Currency	1618
Holland	Tulip bulbs	1634–37
United Kingdom	South Sea shares	1719–20
France	Mississippi shares	1719–21
UK	Railways, mining	1820s–40s
UK, Germany, USA	Banks	1820s–50s
USA	Plank roads	1846–50s
USA	Ponzi (Postal coupons)	1919
Mauritius	Sugar	1920–22
USA	Florida property	1925
USA	Stock market	1927–32
USA	Bowling	1957–63
Hong Kong	HK shares	1970–74
Mexico	Mexico shares	1978–81
USA/UK	Black Friday/Monday: shares	1987
Japan	Tokyo property	1989–92
USA	Nasdaq stock	1991–99
'Asian tigers'	Property & banks	1997–98

In the early 1800s, global finance remained a challenge. Tobacco and wampum were common currencies in North America, while unregulated 'wildcat' banks flooded the states with hundreds of rival paper currencies. Speculators swamped the Ugandan money markets with imported cowrie shells. Singapore, ever the pragmatic global entrepôt, accepted half a dozen currencies as legal tender. In England, during the vast expenses of the Napoleonic wars, the circulation of tokens, foreign coins, and other currencies exceeded official coins of the realm. Average incomes in Europe were rising, but in 1820, gold remained so scarce that there was just 32 grams for each person in the world – less than half the amount there had been 300 years earlier.

In these unsettled circumstances, London-based bankers steadily emerged as leaders in global finance. In 1803, when cash-strapped Napoleon put Louisiana up for sale, the United States offered to buy it for $15 million (about $250 million in today's prices), but didn't have the cash. Their first choice was to borrow the money from Barings (founded 1762) and other London banks. Barings was only too happy to oblige – a state of war with France was no obstacle to these international financiers. Meanwhile, Nathan Rothschild was establishing a London branch of the Frankfurt family bank. Britain was soon responsible for over half of the world's foreign investment.

While the international reach of these banks grew rapidly, they remained well insulated from banks in other countries. Bank crises in England (1826), the USA (1837) and France (1847) had limited international impacts. In 1816, the Coinage Act attempted to streamline the London money bazaar by declaring a new £1 gold sovereign as the sole standard of value and unlimited legal tender. Britain's gradual drift towards a gold standard was made formal in 1844. But if more gold was not brought into circulation, sterling's link with gold would become excessively tenuous, relegating London to a secondary position on the global stage.

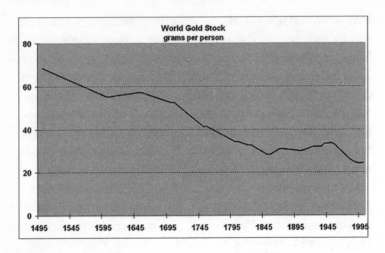

When a farm labourer picked up a gold nugget near his sawmill in California in 1848, Swiss settler John Sutter (1803–80) feared the discovery would ruin his utopian colony. He tried to keep the gold a secret, but failed. The subsequent Gold Rush transformed California. In 1847, world gold output had been 35 tonnes a year. In 1852, after gold strikes in Australia, it was 265 tonnes, and annual production continued at a high rate for the next 30 years. The spread of Californian and Australian gold changed the prospects of Britain's gold-backed money as a global currency. It is no coincidence that the first banking crisis to have transcontinental impacts began in the US in 1857 and spread rapidly to London and Germany.

The gold rushes led to a rapid switch from silver to gold. In 1865, France, Italy, Belgium, Switzerland and Greece had set up a Latin Monetary Union accepting all coinage – silver and gold – as legal tender. At the 1867 International Monetary Conference in Paris, France and the USA aggressively pushed for both silver and gold, but most other countries favoured silver alone. Only Britain, Egypt, Canada, Australia, Chile and Portugal were committed to gold.

When Germany united its currency in 1871, it was based on a gold standard, and the Scandinavian Monetary Union followed suit in 1873. The tide turned rapidly, with silver losing value and causing serious losses to the pro-silver Asian economies – China, India and Japan. In the late 1870s, France moved across to gold, something of a formality since it had been accumulating large quantities of the new gold arriving from California since the mid-1850s. During the global contraction of the 1880s, gold became for the first time a genuinely global currency, circulating widely among ordinary people across the continents, as well as being the reserve of choice within central banks.[239] Hence Nellie Bly's uncertainty about whether the countries she was to visit would accept silver dollars.

In the 1890s, gold was formally adopted by Japan, India and, most grudgingly, by the USA. By the turn of the century only China and a few Central American countries remained loyal to silver. As a result of mining, the world gold supply kept pace with population all the way through to 1955 at around 30 grams per person. Although paper money in circulation was soon many times the gold reserves held by central banks, the link with gold and Britain's dominance of world trade helped maintain faith in exchangeability.

For British free traders, the Gold Standard became the essential complement to lowering tariffs. Economist Robert Mundell described the Gold Standard as a 'self-regulating rudder that guided policy makers toward equilibrium.' The smooth operation of the system has been exaggerated. London was forced to make at least 200 domestic adjustments over the thirty years to 1914 to maintain exchange rates. But even if it was a little creaky, the gold standard facilitated a surge in foreign investment. Foreign investments in Africa, Asia and Latin America increased six-fold from 1870, reaching $235 billion in 1914. On the eve of the Great War, this foreign capital equalled almost a third of recipient countries' economic production.

The foreign investment boom was coupled with economic growth. Average incomes per person worldwide increased from $870 in 1870 to $1,500 in 1913 – an annual growth rate of 1.3 per cent.[240] But foreign capital flows were highly selective. Two-thirds of France and Germany's foreign investments was directed to other European countries, the USA, Canada and Australia. The UK and USA invested half or more of their overseas capital in Latin America, Africa and Asia, with Britain alone responsible for almost half of all foreign investments outside Europe. But these investments were heavily concentrated in a handful of attractive prospects. Argentina, Australia, Brazil, Canada, China, India, Mexico and South Africa accounted for the lion's share of global investments. Many countries failed to attract any global investment whatsoever during the Gold Standard era.

So the benefits of global finance were patchy. By 1913, Americans, Australians and Canadians had average incomes in excess of $5,000 a year, closely followed by the British. Incomes grew fastest in Latin America and Japan, North America and Europe, but much slower than the world average in Africa and Asia. The result was growing inequality in standards of living. The gap between the richest and poorest regions had been three to one in 1820, but regional inequality had trebled to nine to one by 1913. The typical Indian was earning under $2 a day, with once-dynamic sectors like weaving forcibly reduced to the status of cottage industries. Africans, now almost entirely subjects of the European empires, were subsisting on $1.60 a day when they were paid at all. China was the biggest loser from the 1880s–90s global contraction, however. Despite lavish foreign investment in enclaves like Hong Kong, Shanghai and Tsingtao, the average Chinese income was just £1.50 a day in 1913. Ravaged by enforced imports of opium and the European stranglehold over trade, the standard of living was lower than it had been a hundred years before.[241]

If global finance was mixed in its benefits worldwide, life was good for Britain's gentlemanly capitalists. 'The inhabitant of London could adventure his wealth in the natural resources and new enterprises of any quarter of the world, and share, without exertion or even trouble, in their prospective fruits and advantages;' wrote John Maynard Keynes, who combined his economics with a keen enthusiasm for speculation. 'Or he could decide to couple the security of his fortunes with the good faith of the townspeople of any substantial municipality in any continent that fancy or information might recommend.'[242]

Adventuring wealth like this was not risk-free. In 1890, rash investments in railways in Argentina almost destroyed Barings Bank. Despite the risks, City investors were obsessed with the high returns available from global investment opportunities in this period, and especially infrastructure projects like railways. These investments did little to support the development of domestic industry, which was growing sluggishly. The slower British industry grew, the more City investors looked elsewhere. Germany, France, the USA and several other countries were actually growing faster in this period than the UK. Richard Cantillon would have detected something of the wealthy indolence of seventeenth-century Madrid in early twentieth-century London. Being banker to the world turned out to be a mixed blessing.

Tarnished globe (1914–48)

'The global economy that had emerged before 1914 fell apart over the next thirty years. The Great Depression that followed the Wall Street Crash of 1929 finally killed it off.'
Philippe Legrain, *Open World*[243]

In 1931, the concerned citizens of Cameroon clubbed together and sent the starving people of New York the generous sum of $3.77.[244] The impacts the Great Depression were felt around the world. For free-market enthusiasts, it is a potent symbol of how vulnerable the fruits of globalization can be. As we have seen, the Gold Standard era was far from open-handed in its global reach and benefits. Many of the financial problems of the 1920s and 30s were part and parcel of that very same global system.

As the wartime devastation subsided in 1918, the world's finance ministers and central banks tried to patch the Gold Standard back together. The major challenge was to face up to the new balance of power arising from massive migrations of gold that paid for the war, differing experiences of wartime inflation, post-war hyper-inflation in Germany, and the newly revealed might of the US economy. When Britain moved back on to gold in 1925, it was a flawed gold bullion standard pegged at pre-war levels. In the view of John Kenneth Galbraith, this was 'perhaps the most decisively damaging action involving money in modern times.'

Nevertheless, by 1930 forty countries had rejoined, making it the most extensive financial system yet seen. But finance ministers and central bankers were reluctant to follow pre-war global rules, not least because they were nervous about im-posing deflationary adjustments on newly-enfranchised and vociferous working-class electorates. The USA and Canada experienced their first 'general strikes' (in Seattle and Winnipeg, 1919). Britain had its own General Strike in 1926. Best known today for its folk songs, the radical labour organization Industrial Workers of the World had hundreds of thousands of members – and global organizing ambitions – in the early 1920s. Overall, five million US workers were members of trade unions in 1920.

France and the USA in particular were backing several horses in the 1920s, happy to build up gold reserves that left London exposed. But having rejected the League of Nations, the USA had no intention of itself taking up the role of global lender of last resort. Indeed the Federal Reserve's decision to increase interest rates in 1928 helped prick the bubble on Wall Street the following year. But international speculation was largely responsible for that bubble in the first place. In his controversial *Theory of Business Enterprise*, Thorstein Veblen (1857–1929) had identified an inherent tension between the business firm, whose objective was making profits, and the industrial process, whose objective was making goods. By the 1920s, this equation also included millions of ordinary investors looking for the easy profits hitherto reserved for gentlemanly capitalists.

In December 1919, short, fast-talking Italian immigrant Charles Ponzi (1882–1949) started telling thousands of working-class Bostonians that he had worked out a way of making fabulous profits from US postal reply coupons. These coupons had been introduced as a well-meaning innovation – a way for immigrants to remit a sum of money to poor relatives in Europe sufficient to enable them to reply to letters. Ponzi claimed he could make easy profits on exchange rates if he traded enough coupons.

Ponzi became an overnight celebrity and pillar of Boston

society, with a controlling stake in the Hanover Trust Bank and a mansion in Lexington. But his business, whether he knew it or not, was a pyramid scheme relying on new investors to pay the promised returns to previous ones. In all, he took $15 million before the scam was exposed. 'A huge line of investors, four abreast, stretched from the City Hall Annex all the way to my office!' gloated Ponzi. 'Hope and greed could be read in everybody's countenance. Guessed from the wads of money nervously clutched and waved by thousands of out-stretched fists! Madness, money madness, was reflected in everybody's eyes! To the crowd there assembled, I was the realization of their dreams – the "wizard" who could turn a pauper into a millionaire overnight!'[245]

Swedish entrepreneur Ivar Krueger (1880–1932) had an even more dramatic rise. The so-called 'Match King' as-sembled a string of national monopolies on matches and at his peak controlled two-thirds of the world match industry, as well as some 200 telephone companies, banks, pulp mills and ball-bearing makers throughout Europe, in the USA and beyond, making it one of the largest multinational enterprises of its day. Krueger was a hero with investors. The Wall Street crash made Krueger's pyramid empire teeter, but it did not fall until his suicide in 1932 – which set off a further financial crash in Sweden.

Hustlers and money-mad investors were centre stage in the desperate optimism of the roaring 1920s.[246] 'Speculators may do no harm as bubbles on a steady stream of enterprise,' wrote Keynes in his *General Theory of Employment, Interest and Money*. 'But the position is serious when enterprise becomes the bubble on a whirlpool of speculation. When the capital development of a country becomes a by-product of the activ-ities of a casino, the job is likely to be ill-done.'[247]

When the casino-like bubble on Wall Street finally burst, the

Gold Standard came down with it. Global finance in the 1920s was still dominated by a small clique of countries, and suddenly they all wanted to exchange their money for gold. A Bank for International Settlements in 1930 could do little to reverse the run on gold and rapidly became a talking shop for central bankers. The collapse of the Credit Anstalt Bank in Austria in 1931 had immediate knock-on effects on German banks and then in London, which was known to have been lending heavily to Germany. In 1931, Britain was forced to come off the Gold Standard to stem the exodus of gold. It was soon followed by most of the Commonwealth, Ireland, Scandinavia, Iraq, Portugal, Japan, Thailand, and some South American countries. In 1934, the USA unilaterally set an official price for gold at $35 an ounce. The global Gold Standard was finished.[248]

The Depression saw trade levels stagnate or even fall in many countries, and migration slowed. The value of British exports halved and unemployment climbed to 2.5 million. The UK only escaped the worst excesses of depression thanks to a house-building boom, a marginal improvement in terms of trade once it abandoned the Gold Standard, and later spending on armaments. Rubber and tin workers in Asia saw markets dry up, and Australia was hit hard. In France, the economy entered a steady decline that did not hit rock-bottom until 1937. The impacts in Germany were immediate and catastrophic.

In the USA, the suicides on Wall Street were followed by the privations of farmers in the Midwest Dust Bowl and mass lay-offs of industrial workers. Unemployment reached 25 per cent in 1933. A whole generation lost faith in the stock market as a means of saving. The Smoot-Hawley Tariff Act of 1930, which raised import duties on a wide range of goods, was intended as a beggar-thy-neighbour policy, but had limited international repercussions and supported many US businesses that were just beginning to look to export markets.

Indeed those US businesses that weathered the initial storm actually increased their productivity during the Depression, investing in scientific research, taking advantage of techno-logical innovations in electricity and chemicals, and benefit-ing from New Deal government investments in urban, energy and transport infrastructure. According to one estimate, the period 1929–41 saw the fastest growth in US productivity recorded, before or since, despite the introduction of mini-mum wages and corporate regulation like the Robinson-Patman Act on resale price maintenance and state-level attacks on chain stores like A&P and Woolworth's. Ironi-cally, these large retailers were able to drive out smaller stores because they took advantage of the new federally-funded telephone and highway networks to develop more efficient distribution systems.[249]

The impacts of the Depression on global finance were a mixture of the predictable and the unexpected. German overseas investment fell through the floor as the country turned in on itself. French capital invested abroad fell to half its 1914 levels, most of what remained within Europe or in its African and Indo-Chinese colonies. British investments also fell, but to a more limited extent, and actually increased in Latin America and Asia. The USA quietly invested its domes-tic surpluses abroad and increased its share of global capital from under a tenth of the total in 1914 to a quarter by 1938. The USA had a more diverse portfolio of capital investments than any other rich nation, except in Africa, where it found few opportunities. But the US overseas portfolio was still a very small proportion of the huge US economy (about 1.4 per cent of total output) compared to Britain's investments (6 per cent of output). In the late 1930s, then, global financial hegemony still rested with the City of London. But Wall Street was waiting in the wings.

The Second World War strengthened US trade enormously and gave the country a global awareness. It was the national equivalent of Andrew Carnegie's round-the-world-trip. The war also created a *tabula rasa* for worldwide investment, because the rich nations pulled three-quarters of their investments from Latin America, Asia and Africa to pay for the war effort. In the late 1940s, the standard of living across Europe was half that of the USA; in Italy, Germany and Greece it was a third. Incomes had barely grown in Africa and had actually fallen in Asia compared to 1913. In China and many parts of Africa, people were living on less than $1 a day. The inter-regional spread in income between richest and poorest regions had climbed to fifteen to one.[250] The world had never been more economically divided. In Washington and Moscow, strategists started to view these imbalances with increasing concern.

US President Harry S. Truman (1884–1972) made his inaugural address in January 1949, calling for 'a bold new program for making the benefits of our scientific advances and industrial progress available for the improvement and growth of underdeveloped areas . . . More than half the people of the world are living in conditions approaching misery. Their food is inadequate. They are victims of disease. Their economic life is primitive and stagnant. Their poverty is a handicap and a threat both to them and to more prosperous areas.' By 1954, the US was talking of these 'underdeveloped' nations as a set of dominoes stood on end. If one piece were to topple, in Indo-China for example, the whole set could fall into Communist hands. The world, which to the City of London had seemed so united in 1913, was split in three.

The Bretton Woods System (1944–71)

> *'In the past seven years, there has been an average of one international monetary crisis every year. Now who gains from these crises? Not the workingman; not the investor; not the real producers of wealth. The gainers are the international money speculators. Because they thrive on crises, they help to create them'.*
>
> US President Richard Nixon
> addresses the nation, 15 August 1971[251]

Truman's vision for a new world order was more pragmatic, more geopolitical than Roosevelt's talk of peace-loving and united nations. Secretary of State Dean Acheson positively loathed the idea of the United Nations, dismissing it as a nineteenth-century idea (a recurrent strain in US diplomacy which recently resurfaced in taunts about 'Old Europe'). If there had to be a United Nations, it would have to be amenable to US interests. At the 1945 San Francisco conference to agree the UN charter, chief US negotiator Edward Stettinius used bribery, bully tactics and phone taps to ensure the US got its way in the Security Council and that the General Assembly was suitably weak.[252]

The parallel meeting in 1944 at Bretton Woods in New Hampshire was to agree a successor to the Gold Standard. Britain's negotiator Keynes argued furiously with Harry Dexter White for the US on the need for and nature of a global financial reserve fund to act as a lender of last resort to assist countries with temporary balance of payment problems. But they were both agreed that international speculators were a curse that had caused the Great Depression. Global casino capitalism would be limited by national regulation of finance, successfully quashing

Wall Street and the City of London's demands for freedom from controls on international capital movements.

Two new financial institutions were created at Bretton Woods: the International Monetary Fund (IMF) and an International Bank for Reconstruction and Development (IBRD, later the World Bank). Their task was to oversee and enforce rules for a new system of convertible currencies, at more-or-less fixed but adjustable exchange rates, based on a constant value for the dollar of $35 per ounce of gold. Ambitious plans for an International Trade Organization to reduce the 1930s tariffs were rejected by the US Congress in a reprise of the 1919 rejection of the League of Nations. As a pale substitute for such an organization, negotiators in Havana managed to slip an agreement past Congress (the General Agreement on Tariffs and Trade or GATT). Plans to create bodies to stabilize international commodity prices and seek full employment never got off the drawing board.

The overall goal of the Bretton Woods system was to facilitate global trade, but keep capital movements under tight control. Despite its 44-nation membership, the physical location and convoluted governance arrangements of the new institutions reflected the new balance of economic power – the US had amassed 70 per cent of the world's gold reserves during the war. This would later become an Achilles heel for the system. One of the most important tools of the new international financial order was a method for measuring national economic performance called Gross Domestic Product (GDP). Like the spread of double entry book-keeping in the late fifteenth century, standardized GDP enabled consistent comparisons of economic performance between countries. Simon Kuznets (1901–85) created GDP virtually single-handed, beginning in his native Russia at the age of 20, and thereafter at the University of Pennsylvania.

After the war, GDP allowed for the first time a careful examination of the impacts of economic growth on income. Without this tool, the new Washington-based institutions would simply not have been able to exercise the power of oversight and enforcement that they came to acquire on rich and poor national economies alike. Reliance on GDP as a guide to national progress had several important drawbacks. It counts spending on negatives like crime prevention and ill-health but does not count positive contributions like unpaid labour in the home. Nor does it take account of uncosted problems (which economists call 'externalities') like environmental damage.[253] Like nuclear physicist Robert Oppenheimer's disavowal of the atomic bomb, Kuznets himself was the first to argue that GDP is a highly misleading measure of national progress or economic welfare. But because it existed, he could not prevent Washington economists and policy-makers from using it.

The immediate post-war challenge for the new Washington-dominated world economic order was how to pay for rebuilding European economies. Hyper-inflation in Europe had seen the return of barter and tobacco as currencies, and in many countries socialism was on the rise. The 1949–50 Marshall Plan was the US response, steering around $90 billion towards 16 European countries provided they moved towards currency convertibility, lowered trade tariffs, promoted exports to the US – and were tough on communism. This investment was significantly supplemented by military spending during the Berlin airlift (1948) and Korean War (1950–53).

By the late 1950s, the Bretton Woods system and US investments had been reasonably effective: the main European economies were back to their pre-war levels and ready to declare their currencies fully convertible. If foreign trade and investment were at modest levels, the richer nations were not unduly worried. In 1954, the Dow Jones index of US stocks returned to its 1929 level. The appearance of a US balance of payments deficit was seen more as an opportunity than as a problem.

The broader global implications of the system became apparent when Britain and France made their ill-fated incursion into Suez in 1956. As the costly invasion ran into logistical and tactical trouble, speculators punished the pound and franc, leaving Britain and France nowhere to turn but to the US-dominated IMF. Eisenhower was in a position to demand that the British withdraw unconditionally from Egypt before approving a $1.2 billion rescue loan. France received an additional $260 million.

This marked a turning point in the hitherto halting process of decolonization. Ghana and Malaya rapidly gained independence in 1957, and the late 1950s and 1960s saw a rapid growth in the number of new nations. Recent studies show how brutal and precipitate the exit from empire often was, as in Algeria or during the repression of the Mau Mau rebellion of 1952–60.[254] The membership of the United Nations doubled from 60 member states in 1954 to 122 in 1966. In this same period, almost all primitive forms of money – manillas, cowries – disappeared from use, with the sole exception of the huge *fei* stone coins on the island of Yap. By the early 1960s, world trade topped $100 billion, fuelled by returning prosperity in Europe and the US consumer boom. Gold could simply not be mined fast enough to keep up with the demand for liquidity. The dollar and, to a lesser extent, the pound were becoming reserve assets in their own right. Neither country wanted falling gold reserves and rising inflation. But the alternative – limiting the supply of money in circulation – 'could permit a crisis to develop', warned IMF managing director Pierre-Paul Schweitzer in 1964, 'in which most of the world would tend toward economic stagnation and would suffer from declining trade.'

In 1964, Auric Goldfinger hatched a dastardly plan to irradiate all the gold in Fort Knox and cause global financial meltdown. There is a problem with the story line of the classic James Bond film, however. By the mid-1960s, the US had hardly any gold: just $3 billion of bullion to cover foreign central bank and government holdings of $14 billion. What would happen if a foreign government lost faith in its dollar holdings? Through the 1960s, the Western nations made unsuccessful efforts to pool gold, and the US government tried to stem the outflow of dollars through the 1965 Voluntary Capital Control Program, where US corporations were actively discouraged from investing abroad, as well as controls of foreign purchases of US stocks. These Spartan efforts to limit overseas capital flows were undermined by massive military spending, however. Not least of these investments was the Space Race sparked off by Sputnik.

By the late 1960s, the drain on gold was so desperate that the US would no longer redeem dollars from private investors. But gold hoarding and speculation continued, even after the IMF invented an entirely new form of global currency called the Special Drawing Right. As first individuals and then central banks began another run on the dollar in August 1971, President Nixon made a snap decision at Camp David and made a historic announcement. 'In recent weeks, the speculators have been waging an all-out war on the American dollar,' he told the nation. 'Accordingly, I have directed the Secretary of the Treasury to suspend temporarily the convertibility of the dollar into gold or other reserve assets.'

Nixon mentioned 'fairness' half a dozen times in his address to the nation, but this was an undisguised protectionist package. Nixon reduced US car sales tax, cut foreign aid, froze price increases and slapped an across the board 10 per cent increase on import tariffs. 'If you want to buy a foreign car or take a trip abroad, market conditions may cause your dollar to buy slightly less', Nixon warned unpatriotic consumers. 'But if you are among the overwhelming majority of Americans who buy American-made products in America, your dollar will be worth just as much tomorrow as it is today.' The US could only get away with such drastic measures because in 1971, despite having the *de facto* world currency, the US economy was still largely domestic in focus.

For 100 years, much of the world had been operating on currencies tied to gold. By 1973, currencies were floating free of any link to the physical world – as currencies in the Communist Bloc had been for some time. Without the pull of gold, currencies gravitated to regional or post-colonial loyalties, and attempted to peg their currency within certain limits. The irony was that the troubled teenage years and collapse of the Bretton Woods system coincided with what is widely considered to be the 'golden age' for the world economy, from 1950 to 1973.

In this period of global contraction, average world income per person grew twice as fast as it had in the previous contraction of the 1880s and 90s. The annual growth rate topped four per cent in Europe, 3.5 per cent in the Soviet Union, two per cent in Africa, a staggering eight per cent in Japan and six per cent in Korea and Taiwan. Many parts of the world seemed to be catching up with the USA, where growth was running at a comparatively modest 2.5 per cent. Although there was still a massive gap between the income of the average Asian ($1,200), African ($1,400) and Latin American ($4,500) compared to the rich nations ($11–16,000), income inequality between the world's regions actually fell for the first time in history.

Surprisingly, this global contraction took place with only modest levels of global financial exchange. Many countries in this period, from China to the USA to Latin America, did their utmost to limit rather than increase their participation in global financial markets. This is not to say that foreign investment – and its alter ego currency speculation – was altogether absent. Some of the earliest global investors were the pension-fund managers of the World Bank and those US corporations who realized they had built up large foreign payrolls and wanted to hedge against their pension commitments. In general, however, finance was far from global when the gold-backed dollar collapsed in the early 1970s.

'Greed is global' (1973–2005)

> *'Investment bankers are always telling me – usually late at night, when they're pretty well oiled – that Gordon Gekko is the reason they got into the business. Which is a little scary.'*
> Michael Douglas[255]

Michael Douglas won an Oscar for his role as ruthless investment banker Gordon Gekko in the film *Wall Street* (1987). Gekko's mantra – 'greed is good' – entered the vocabulary. The main impacts of corporate raiders were still seen at the national level, but in the late 1980s, cross-border equity investments were approaching $2 trillion – almost a fifth of the total value of the world's stock markets. In the 'Roaring Nineties', cross-border investments passed the fifty per cent mark of world stock market capitalization.

By 2000, foreign equity investments reached a staggering $26 trillion, accounting for over three-quarters of the world's stock market value. This was not just a US investment spree:

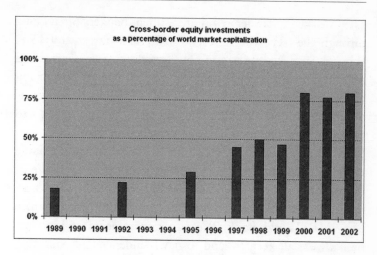

Cross-border equity investments as a percentage of world market capitalization

foreigners owned 12 per cent of US equities and 25 per cent of US corporate bonds, up from just four per cent and one per cent, respectively, in 1975. 'With a few exceptions', says Diana Farrell, director of the McKinsey Global Institute, 'it is no longer accurate to think in terms of national financial markets. Instead, individual markets are becoming increasingly integrated into a single global market for funding.' For today's Gordon Gekkos, greed is global.[256] How did it happen and what are the implications?

Global capital flows began to increase modestly in the 1970s with the breakdown of the fixed exchange rate system and capital flow controls that had been introduced by Bretton Woods. Until that point, national financial markets had been largely independent. In the late 1960s, only a dozen US banks had an international presence, and they had just 200 foreign branches between them. After Nixon's devaluation, desperate efforts were made through the 1970s to avoid what seemed to be a terrifying concept: freely floating currencies.

But by 1978, the IMF, the US Treasury and Wall Street had shaken off the anti-speculation mindset of Keynes and White.

They worked in tandem, with investment bankers often going through the 'revolving doors' at 700 19th Street and 1500 Pennsylvania Avenue to promote free-floating currencies and deregulation of national controls. Global capital flows soon followed. In the mid-1980s, over 200 US banks had international operations, with 800 overseas branches. European and Japanese banks built up a strong presence on Wall Street, too. Elites in many developing countries started to ask for large sums to fund industrial and infrastructure projects, military expansion – and plain old-fashioned corruption. Most of these loans were at variable interest rates from commercial banks. The IMF, World Bank, Western governments and private banks were all keen to lend to newly-independent countries, particularly if they were tough on communism. Thanks to 'petro-dollars', they had the money to do so.

The weakness at the core of the post-war institutions led to the formation of new interest groups of all sorts. One of the earliest was the Bilderberg Group – a private network of industrialists and politicians (1954). Some were governmental alliances, like the small group of oil-producing nations that met in Baghdad in 1960, or the formation of the Non-Aligned Movement by India, Yugoslavia, Indonesia and Egypt from 1961–66. Others were non-governmental organizations (NGOs), such as the conservationists who founded the World Wildlife Fund in 1961 or the British and Irish churches that formed Christian Aid in 1964 to tackle world hunger. The new NGOs used improved communications and were funded by donations from rising incomes to represent many different interests. The year 1971, for example, saw the foundation of Médecins Sans Frontières, Greenpeace, and the World Economic Forum.

OPEC was the first group to flex its global muscles. In 1974, this cartel of petroleum exporting countries with members in

Latin America, Asia, Africa and the Middle East decided to raise oil prices as a direct response to Nixon's devaluation of the dollar. The US and Europe were anguished but because their economies were largely reliant on oil, they were incapable of reducing consumption to any significant degree. In 1972, oil exporters had gained $23 billion in oil revenues. By 1977, they were receiving $140 billion, and could hardly spend their new earnings fast enough.[257] Petro-dollars began accumulating in European and US bank vaults, sparking inflation. Finance ministers and central banks responded by raising interest rates.

The result was that the debt repayments of many developing countries spiralled beyond their ability to pay. Poland and Mexico were in trouble by the early 1980s. By the end of the decade, dozens of countries had debts greater than their national income. Mozambique owed its entire output four times over. Although to many development experts these debts looked unpayable, the IMF insisted on the strong medicine called Structural Adjustment, which demanded major cutbacks in government spending. Much of the money had been either embezzled, spend on armaments or invested in ill-fated projects that generated little income, leaving many poor countries with debt obligations that they could meet only by cutting education and healthcare.

Despite the problems of the 1980s, when the Berlin Wall fell in 1989, and the Soviet Union imploded two years later, global financiers were in triumphant mood at the victory of capitalism and 'the end of history'. The IMF's standard package – liberalization, privatization and foreign investment – was applied in even more of a rush. The impacts of this 'shock therapy' in the former Soviet Union and Eastern Europe were devastating: hunger and riots, mass job losses, *mafiosi* business oligarchs, organized crime, deteriorating social services, a resurgence of extremism.[258]

There were over 100 financial crises from 1970 to 1995, from Finland and Sweden to Argentina and Indonesia. In the Roaring Nineties, the rate actually accelerated from 2.6 to 3.1 crises a year.[259] In 1995 Barings Bank fell victim to a lone Hong Kong speculator, 105 years after its narrow escape from bad Argentine loans. In the mid-1990s a string of Japanese bank crises soon followed. The 'Asian Tigers' ran into serious trouble in 1997, as over $100 billion in foreign cash looking for quick profits first flooded in and then was rapidly withdrawn. In Korea, the government was forced to beg its citizens to hand in their 'hoarded gold' (including jewellery) in exchange for government bonds. The dutiful Koreans responded, handing over 300 tonnes of gold: some 65 grams each.[260] In 1999 came the US tech stock bubble, when global speculators ignored Federal Reserve chairman Alan Greenspan's memorable 1996 warning about irrational exuberance. Many dot.-com companies disappeared almost overnight.

Global speculation was getting easier all the time, with transaction costs plummeting as a result of automated trading platforms, 24 hour trading across time zones, high-tech settlement and clearing systems, and new media outlets exclusively putting out investment news. As money-mad investors sought out profits in a low inflation global system, their strategies converged. Bubbles grew faster, and burst faster. The 1929 Wall Street Crash took months or even years to reach across Europe. In October 1987, Black Friday on Wall Street led directly to a Black Monday in the City of London. As stock markets became computerized, 'contagion' no longer took a weekend to transmit. The 1997 Asian stock markets influenced each other in minutes.

'With globalization increasing,' warned John Meriwether of Long Term Capital Management (the hedge fund which collapsed in 1998 as a result of over-investment in Russia), 'you'll see more crises.' He was right. There followed a spate of corporate scandals involving derivatives, false accounting, insider trading and mutual funds in all the major economic centres. The 2001 melt-down in Argentina, considered a star pupil of the IMF, caused mass unemployment and the return of barter to replace currency. Other countries that followed the prescriptions, like Armenia, Georgia, the Kyrgyz Republic and Moldova, saw their incomes halve and their debt burdens swell from zero in 1991 to unmanageable proportions. Many analysts in 2005 believed property bubbles had developed in a number of countries and were ready for bursting.[261]

Supporters of global money markets don't talk about speculative bubbles, but about crises that they can blame on 'a few bad apples' – nepotism in East Asia; cronyism in Japan; accounting loopholes in the US. But some insiders like Robert Monks and George Soros began to see something systematic about these global events. Reformed currency raider Soros founded an NGO, the Open Society Institute; Michael Milken founded a think-tank. Former World Bank chief economist Joseph Stiglitz asked himself how an organization like the IMF, 'with such talented (and highly paid) government bureaucrats [could] make so many mistakes?'

The answer is that from the late 1970s, the IMF, like the US Treasury, Wall Street, the City of London and a credulous investment community developed what psychologist Irving Janis called 'groupthink' – the tendency to recruit like-minded people, to develop a sense of infallibility and dislike of debate, and the ability to erase or rationalize away counter-evidence. They also developed 'mission creep', gradually moving from the task of promoting global economic stability to the rather different job of promoting capital market liberalization. Money became a tradable commodity in its own right.[262]

This global economic groupthink was blatantly obvious in

the annual ceremony known as the Nobel Prize in Economics. This prize – the Oscars of the Dismal Science – was not actually founded by guilty pacifist Alfred Nobel, but invented in 1969 by the Bank of Sweden to mark its 300th anniversary (it should really be called the Bank of Sweden Prize in Economic Sciences in Memory of Alfred Nobel). Over the last 35 years most of the prizes have gone to US neo-liberal economists, eight of them alumni of the Chicago School of Economics. Alfred Nobel would have exploded if he had seen a prize bearing his name going to an economist who denies that corporations have social responsibilities (Milton Friedman, 1976) or to someone devising better ways of speculating on the stock market (like Myron Scholes, 1997). It's surprising that Gordon Gekko didn't get one.

In 1980, a Swedish-German stamp collector turned activist called Jakob von Uexkull took matters into his own hands. He sold his stamp collection and endowed an 'alternative' Nobel Prize called the Right Livelihood Awards (RLA). Most of the winners have been green, pacifist and critical of globalization. Unlike Nobel prize winners, they come from all corners of the world and are often women. Wangari Maathai won the RLA in 1984 for her pioneering work combining women's empowerment and tree planting in Kenya. She went on to win a Nobel Peace Prize twenty years later. As of 2005, on the other hand, a Nobel Prize for Economics winner has yet to receive a Right Livelihood Award.[263]

A direct response to the 1974 oil crisis was the formation of a very different informal group, this time of six leading industrial nations (France, West Germany, Italy, Japan, the UK and USA), convened at the invitation of French President Valérie Giscard d'Estaing in 1975. It was not the oil crisis but third-world debt that soon became a permanent agenda item for the G8 (Canada joined in 1976, Russia in 1998). This self-appointed group was seen as holding the purse strings of the Washington institutions by increasingly vociferous NGOs calling for debt cancellation.

The first large-scale 'anti-globalization' protests took place at the G8 Summit in Birmingham in 1998, with 50,000 debt-relief campaigners creating a human chain around the world leaders. Piecemeal steps have grudgingly been taken to alleviate the worst excesses of the debt crisis. By 2005, African countries had already repaid $550 billion against original loans of $540 billion. But because of high interest rates, $245 billion was still outstanding. The most recent G8 debt relief agreement, at Gleneagles in July 2005, offered to write off the equivalent of $1.5 billion a year in repayments from around 20 of the worst-affected counties. The Gleneagles deal provided a lot of self-congratulation among G8 finance ministers, pop stars and non-governmental organizations. To put the largesse in context, the sum the G8 leaders grudgingly agreed in 2005 is equivalent to half an hour's economic activity by G8 countries.[264]

Imagine what could be achieved in a couple of hours in a world now worth $118 trillion. The world's capital assets, as calculated by McKinsey Global Institute, have grown tenfold since 1980. Shared evenly, every man, woman and child on the planet would have $20,000 of capital. We have come a long way since gold was our currency: the global gold stock would supply just 23 grams per person worth about $325. But the world's wealth is far from evenly shared. People in the USA, Europe and Japan own 83 per cent of it. China, with over a fifth of the world's population, has just four per cent of its financial capital. Latin America has just two per cent, and Africa doesn't even register. This extreme concentration of wealth – which is widely forecast to become more extreme in future – oils not the wheels of trade but the roulette wheels of the global casino.[265]

Lycurgus of Sparta, Isaac Newton, John Maynard Keynes and Richard Nixon all battled money-mad currency speculators – and lost. More recently, individual nations such as Chile and Malaysia have put controls on short-term capital influxes, with surprising success and widespread condemnation from global financiers. Negotiations on a Multilateral Agreement on Investment (MAI), a missing piece of the financial globalization jigsaw, collapsed amid NGO activism and growing unease from national policy-makers in 1998. But unilateral action and the failure of the MAI did little to limit foreign investment, and nor did the blip in world trade that occurred in 2001.

Could the market itself be used to tame speculation? The first call for a tax on currency speculation came from US economist James Tobin (1918–2002), in a paper he wrote in 1972, spurred on by Nixon's vitriolic attacks on international currency speculators. At that point, foreign exchange markets were turning over $15 billion a day – a sum which seemed dangerous and out of control to many economists and policy-makers. Tobin's idea was to levy a small tax on every transaction, to damp down levels of unhelpful speculation.

In 1997, Ignacio Ramonet wrote an editorial in France's left-wing journal *Le Monde Diplomatique* dusting off the idea of a Tobin Tax.[266] Tobin, himself a winner of the Bank of Sweden prize in economics, was unhappy that his idea was later 'hijacked' by the burgeoning anti-globalization movement as a way not to damp down speculation but to raise large sums stealthily and use them for worthy causes such as aid to developing countries. But the idea was taken up enthusiastically by French civil society, which soon formed a new NGO called ATTAC (the Association for the Taxation of Financial Transactions for the Aid of Citizens). The Tobin Tax received some parliamentary support in Belgium and Canada, and was toyed with by Presidents Lula of Brazil and Chavez of Venezuela. Today it remains a popular platform of the alternative globalization movement.

With foreign exchange transactions now running at $2 trillion a day, a tax pitched at 0.01 per cent would raise $50 billion a year.[267] That could make an important contribution to pressing global needs for poverty alleviation, healthcare, education, infrastructure and environmental protection. In 2005, the UN warned that rich nations would need to double current aid flows from $50 to $100 billion to stand any chance of meeting these 'Millennium Development Goals' by 2015. Ironically, the very automation that makes global speculation so rapid would make the tax easy to collect. Some economists argue against a currency tax, insisting that most currency transactions are not speculative assaults but routine hedging designed to stabilize transactions. Others argue that development aid should be provided willingly by individual tax-payers, or by a tax on international air passengers, rather than by a global currency tax.

The debate on the Tobin Tax shows how far the dollar is from being a global currency. If it was, there would be no foreign exchange transactions to tax. In 1860, Guernsey newspaper publisher and stationer Thomas De La Rue took on a stopgap job – printing some £5, £1 and 10 shilling banknotes for the Government of Mauritius. As countries experimented with monetary unions and the sterling gold standard system emerged, printing foreign banknotes didn't sound like a promising business in the mid-nineteenth century. Despite the advent of the euro in 1999 and the adoption of the US dollar by the world's newest country Timor Leste in 2002, national currencies are far from endangered species.

Today, De La Rue still prints banknotes for 150 countries, as many as when I worked for the company in the mid-1980s. Although 90 per cent of all foreign exchange transactions involve the US dollar, the euro accounts for over a third, the yen another fifth and the British pound 17 per cent.[268] As the Chinese yuan begins to float more freely, it will soon be among those top currencies. Malaysia and Iran recently proposed relaunching an Islamic gold dinar. There is even the possibility that some European currencies will reappear in a tide of anti-European Union sentiment. Meanwhile, thousands of alternative currencies like time dollars have been launched at subnational level. The Tobin Tax could work, because a single global currency is less likely today than in the 1970s, when it was seriously mooted by US economists; or when the British sovereign commanded a third of world trade in the late nineteenth century; or even under the thirteenth-century Mongols for that matter. The only convincing candidate is a carbon-based currency.

The climate casino (1973–2005)

'Does the flap of a butterfly's wings in Brazil set off a tornado in Texas?'

Edward Norton Lorenz, 1972

'It's almost trite to compare the stock market and the weather and speak of storms and hurricanes on Wall Street. For a while the market is almost flat, and almost nothing happens. But every so often it hits a little storm, or a hurricane. These are words which practical people use very freely but one may have viewed them as idle metaphors. It turns out, however, that the techniques I developed for studying turbulence – like weather – also apply to the stock market.'

Benoit Mandlebrot, 2004[269]

When weather forecaster Lewis Fry Richardson was totting up the body count of deadly quarrels, he wanted to know if neighbouring countries with a common border were more likely to fight each other. He couldn't find reliable information on the lengths of international frontiers – even easy ones like the Franco-German border. Richardson got out his dividers, unfolded the most detailed maps he could find, and tried to come up with some definitive measurements of national frontiers. But when he came to double-check his results, he got a different answer depending on how he set the dividers. If he followed the border using closely spaced dividers, the result was much longer than if he calibrated his dividers broadly. He wrote up his results on the expanding length of frontiers and coastlines in an obscure journal and got back to his deadly quarrels.

Little did he know he had started to uncover a strange connection between two global processes: financial speculation and climate change. IBM researcher Benoit Mandelbrot stumbled across the coastline paper in the 1960s. The expansibility of coastlines was deeply influential in his theory of fractals – the infinitely repeating geometric patterns that underlie apparent roughness and chaos. Over the past 40 years Mandelbrot has studied ferns, cauliflowers, Hokusai's Great Wave, climate – and the workings of the stock market.

Mandelbrot tried (and failed) to make sense of cotton prices in 1963, and came back to the stock market in his book *The (Mis)behavior of Markets* (2004) co-written with former *Wall Street Journal* editor Richard Hudson. They argue that stock market movements are far more chaotic than most people believe. Most investors grossly underestimate the risks they are taking. Few people heed warnings against speculation, least of all John Maynard Keynes, who lost and won fortunes on the London stock market. Investors believe themselves rational and prudent; but they also want something for nothing.

Pioneer climate modeller Edward Lorenz developed the theory that small changes could lead to radical upheavals in climate with his famous question about the butterfly's wing. Global finance and the global climate turned out to be more closely connected than Richardson, Mandelbrot and Lorenz realised. Oil was behind the massive growth of global finance from the 1970s. It is also behind global warming. Over the next 100 years, rising sea levels will make coastlines shorter and far more chaotic. Dealing with climate change will also test global economic and social arrangements to the limit.

The first phase of global capital flows was the story of gold; the second was the story of the dollar. The third global currency was black gold – oil. Today, more people around the world are directly affected by the price of petrol than the value of an ounce of gold or the dollar–euro exchange rate. In 1859, oil was drilled for the first time at Titusville, Pennsylvania. Speculators were initially less interested than they had been by the gold rush a decade before. But by 1870, Standard Oil dominated the fledgling oil business, and petroleum exports to Europe provided a large enough trade balance to pay the interest on US bonds held abroad. In the 1890s more oil was found in California, in 1901 in Texas, and by 1913, the USA was producing more than half the world's oil.[270]

The rise of the automobile and then the airplane gave a major boost to the oil business in the early twentieth century. But when the US used up six billion barrels of oil during the Second World War, the realization dawned that the US oilfields were far from inexhaustible. Oil was by now the linchpin of the US economy, so securing new supplies became a top priority, dictating US policy in the Iran (1950–54) and Suez (1956) crises. With the formation of OPEC in 1960, the USA was on a collision course with Arab oil producers unhappy with the country's support for Israel. Far more damaging than the 1973 Arab oil embargo of the USA and Netherlands was the four-fold price rise that OPEC enforced in the same year – in retaliation for the devaluation of the dollar.

Despite efforts to reduce demand and develop alternative sources of energy, Western nations were unable to wean themselves off oil and natural gas, either in the mid-1970s or in the Iran crisis (1979–80). Oil had thoroughly permeated global industry and trade, and became the key global commodity in its own right. Today, the United States still consumes two-thirds of global oil production.

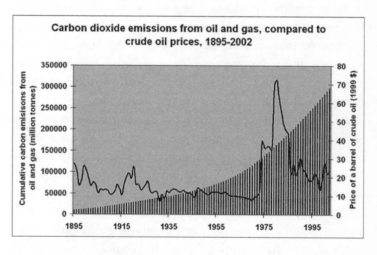

The chart compares global oil consumption (measured as cumulative carbon dioxide emissions from oil and gas) against oil prices (the black line). Carbon dioxide emissions from oil and gas built up slowly from 1895, but started to accelerate in the global contraction of the 1950s. Oil prices were on a downward trend. But the sharp price increases of the 1970s made no discernible impact on oil consumption.[271] No wonder OPEC countries were awash with petro-dollars in the 1970s and 1980s. The doubling of oil prices to over $60 a barrel in 2005 again caused anguish, calls for 'energy security', but no real change in consumption patterns. Today, proven reserves of oil amount to over one trillion barrels and their current market value would equal half of all the financial wealth on the planet. As we saw in Chapter Four, oil companies make more money than most of the world's nations, and will carry on doing so until the oil runs out.

The extent to which changing climate has affected past civilizations has only recently been appreciated. From the disintegration of the prosperous city of Ur in around 2000 BC as a result of prolonged drought to the collapse of the Mayan dynasty and the disruption of medieval Europe's Little Ice Age to the catastrophic famines of the late nineteenth century in India, Northern China, and North Eastern Brazil, human societies have always been vulnerable to changes in climate.[272] But these crises were not manmade.

In 1859, British physicist John Tyndall discovered that carbon dioxide (CO_2) helped trap heat in the atmosphere, keeping the planet warm and cozy. Swedish chemist Svante Arrhenius in 1894 started to ponder what would happen if there was too much CO_2. After a year of gruelling calculations, Arrhenius concluded that carbon dioxide emissions from coal burning could enhance the Earth's natural greenhouse effect and lead to global warming. Wood and coal were the fuels of nineteenth-century globalization; oil and gas had contributed less than two per cent to the cumulative man-made burden of carbon dioxide in the atmosphere in 1900. Arrhenius was no alarmist – he thought it would take 3,000 years to double the amount of carbon in the atmosphere.

He was wrong. Carbon dioxide concentrations were already climbing steadily from their natural level of around 280 parts per million (ppm). Thirty years later, US physicist Alfred Lotka claimed coal burning could double atmospheric CO_2 in 500 years. Coal was still by far the most important fuel; oil and gas were responsible for just five per cent of the carbon in the atmosphere, which was up to about 300 ppm in 1930.

In 1949, British scientist Guy Callendar linked increasing amounts of CO_2 in the atmosphere to the observation that northern Europe and North America had been getting warmer since the 1880s. In the 1950s, biologists warned that deforestation would increase atmospheric CO_2, while oceanographers feared the world's oceans would simply not be able to absorb much of the additional carbon. In 1958, scientists made the first robust measurements of atmospheric carbon dioxide at the Mauna Loa Observatory in Hawaii: 315 parts in every million in the atmosphere. As yet, worries about global warming were confined to a handful of scientists. But the 1960s saw the birth of a global environmental consciousness.

The green movement began parochially enough, with protests among East Coast intellectuals against aerial spraying of the insecticide DDT. In 1958, the Sierra Club – a conservationist NGO founded in 1892 – had just 15,000 members. But after the appearance of Rachel Carson's bestselling book *Silent Spring* in 1962, the pesticide protest spread rapidly to middle-class households across the USA, and then to Europe. The 1960s space race also built environmental consciousness, particularly the first photographs of Earth from space. 'The Earth was small, light blue, and so touchingly alone, our home that must be defended like a holy relic,' said Aleksei Leonov, the first man to walk in space in 1965. 'The Earth was absolutely round. I believe I never knew what the word round meant until I saw Earth from space.'

The first Earth Day in 1970 was celebrated by 20 million Americans. Sierra Club membership grew to 114,000. 'A chorus of concern for the environment is sweeping the country,' the President's Council on Environmental Quality reported in 1970. 'It reaches to the regional, national and international environmental problems. It embraces pollution of the Earth's air and water, noise and waste, and the threatened disappearance of whole species of plant and animal life.'

In the early 1970s, that concern became global, with persistent pollutants like DDT found in the remotest places of the planet – in Arctic beluga whales and Antarctic penguins. NGOs like Greenpeace and Friends of the Earth rapidly became international. By then, world oil and gas consumption had already pumped 100 billion tonnes of carbon into the atmosphere, and the concentration had reached 330 parts per million. Scientists also began warning that chlorofluorocarbons (CFCs) could destroy the layer of protective ozone in the stratosphere.[273] The existence of the ozone hole above Antarctica was confirmed in 1985.

Solving the global CFC problem was seen as a great success for international concerted action, but it distracted scientists and politicians from addressing the shocking evidence emerging from climate change models in the late 1970s and 1980s. A 1979 report from the National Academy of Sciences (NAS) warned that a 'wait-and-see policy may mean waiting until it is too late.' It was in the 1980s that humans first exceeded the planet's capacity to provide natural resources and absorb pollution, according to the Worldwide Fund for Nature. In addition to declines in fish stocks, loss of tropical forests and loss of farmland to erosion and urbanization, concentrations of carbon in the atmosphere continued to rise inexorably, to 360 parts per million in 1995 and 378 ppm today. On current trends, they will reach 500 ppm in 2050.[274]

Since 1751 nearly 300 billion tonnes of carbon have been released to the atmosphere from the consumption of fossil fuels and cement production. Half of these emissions have occurred since the mid-1970s, when climate change was already on the environmental agenda. Current annual emissions – almost seven billion tonnes of carbon in 2002 – are an all-time high. The Kyoto Protocol, which entered into force in 2005, is just a first modest step towards radical reductions in carbon emissions, according to most scientists. While many participating countries are not on track to meet their first commitments to reduce using fossil fuels, the most serious weakness of Kyoto is the refusal of the USA, responsible for a fifth of all global emissions, to sign up. The current US administration's position is reminiscent of 1919, when the USA turned its back on the League of Nations and Charles Ponzi assured working-class investors that his pyramid scheme was as good as gold.

Climate scientists almost unanimously agree the globe will warm by between 1.7 degrees Celsius and 4.9 degrees Celsius by the end of this century. Rising temperatures will melt Arctic ice sheets, causing sea levels to rise and drowning low-lying island and coastal communities around the world. Rain patterns will change, causing both droughts and flooding, and more violent storms and hurricanes. No wonder the insurance industry is already counting the cost. Freak weather conditions cost the global insurance industry over $25 billion in 2004, and they are still calculating the colossal costs of the 2005 hurricanes. The world's largest reinsurer, Munich Re, says the frequency of weather disasters has tripled since the 1960s. According to Munich Re's figures, economic losses from natural disasters have doubled every decade, from $53 billion in the 1960s to $480 billion in the 1990s. Losses could reach $300 billion a year by 2050, the vast majority caused by weather-related events.[275]

Lawyers are also beginning to talk about tort actions against rogue emitters – which could be either companies or countries. How long before an international court tries a case of 'culpable climacide'? Action on climate change is being delayed by intransigence. The US and Australia argue that large nations like India and China must also agree to reduce emissions. Developing countries argue that rich nations have already industrialized using the carbon economy and that it is their turn next. For a while yet, rich nations will battle the developing world over proportionate emissions rights. How, asked former Indian Prime Minister Atal Bihari Vajpayee can 'the ethos of democracy support any norm other than equal per capita rights to global environmental resources?' Poor nations are starting to talk about repayments for 'ecological debts' incurred in previous rounds of globalization.[276] That democratic ethos has yet to penetrate global institutions such as the IMF and United Nations. If and when it does, the financial ramifications of equal rights to carbon emissions will make 1990s currency raids look like storms in a teacup.

Despite the potential of technical fixes, it is hard to see how global warming will be effectively tamed without some form of worldwide carbon rationing. An emerging carbon economy is already discernible in the fledgling European emission permit trading system. Carbon rights will inevitably be hard-wired into the next global currency.

7

A WORLD OF IDEAS: RELIGION, LANGUAGE, CULTURE AND COMMUNICATION

'All thought draws life from contacts and exchanges.'
Fernand Braudel (1902–1985)

Global trade, labour and financial flows directly involve at least one in ten people around the world, and their impacts are felt still more widely. The world of ideas, from religion and language, to art, football and pop music, is the daily experience of globalization. There have been many benefits to cultural mixing and openness, speeded by waves of innovation in communication. But global contacts and exchanges have also exacerbated the 'clash of cultures', bringing persecution, dependency and bland uniformity.

Cultural globalization ranges from the spiritual and high-brow – the rise of syncretic religions and the influences on Picasso's masks – to the trivial, tracing the 2005 European rush for Crazy Frog ring-tones, which co-creator Erik Wernquist called 'the most annoying thing in the world'. We have so far charted the globalization of exploration, trade, migration and money – all tangible and measurable phenomena. These chapters point to four great periods of contraction when the ever-present tension between the exotic and the uniform became intense. The rich and intangible history of ideas poses far greater challenges. Is there any evidence to support the notion of global contractions? One starting place is football – the universal sport *par excellence*, where fans have kept meticulous records. There is some historical precedent for taking sport as a gauge for global culture. By far the most famous inhabitant of sixth-century BC Croton was not the globe-imaging boffin Pythagoras, but the mighty wrestler Milo, six times an Olympic medal winner.

Football: the world's language

'Win or die.'
        Mussolini to Italian national football team, 1930[277]

There are more national members of FIFA, the international football body, than the United Nations. 200 million men and women play the game at competitive level. Football may well be 'the world's language', as FIFA claims, even if the Americans, Chinese and Indians are not yet fluent. Football has long been a crucible for local and global tensions, right back to its medieval origins as a rowdy and sometime murderous inter-village ritual played on Shrove Tuesdays in England.[278]

What is noteworthy is that football was a team sport, unlike other athletic contests that promoted individual prowess. It was also a focus for geographical rivalries. For these reasons, bureaucrats disapproved of the violent, unruly game, which undermined public order while doing little to promote military skills. By the late eighteenth century, various versions of football were endemic to elite English schools such as Harrow and Eton. Hacking, barging and elbowing were allowed; the ball was often shaped like a big cheese. When popular pastimes such as cockfighting, bullfighting and bear-baiting were driven underground by the 1835 Cruelty to Animals Act, cricket, boxing and horse racing first caught the public's attention, but football gradually broke out of its elite niche when educated factory-owners introduced the game to industrial towns like Sheffield and Nottingham.

In 1872, the Football Association turned its attention from rule-making to the organization of an annual cup.[279] The winners were initially teams of well-off amateurs: ex-public school players and army engineers on their way to serve the British Empire. The Old Etonians, captained by Lord Kinnaird, had been runners-up in 1875 and 1876 and winners in 1879, and they secured an easy victory over Blackburn Rovers in the 1882 cup final. The next year, Blackburn Olympic descended to face the Old Etonians at the Kennington Oval. The *Pall Mall Gazette* described the Blackburn supporters as 'a Northern horde of uncouth garb and strange oaths – like a tribe of Sudanese Arabs let loose.'[280] More importantly, the Blackburn team included 'paid men'. One-all after 90 tense minutes, the game went to extra time. Blackburn secured a second goal. The cosmopolitan Old Etonians never won again. The first Football League, formed in 1888, was made up of a dozen teams from the Midlands and North.[281] West Bromwich Albion won the FA Cup with a team all born in England. Football had become a professional sport dominated by geographic rivalries.

Shortened working hours and cheap railways made it possible for spectators to finish work and get to a match in time for a 3 p.m. kick-off. British mariners and industrialists spread the game to the ports of Italy (Juventus, Bologna), Spain (Bilbao), Argentina and Brazil, and football associations proliferated internationally. In 1904, Robert Guérin pulled to-

gether the Fédération Internationale de Football Association
(FIFA) in Paris with seven members: France, Belgium, Denmark, the Netherlands, Spain, Sweden and Switzerland. Guérin was consciously following the lead of fellow Frenchman
Baron Pierre de Coubertin, the historian who in 1894 had
revived the Olympic Games in modern form as a means of
promoting international harmony. Although the first athletic
games struggled to make headway against surrounding world
fairs, the 1906 games in Athens attracted 900 athletes from 20
nations. England, initially hostile to the European attempt to
universalize football, signed up to FIFA in 1906. By 1913,
South Africa, Argentina, Chile and the USA had also joined,
and in that year China lost to the Philippines in Manila.[282]
Football was a game played on all continents.

Football, like the US economy, had a surprisingly productive
Great Depression. In the 1930s, towns built large numbers of
pitches and better stadia. Crowds of 60,000 became common
at matches, and telegraph, radio and Saturday evening newspapers spread results quickly to those who did not attend. The
global reach of football was given a major boost in 1930 when
Frenchman Jules Rimet almost single-handedly promoted the
first 'world cup', which held in Uruguay. Although only four
European nations braved the two-month sea voyage, football,
like sport more generally, was caught up in the rise of tota-
litarianism, with Mussolini equating goals with national pride
in the same way Hitler sought glory at the 1936 Olympics in
Berlin.

By the 1950s, 73 countries were members of FIFA. Brazil
and Uruguay dominated the world cups in this decade. Football had become global, though still animated by local passion
and rivalry. When Glasgow's Celtic faced Inter Milan in the
Lisbon Stadium for the European Cup final of 1967, every
player was from Glasgow, except for Wallace, an 'outsider'

signed from nearby Hearts a few months earlier. When Celtic won 2–1, Inter's coach, Helenio Herrera described the match as a 'victory for sport'. But it marked a turning point for the focus on local players.

By the early 1990s, the average English Premier League club had two or three foreign players, and some had many more. Players' freedom to move club was highly restricted until 1995, when Belgian player Jean-Marc Bosman made a successful legal challenge against his club's efforts to prevent his move to a French team. Rich clubs used the Bosman ruling as a green light to buy up international talent. By the 1999 season, more than half the players in the English Premier League were foreign, according to the Sir Norman Chester Centre for Football Research at the University of Leicester.[283]

Globalization is sometimes described as a process, not a destination, but on Boxing Day 1999, Chelsea became the first English club to field an all-foreign team, and when they played the Italian side Lazio later that season, not a single English player was present. The press described the team photograph as a 'picture that humiliates the English Game'.

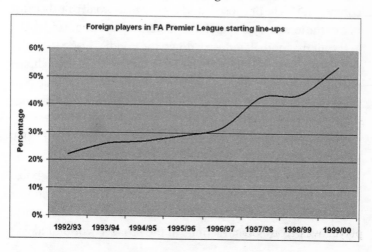

But an anti-global backlash was brewing. The National Fan Survey of 2001 showed that 60 per cent of football fans thought there were now too many foreign players in the English game. There was a 'muscle drain', as wealthy clubs bought up players from around the world, often to the detriment of the clubs that trained them. This was a vicious circle, where better results led to increased revenues, and more money led to further hiring. A similar phenomenon was seen in athletics, with scores of East African long-distance runners repatriated to Europe and the Gulf States, leaving their home countries impoverished. Only a few football clubs, like Athletic Club Bilbao, resisted the tide. 'Athletic remain committed to developing grassroots football in the region and have been doing so for over forty years,' says sports director Andoni Zubizarreta. 'We will continue to develop local players'.[284]

In 2005, European football's governing body UEFA unveiled proposed rules to force clubs to do more to support 'home-grown' talent, suggesting a timetable for introducing a fixed proportion of local players in club squads. But was UEFA legally entitled to set rules to protect local players against global competition? The proposed 'home-grown' football rules became one of the few aspects of globalization to arouse popular debate, and split the football industry down the middle. José Mourinho of Chelsea declared himself broadly in favour: 'I believe in home players'. But Arsenal's vice-chairman David Dein said the proposal would restrict the free movement of workers: 'It's misguided and it will almost certainly be challenged'.[285]

The world of football had come full circle, reminiscent of 1883, when local Blackburn battled the global Old Etonians. Football does present one awkward challenge to the timing of global contractions, because the 1930s were clearly an intense period for the globalization of the game. Enough of football. Were there comparable global contractions in the broader world of ideas?

The late fifteenth-century contraction

*'Are these not men? Have they not rational souls? Must not
you love them as you love yourselves?'*
Dominican friar Antonio de Montesinos, 1511

When did religions acquire their globalizing ambitions? Large-
scale efforts at religious conversion had been a recurrent
feature on the world stage – from St Paul in Asia Minor
and Charlemagne in Europe to the Abbasids of Baghdad
and the Aztecs of Mexico. The twelfth- to fourteenth-century
Crusades were to a large extent a struggle for religious supremacy.[286] But the Spanish confrontation with indigenous
peoples in the Americas escalated both the scale and scope of
these religious tensions. Many Spaniards did not agree with
Montesinos and Las Casas. The debate on forced conversions
took on planetary implications in a world formally divided
between European powers.

Widespread participation in spiritual debate and geographical exploration was severely limited prior to the commercialization of printing by Johannes Gutenberg (c.1400–1468).
A bible took 20 years to transcribe and few could afford them
outside princely and religious elites. So when Gutenberg exhibited a two-volume printed bible at the 1455 Frankfurt Book
Fair, the significance of printing was immediately clear. Printing presses spread rapidly across Europe, to Italy (1465),
France (1470), Spain (1472) and England (1475). Mexico
City had its first press by 1533; the press arrived in Cambridge
Massachusetts in 1638.

In 1494, Italian humanist Aldus Manutius started to intro-
duce affordable half-sized books, in print-runs of 1,000 and
with a compact new Italic typeface.[287] Printing began slowly

to democratize literacy and learning around the world. Similar impacts must have occurred in China and Korea, where printing had developed much earlier, although the results were more muted because of the high costs of printing such complex alphabets. Initially, printing in Europe served to standardize written Latin and assisted its role as a universal language, but as publishers began to publish Dante and other early renaissance writers, the printed book began to weaken the primacy of Latin and led to the flourishing of European vernacular languages. On the other hand, from the 1480s religious fundamentalists like Tomas Torquemada reacted to the proliferation of non-Catholic literature, especially Jewish Talmuds and Arabic texts, by orchestrating public burnings.

'The effect of commerce is riches; the consequence of riches, luxury,' wrote Montesquieu (1689–1755), 'and that of luxury the perfection of arts'. Printing and the increased trade in luxuries certainly helped spread the humanist ideas of the Italian Renaissance across Northern Europe – and to pass Northern innovations in music southwards. Yet the Renaissance defies any effort to pin it down chronologically, nor can it plausibly be described as a global movement. The exchange of ideas did speed up in the late fifteenth century, but a truly global contraction in ideas was building in the next three centuries.

The late nineteenth-century contraction

'A tradition circulates among the Guahibos, that the war-like Atures, pursued by the Caribs, escaped to the rocks that rise in the middle of the Great Cataracts; and there that nation, heretofore so numerous, became gradually extinct, *as well as its language. The last families of the Atures still existed in 1767, in the time of the missionary Gili. At the period of our voyage an old parrot was shown at Maypures, of which the inhabitants said, and the fact is worthy of observation, that they did not understand what it said, because it spoke the language of the Atures.'*

Alexander von Humboldt,
Personal Narrative of Travels to the Equinoctial Regions of America (1799–1804)

Enlightenment thinking gathered force in Europe in the 1750s, but this was far from being an era of 'godless' liberal capitalism. Indeed, the nineteenth century was a period of 'triumphal re-emergence and expansion' of world religions, under the aegis of supposedly secular trends – imperialism, trade and labour migration.[288] The great religions – Christianity, Hinduism, Islam, Buddhism, Judaism – retrenched for global expansion, while a number of smaller faiths like Baha'i also extended their scope worldwide.

The world religions streamlined their bureaucracies, formalized their doctrines and exploited mass printing, cheap and secure long-distance travel and new building technologies to increase their global reach. Pilgrimages to Benares, Santiago, Guadeloupe, Lhasa and Mecca were an important motive for international travel, as was the spectacular Muslim expansion into Africa, beginning in 1800, and later Christian missions in Africa, Asia, the Pacific and South America. Missionaries were treated with real hostility by East India Company officials because of their propensity to stir up unrest, but the Company failed to stem the numbers of missionaries. By the late nineteenth century, there were an estimated 100,000 Christian missionaries in Africa, and many more Islamic ones.

Frenchman Alexis de Tocqueville identified religion as part

of the key to the vibrancy of US society in his *Democracy in America* (1835–40). He believed that 'Islam will not be able to hold its power long in ages of enlightenment and democracy, while Christianity is destined to reign in such ages'. In the USA, African-Americans built up Baptist and other churches as part of a drive for emancipation, appropriating Scottish Presbyterian slave-owners' church music to suit their spiritual and cultural needs. In 1893, a World Parliament of Religions was convened in Chicago, with the goal of stemming religious conflict. Perhaps it is not surprising that it was less successful than the Meridian Conference convened a decade before. The power of differing religions as world forces was picked up by Max Weber's theory of *The Protestant Ethic and the Spirit of Capitalism* in 1904–5.[289]

Religious expansion and colonialism impacted on the diversity of languages in unexpected ways. Languages were going extinct well before the modern phase of globalization – a result first of the decimation of native peoples by conquest and disease, and then as nation-builders persecuted minority languages in the name of national assimilation. In the eighteenth and nineteenth centuries, linguistic experts like East Indian Company official William Jones and the German Sanskrit expert Franz Bopp had made great strides in understanding the common roots of European, Persian and Indian languages.[290] In the late nineteenth century, both European and non-European languages like Hindi, Urdu, Swahili, Bislama and Malay were grammatically codified and became more uniform, at the cost of local dialects. Meanwhile, new hybrid languages like Creole and Pidgin came into existence, and some missionaries began to document the languages of remote peoples in an effort to assist conversion. This period also saw high-minded efforts to create universal languages. Lazar Zamenhof's *Esperanto* (1887) is the best-known.[291]

From the eighteenth century, European enthusiasts also began to assemble important collections of art and artefacts from around the world. More Europeans went to Asia than vice versa, and many were fascinated with what they saw.[292] Physician Hans Sloane (1660–1753) assembled an impressive collection that on his death laid the foundations for the British Museum. The acquisition of sculptures from the Parthenon in the early 1800s by Thomas Bruce, 7th Earl of Elgin inaugurated a period of intense competition between European nations to assemble national art collections. Napoleon and his generals were ruthlessly acquisitive in stocking the Louvre, the royal palace that re-opened as a public museum in 1793. Europeans were not always driven by aesthetic mission, however – the British deliberately destroyed the Chinese Imperial summer palace in 1860.

The nineteenth-century 'Scramble for Artworks' was exemplified by the acquisition of the Venus de Milo. Unearthed by a gardener on the Mediterranean island of Milos in 1820, the statue became the object of an unseemly transaction between disgruntled islanders, Turkish bureaucrats and a French naval officer seeking to curry favour. Legend has it that the statue lost its arm in a scuffle on the Milos dockside. That the Venus is today one of the most globally recognizable artworks owes much to boosting by French connoisseurs. After France was forced to return the purloined Medici Venus to Italy in 1815, curators sought to elevate the status of the Venus de Milo as a replacement, suppressing evidence that the sculpture was by an unknown Antiochan, Alexandos. Instead they claimed it to be a work of the great Praxiteles.[293]

In this period, painting, sculpture and music were all pressed into the service of nation-building, epitomized by a proliferation of larger than life equestrian statues and triumphal canvases. A US national art collection was unveiled at the

Metropolitan Museum of Art in 1872, and art museums followed in capitals around the world, from Hanoi and Cairo to Bogotá. New art forms were more easily exchanged internationally. First the novel (eighteenth century), then photography (1830s) and finally impressionist (1870s) and abstract art (1900s) were admired, copied and hybridized around the world. 'A century which began with the Spanish painter Francisco Goya's lurid nightmares of war and revolution,' writes Christopher Bayly, 'ended with Japanese sculptors modifying the style of the French master Auguste Rodin, while Indian modernists borrowed Japanese techniques of colour and brushwork'.[294] Commercial printmaking enabled the proliferation of copies of artworks: this was the period when the *Mona Lisa* became a global icon. Literature also became far more accessible with the introduction of the Universal-Bibiothek paperback series in Leipzig in the 1860s. It spawned numerous imitations, culminating in the Penguin paperback series launched by Allen Lane in 1935.[295]

Meanwhile, a broader urban culture was also developing, associated with a whole range of new opportunities for sociable cultural exchange: cafés and public houses; shopping streets, department stores and offices; museums and libraries; places of worship, music halls and sports grounds. Commerce, creativity and philanthropy combined to drive these developments. Architectural innovations also underpinned this increasingly homogenous urban cultural infrastructure, notably the invention of Portland cement (1824) and the rolled steel joist. Architecture, commerce and culture came together in the World Fairs, beginning in 1851 in London, and circulating around European and US cities every few years thereafter. In 1893, some 27 million people visited the Chicago *World's Columbian Exposition*. The World Fairs were competitive opportunities to showcase national cultural and technological prowess. Through industrial and cultural espionage and the power of example, they helped diffuse innovations globally.[296]

Global currents ran in all directions. In the 1880s Scottish lighthouse engineer turned novelist Robert Louis Stevenson settled in Samoa. His novella *Beach at Falesa* (1892) was a harsh commentary on European ideological imperialism in the South Seas. Ex-stockbroker Paul Gauguin sought his inspiration in Tahiti. In the early decades of the twentieth century, Picasso was borrowing heavily from African masks. One conscious challenge to the global hybrid culture can be traced from the 1880s when the Arts and Crafts Movement, first in Britain, then the US, promoted 'authentic' domestic techniques. Yet the movement was inspired in part by Persian weaving, and went on to influence Gandhi's 'swadeshi' movement for home-grown Indian weaving.[297]

What role did communications technologies like the telegraph and newspaper play in this fertile period of global exchange? Technology turns out to have a complex and unexpected 'social life'.[298] The newspaper emerged only slowly as a mass medium. Frederick Marryat estimated that there were over 10,000 locally based newspapers in the USA in 1839. It took Congress five years to fund the first 40-mile stretch of telegraph cable from Baltimore to Washington, and laying the first transatlantic telegraph cable took 14 years, five failures, the biggest steamship ever built, government monopolies on landing sites in Nova Scotia, a unique insulating material from the forests of Malaysia, and repeated injections of US capital and British technology. Only in 1866 did these efforts finally pay off.[299] A telegraph message from Bombay to London in 1880 cost over £12 a word in today's prices, and was delivered by hand across London.

Thomas Edison, looking for uses for his phonograph in

1877, wanted to use it to record people's dying words or to announce clock time. For twenty years he steadfastly refused to allow its use for playing music.[300] Without the dogged determination and downright egotism of men like Cyrus Field, Theodore Judah and William Randolph Hearst, the commercialization of the telegraph, railroad and popular press could have taken decades longer. Global communication also relied on influential early adopters: Queen Victoria was an enthusiastic telegraph 'geek' who checked her in-box daily and sent a 17-hour birthday greeting to US President McKinley.

Many people actively resisted the spread of this global communications infrastructure, from the saboteurs of transatlantic cable-laying and the destructive competitiveness of rival railroad laying teams, to the efforts of telegraph companies to kill the telephone and resistance of naval officers to the introduction of ship-to-shore radio. The self-confident white bureaucrats in the Indian Civil Service often ignored telegraphic instructions from Whitehall. It took about 50 years for the package of technologies to finally become global. In July 1903, US President Theodore Roosevelt wished 'a happy Independence Day to the US, its territories and properties'. It took nine minutes for the message to travel by telegraph from San Francisco to Honolulu, to Midway, Guam, Manila, China and westwards.[301]

One episode in particular captures the unexpected pathways of global exchange in this period. In 1892, US President William McKinley (1843–1901) wanted to sound out Cuban revolutionary leader Calixto Iñigues García about helping topple the Spanish in Cuba. The rebel leader was hiding out in mountainous jungles so the new-fangled telegraph was no use. If the Spanish caught the messenger, they would kill him without compunction. Even if the messenger evaded the Spanish, his safe reception by the notoriously hot-heated

García was far from certain. To make matters worse, US public opinion was sharply divided on the prospect of a Spanish adventure. 'War with Spain would increase the business and earnings of every American railroad', urged Senator John M. Thurston of Nebraska, 'it would increase the output of every American factory, it would stimulate every branch of industry and domestic commerce'. But Mark Twain and many others were vociferous pacifists and non-interventionists.

'Where can I find a man who will carry a message to García?' McKinley asked his head of military intelligence. 'There's a fellow by the name of Rowan will find García for you, if anybody can', responded Colonel Arthur Wagner. 'Send him!' barked the President.[302] Getting the message to García was an epic adventure that made first lieutenant Andrew S. Rowan, graduate of West Point, a hero. Without asking any questions, he braved his way by boat, foot and horseback to the rebel camp, delivered his message, and found his way back safely. It was a small world if you were determined enough.

The 'yellow journalism' of William Randolph Hearst and Joseph Pulitzer about Spanish atrocities and noble Cuban rebels embroiled the US in further interventions, paving the way for the Panama Canal, the blatant acquisition of Puerto Rico and Guam, and a 16-year period of bloody occupation in the Philippines. A probably apocryphal story has Hearst sending a telegram to illustrator Frederic Remington: 'You furnish the pictures and I'll furnish the war'. Rowan's adventure became a worldwide bestseller, not through the New York press barons, but by an obscure publication out of Aurora, NY.

The Roycroft Press was run by Elbert Hubbard, an ex-soap-salesman from Buffalo who was influenced by the Arts and Crafts Movement of John Ruskin and William Morris. It put

out a number of successful small-circulation magazines, and
Hubbard was its most prolific writer, penning over seven
million words before his death on the *Lusitania* in 1915.
Hubbard's enduring legacy was a short 'literary trifle' that
he dashed off one evening inside an hour after dinner one night
in February 1899. It was intended to fill some space in the
forthcoming issue of the Roycroft magazine *Philistine*. The
article was called *A Message to García*. Hubbard recounts
how the tenacious lieutenant 'took the letter, sealed it up in an
oil-skin pouch, strapped it over his heart, in four days landed
by night off the coast of Cuba from an open boat, disappeared
into the jungle, & in three weeks came out on the other side of
the Island, having traversed a hostile country on foot, and
delivered his letter to García'.

A Message to García became the first management bestseller
at a time of growing tensions between managers and labour in
the new corporations. 'The hero is the man who does his
work,' writes Hubbard, 'who carries the message to García
without having to petulantly ask "Where is he at?"' Hubbard's sympathies are firmly with 'the employer who grows
old before his time in a vain attempt to get frowsy ne'er-do-
wells to do intelligent work'. Managers loved it. Orders for
extra copies of the March 1899 edition of *Philistine* begin to
flood in. 'When the American News Company ordered a
thousand'; Hubbard recalled, 'I asked one of my helpers which
article it was that stirred up the cosmic dust. "It's the stuff
about García," he said.'

George Daniels at the New York Central Railroad asked
Hubbard for 100,000 copies – with an advert of the Empire
State Express on the back. *A Message to García* predated and
outsold F.W. Taylor's famous treatise on 'scientific management' (1911). Daniels eventually distributed one and a half
million copies to employees and customers; and the story was

reprinted in hundreds of magazines and newspapers. The director of the Russian railways, visiting Daniels in the US, decided to translate *A Message* into Russian and give a copy to every Russian railway worker. Lenin must have been furious. His monumental *Development of Capitalism in Russia* (1899) had a print-run of 2,400.

A Message spread from Russia to Germany, France, Spain, Turkey, India and China. During the Russo-Japanese war (1904–05), Russian troops were given a copy on the way to the front. The Japanese found the booklet on Russian prisoners and concluded it must be a good thing. It was translated and given to every Japanese soldier and civil servant. The Japanese victory in 1905 owed much to their openness to new ideas, and sent shock waves around the world, marking a resurgence of Asian confidence that Europe was not invincible. In remote Indian villages, babies were named after Japanese generals.[303] All in all, some 40 million copies of *A Message To García* were printed and distributed.[304]

A Message captures some of the complexity of cultural exchange on a shrinking planet: the importance of the individual in geopolitics; the sabre-rattling power of the popular media; the unpredictable transmission of cultural fashion; the limitations of technology. And what was García's reply to McKinley's message? Far from welcoming US intervention with open arms, García dispatched three trusted emissaries to Washington to test the water. Global exchange is a two-way process.

Phoney globalization (1920s–40s)

In 1928, Brazilian poet Oswald de Andrade wrote his *Cannibal's Manifesto* (1928), urging Brazilian artists to draw their inspiration from around the world. The balance between home-grown culture and global cannibalism see-sawed through the inter-war period. In many ways it was a period of 'Phoney Globalization'. Josephine Baker, the exotic dancer from St. Louis, Missouri, vied with Parisian-born singer Edith Piaf for the limelight in Paris before and during the Second World War. International sport became the expression of geopolitical conflict in the 1930s. The Nobel prizes in literature stayed mainly in Europe but some token efforts were made to embrace other literary traditions. The prize went to Bengali Rabindrath Tagore (1913), to a clutch of Americans in the 1930s, and to Gabriela Mistral of Chile in 1945.

This period was a mixed one in world religion, marked by both secularism and growing evangelism. In Turkey, for example, modernizer Mustafa Kemal Atatürk (1881–1938) abolished the 1,300-year-old Islamic caliphate in 1924 and established a clear separation between mosque and state. But the Muslim Brotherhood was founded in Cairo in 1928. In this same period, Protestant churches in the USA began to debate in earnest the challenges of modernity, and especially the implications of Darwin's theory of natural selection, inspired by a series of books published by the Bible Institute of Los Angeles called *The Fundamentals*.

Cultural tension was also evident in early cinema, with the parochial (Edwin Porter's *Great Train Robbery*, 1903) vying with the nationalistic (D.W. Griffith's *Birth of a Nation*, 1915) and the extraterrestrial (Georges Méliès' *Le Voyage dans la Lune*, 1902). By the 1920s, the US and European film industries were borrowing extensively from each other – both themes and people. At the same time, European regulators made efforts to combat the influence of Hollywood – both because of its depravity and out of jealousy.[305]

Hybridization reached its climax with *Steamboat Willie*, the

1928 sound cartoon featuring Mickey Mouse, parodying
Buster Keaton, and using technology pioneered by Al Jolson's
The Jazz Singer the previous year. But paradoxically, the
'Golden Age' of 1930s cinema was distinctly unglobal, because
the introduction of soundtracks imposed linguistic constraints.
In the 1940s, this divide between English-speaking and other
cinematic traditions was enshrined when the Oscars intro-
duced a special award for foreign-language films.

The literary genre of the nightmarish world state first
appeared in this period, beginning with Yevgeny Zamyatin's
We (1920) and H. G. Wells' *Men Like Gods* (1923), and
continuing with Aldous Huxley's *Brave New World* (1932)
and George Orwell's *Animal Farm* (1945). Film on the other
hand was shamelessly appropriated to serve nation-building
and international propaganda. In 1936, George Marshall
directed an unashamedly patriotic movie version of *A Message
to García*, and in 1939 the British celebrated empire with *The
Four Feathers*. Leni Riefenstahl won a gold medal at the 1937
World Exhibition in Paris for her fascist documentary *The
Triumph of the Will*. Fascists regimes also responded to
'degenerate' art and literature by burning it. The mass movements and disruptions of the Second World War smoothed the
way not just for trade and finance, but for a less propagandist,
more popular and creative era of ideological exchange.

The Sputnik contraction (1950s–60s)

*'Men on frontiers, whether of time or space, abandon their
previous identities. Neighbourhood gives identity. Frontiers
snatch it away.'*
                    Herbert Marshall McLuhan, 1911–1980[306]

A package of artistic and technical innovations in the early 1950s opened up a new phase of cultural exchange. The roots of rock 'n' roll, portable radio and electronic television can all be traced back to the 1920s or earlier. But television sets cost about a year's wages in the 1930s and there was little demand for portable radios. The following for rhythm and blues was strictly and racially limited until Bill Haley's *Rock around the Clock* (1954). The development of the cheap pocket transistor radio in 1954 came at just the right time for teenagers. *The Catcher in the Rye* (1951) and *Rebel without a Cause* (1955) expressed teenage angst, but the simultaneous arrival of network TV, pocket radio and rock 'n' roll facilitated a more positive expression of teenage cultural exuberance, at least in the West. Each decade since then has seen extensions of – but not radical departures from – this 1950s cultural package, like the compact audiocassette (1963), Walkman (1979), MTV (1981), mainstream hip-hop (1980s), mobile phone text-message (1992) and iPod (2001).

The interplay between global and local culture was evident in the Eurovision song contest. From its origins in Monaco as a seven-country competition in 1956, it appeared at first glance to be quintessentially globalizing. But the contest developed strong anti-global undercurrents. Organizers insisted on the use of 'national' language from 1966 to 1972. Over the years, songs were sung in Lithuanian, Alpine, Romansch, Breton and Corsican languages and dialects, as political statements. On contest night in April 1968, these tensions came to a head at the Royal Albert Hall. Austria's entrant was Karel Gott from Czechoslovakia; and Germany was represented by Norwegian Wencke Myhre. Spain's original entrant Juan Manuel Serrat wanted to sing in Catalan but was forbidden by dictator Francisco Franco. He was replaced by the more photogenic Massiel, who cost British crooner Cliff Richard victory after

Germany – still smarting after their defeat by England in the football World Cup two years previously – gave their points to Spain.[307]

From the 1960s, cultural cannibalism took off in the developing world, too. In Brazil, this was epitomized by Gilberto Gil's song *Chuckberry Fields Forever*, which mixed The Beatles and Chuck Berry with Afro-Brazilian beats into the uniquely Brazilian style of *tropicalismo*. Other examples of this hybridization process in the field of popular music ranged from Jamaican reggae to Senegalese griot.[308]

In film, a mould-breaking contribution was *For a Fistful of Dollars* (made 1964, released 1967), Italian director Sergio Leone's great Western. An anonymous gunslinger rides into a lawless and dusty frontier town on a mule. San Miguel is being torn apart by the bloody rivalry of two gangs, the Baxters and the Rojos, fighting to win a monopoly on the trade in guns and liquor. 'There's money to be made in a place like this', muses the Man with No Name. He ruthlessly plays the two gangs off against each other, getting rich and restoring order to the town into the bargain.

For a Fistful of Dollars is a sombre tale of crony capitalism, shady multinationals, culture clashes, intellectual property piracy, fake branding and labour exploitation. It's also about creative destruction, amazing technical innovation, huge profits and sheer exhilaration. It was the very essence of 1960s globalization. And that was just the making of the movie. Originally titled *The Magnificent Stranger*, it was basically a rip-off of Japanese director Akira Kurosawa's 1961 samurai film *Yojimbo*. Indeed its US release was delayed three years while Kurosawa sued Leone for breach of copyright – successfully.

Dozens of 'spaghetti westerns' had already been made by Italians but failed to attract audiences outside Italy. So it was dressed up as an 'authentic Western', with dozens of European actors and crew adopting American names on the credits. Sergio Leone styled himself 'Bob Robertson', Ennio Morricone was 'Dan Savio', and Mario Brega – a major leap of the imagination this one – became 'Richard Stuyvesant'. *Per Un Pugno di Dollari* – as it was called on its first Italian release – was mainly filmed in and around Los Albaricoques in the Southern Spanish region of Almería. Dry and dusty, the region bears a striking resemblance to the American West – far more than any location in Italy.[309]

For a Fistful of Dollars was a sweatshop. Clint Eastwood had to buy his own black jeans and received just US$15,000 (about US$80,000 in today's prices). He only agreed to the project because he recognized the plot from *Yojimbo*, which he had seen and liked. 'Over I went, taking the poncho with me – yeah the cape was my idea'. He had to wear the same unwashed poncho throughout the trilogy of Man with No Name films. Leone used dazzling electric arc lights over and above the harsh Almería sun to give Clint his trademark squint. The set was a linguistic Tower of Babel. Each actor spoke his or her native tongue, with only the stuntman Benito Stefanelli able to act as informal interpreter between Leone and Eastwood. The unintended side effect of the dubbing is that the taciturn Man with No Name emerges as the only plain-talking character in a town of rogues. The film's score launched Ennio Morricone's international career, but he got the job mainly because he had been in the same class as Leone at school.

When it appeared in the US, the film was unpopular with US critics. Leone had broken Hollywood's unwritten rules for Westerns: stylized violence, stereotyped 'Indians', the hero playing guitar by a campfire. But audiences loved it. *For a Fistful of Dollars* touched a raw nerve in its reframing of the frontier myth as a tale of cynicism, greed and violence. According to Leone's biographer Christopher Frayling, early viewers responded to the film because of disenchantment driven by the assassination of Kennedy and military escalation in Vietnam. In the early 1970s, ABC made a misguided effort to blur the mercenary tone of the film by adding a prologue.[310] The original film went on to influence Hong Kong martial arts movies and Westerns right through to the recent *Deadwood*.

By the end of the 1960s, cultural exchanges had become markedly more global. But the hand of the corporation was becoming clearly visible. When the clean-cut New Seekers wanted to 'teach the world to sing, in perfect harmony' (1971), they were adapting a song that had first been written for a Coca-Cola advertisement.[311]

The emergence of global culture?

'New technologies are part of a powerful civilization which is rapidly transforming the world around us. Sometimes that change is empowering. But all too often it endangers precious human ways of life, just as surely as it endangers the environment within which those ways of life flourish.'
Mickey Hart & Alan Jabbour

In the mid-1990s, Russian artists Vitaly Komar and Alex Melamid ran a series of surveys asking people around the world about their artistic preferences. The surveys, conducted under the auspices of New York's Dia Center for the Arts and funded by Chase Manhattan Bank, showed that people from 14 different countries had surprisingly similar tastes in painting. Most people, it transpired, liked the colour blue and preferred their paintings to be 'dishwasher-sized'. Komar and Melamid painted interpretations of what people said they most and least wanted.

The result caused uproar. Harvard psychology professor Steven Pinker claimed it showed evidence of the existence of genetically-programmed universal artistic tastes. Others saw the whole exercise as an elaborate and subversive practical joke. To Michael Govan, director of the Dia Center, Komar and Melamid's project posed 'relevant questions that an art-interested public, and society in general often fail to ask: What would art look like if it were to please the greatest number of people? Or conversely: What kind of culture is produced by a society that lives and governs itself by opinion polls?'[312]

After the three global contractions of the 1490s, 1880s and 1950s, the globe remains highly diverse. There is no 'most wanted' painting, literature, movie genre, music or airline, let alone religious belief, cultural norm or political ideology. The world's 200 plus countries hold over 5,000 ethnic groups speaking nearly 7,000 languages. In two-thirds of those countries, at least one significant ethnic minority makes up ten per cent or more of the total population. Can this diversity last in the face of the fourth great contraction?

Persecution of diversity is a persistent and perhaps growing problem, with some 360 million people suffering exclusion as a result of religious beliefs, according to the *Minorities at Risk* database at the University of Maryland's Centre for International Development and Conflict Management. Religion, culture and poverty often go hand in hand. Altogether 890 million people experience cultural, economic or political exclusion – and for around half of these, according to researchers, the exclusion has its roots in historic neglect. In Iran, for example, the 300,000 strong Baha'i community are considered non-persons in the constitution. Cultural exclusion can be a matter of life or death: the Dalit population of Nepal lives 20 years less than the average Nepalese – a scandalous gap. Global media helps highlight these injustices, and to some extent even helps challenge them. There is now an online resource centre working to support the 'untouchable' caste of Dalits (www.dalitstan.org), and another to coordinate information on human trafficking in South-East Asia (www.tipinasia.info). Mobile phones helped coordinate the 'People Power II' revolt in the Philippines in 2001, and are giving Indian spice growers access to world market prices.

In the 1990s, ideas and information were exchanged between greater numbers of people than ever before. The results are as difficult to interpret as Komar and Melamid's 'most wanted painting'. Some argue that religious fundamentalism is on the rise, aided by modern communications technologies like the internet. Others suggest that Muslim madrassas, Hindu extremists and Southern Baptist preachers simply receive more media coverage than they used to, while globalization is actually spreading secular values and encouraging more spiritual diversity. Few doubt the global impacts of Al-Qaeda, but is it a genuinely worldwide movement, or a collection of 'super-empowered' angry individuals using global technologies to fight for regional goals?

Linguistic diversity is another area of controversy. Throughout the twentieth century, three languages dominated: Mandarin Chinese, Arabic and Hindi. But although spoken by fewer people as a first language (some 340 million), English steadily eclipsed its rivals as the global *lingua franca*. It is now spoken by an estimated 600 million as a second language, and heading for one billion speakers altogether. Some estimate that half the world's population will be able to speak it by 2050. Many minority languages will not be able to withstand the assault of the five big languages.

Malayalam, the language of the black pepper lands of Kerala in South-West India, still has 35 million speakers. But others are in serious trouble: only 300 people on Vancouver island in west

Canada can still speak Nuuchahnulth, while in north Australia, Patrick Nudjulu is one of just three remaining speakers of Mati Ke. One of the other speakers lives far off, and the other is Patrick's sister, but aboriginal tradition forbids siblings from speaking to each other after puberty. Languages are vanishing at the rate of one a fortnight.[313] Of an estimated 14,500 languages that existed in the 1490s, the number had fallen to 10,000 by the early nineteenth century, and 7,500 by 1900. Today there are around 6,900 living languages, according to the linguistic database Ethnologue.[314] This database is run by SIL International – formerly the Summer Institute of Linguistics, which like other religious missions did much to homogenize language around the world in the quest for conversions. Experts predict the number of languages in the world will fall by 50–90 per cent over the next 100 years.

What are the implications of the globalization of language? In thirty African countries, most people don't speak the official language and seven children out of eight are not taught in their mother tongue. In Eastern Europe and the former Soviet Union, one in four children studies in a foreign language.[315] Learning is more difficult if it is not in the mother tongue. But defenders of global language argue that ability to speak one of the world's main languages enhances economic and cultural opportunities. Global languages are in a constant state of flux, and are highly adaptable to local needs. The internet can also facilitate the revival of languages such as Occitan and Welsh by joining up geographically dispersed speakers.

Global exchange of culture was severely limited prior to the lifting of the immensely destructive Cultural Revolution in China in the mid-1970s and the opening up ('glasnost') of the Soviet Union from 1985. In the 1980s and nineties, world trade in cultural goods (printed matter, literature, music, visual arts, cinema, photography, radio, television, games and sporting goods) almost quadrupled, to an estimated $390 billion. But the globalization of culture remained a limited process, with a few major players and many non-participants. In 1990, Japan, USA, Germany and UK exported over half of all cultural goods; those countries and France accounted for half of all imports. By the late 1990s, China had also become a significant exporter, and the stranglehold of this cultural 'gang of six' had actually increased.[316]

The international trade in cultural goods is growing. 100,000 new songs are released each year, according to the industry body IFPI. Culture around the world is still stunningly diverse. The most popular Brazilian musical form, *sertaneja*, is hardly known outside the country; while Indian music still commands 90 per cent of the market in India. Yet amid this diversity, there is also growing homogeneity. The USA and UK alone account for almost half of total CD sales worldwide. Only eight albums sold more than five million copies worldwide in 2004 – all bar one by Anglo-Saxons.[317] The top ten bestsellers are actually increasing their share of the $34 billion global music market – and it is unclear whether the proliferation of music piracy and pay-as-you-go downloading will promote musical diversity or homogeneity.

Bollywood produces far more films than Hollywood each year, but American films have an estimated 85 per cent monopoly of screenings worldwide. Hollywood is cosmopolitan, open to talented directors and actors from around the world. But critics see it less as a global melting pot than as an industry steeped in American values but tolerant of the occasional foreign fad: Scottish swashbucklers *Braveheart* and *Rob Roy* in 1995; Chinese martial arts epics *House of Flying Daggers* and *Hero* ten years later.

In 1980, CNN introduced 24-hour news, but the concept of instantaneous live news came to prominence during the coverage of the 1991 Gulf War and the introduction of news websites in 1995. Over this period, the ownership of entertainment, newspapers, television, film and advertising came to be concentrated in the hands of ten major corporations, which jointly control some two-thirds of the global communications industry. These media conglomerates are criticized for creating bland, sanitized 'infotainment' and saturating households with television and commercials, first in the USA and Europe, and then worldwide. On the other hand, news reporting is arguably more balanced than it was in the 1840s, when 10,000 US newspapers vied for readers.

STAR TV, founded by Li Ka-Shing in Hong Kong in 1991, was intended to follow this model, broadcasting English-language, western programming to Asia's upper-middle classes. But STAR gradually metamorphosed into thirty local, more popular channels with programming in eight languages. 'It is widely believed that globally standardized product varieties are displacing locally customized ones in many product categories,' says Pankaj Ghemawat of Harvard Business School. 'But there is actually no systematic evidence on this subject'.[318] The phenomenal recent growth in independent web-logs promoting alternative views, news and photos will to some extent balance the concentration of communications media. There were 15 million blogs in mid-2005, with increasing numbers from China and other countries where censorship remains overt.

Mickey Hart, ex-drummer of the Grateful Dead, and Alain Jabbour, Director of the American Folklife Center recently collaborated to re-release a series of unique early recordings from West Africa, the South American rainforests and islands of Indonesia under the Endangered Music Project.[319] Such efforts to protect traditional cultural forms in the face of a global onslaught are becoming more widespread. France and Canada both require a minimum amount of domestic musical content on radio. China limits the screenings of US films. The UK Film Council recently decided to use money from the national lottery to subsidize a digital network for cinemas, provided they increase screenings of 'art house' films. In 2005, the BBC made fresh recordings of the entire works of Beethoven freely downloadable on the internet. 'Putting things on the web, where they are available to the whole world, does not make the world more homogenous', says journalist Andrew Brown. 'It is the sort of globalisation that sharpens the distinctiveness of nations and societies'.[320]

Global cultural exchange has contradictory tendencies, then. On the one hand it creates homogeneity. On the other, it can enhance cannibalistic creativity and rescue vulnerable artefacts. In the 1970s, popular culture was pressed into service by environmental and anti-war protesters, for example John Denver's *Whose Garden Was This?* and Edward Abbey's cult novel *The Monkey Wrench Gang*. In 1985, Western pop stars came together as Band Aid to draw attention to famine in Ethiopia. After an apolitical period, artists and musicians are once again being pressed into service in global protest movements. Works by Sebastiao Salgado, Damien Hirst and Andreas Gursky have been adopted by anti-globalization activists. In 2005, at the World Social Forum in Porto Alegre in Brazil, the show was opened by Brazil's minister of culture, none other than Gilberto Gil, and closed by musical cannibal Manu Chao, with the rallying cry 'another world is possible'.

In summer 2005, dozens of musicians attempted to pressurise the G8 meeting in Scotland to go further on debt relief and international aid. 'What we do in the next five weeks is seriously, properly, historically, politically important,' said Bob Geldof in the run-up to the concerts. 'There's more than a chance that the boys and girls with guitars will finally get to turn the world on its axis'. As we saw in the last chapter, the songs helped win some modest concessions but weren't quite enough to rock the world. Cynics point out that anti-global culture has its global market, from coffee-table books to increased record sales. In 2002, Gursky's photo of rows of trainers sold in London for £432,750, a record for a photograph.[321] But what these high-profile interventions showed was the inability of global agencies, governments, NGOs, mainstream media and businesses to engage ordinary citizens in the globalization debate.

Large majorities in almost every country feel their traditional way of life is being lost. Although they welcome many aspects of globalization, most people believe that their way of life should be protected against foreign influence.[322] In the world of ideas, globalizing tendencies have long been in tension with local preferences. Today, global exchanges apparently have the upper hand. But whether it is religion, high art, music, football or surfing the net, the process has been complex and patchy, both in the benefits it brings and the extent of the phenomenon. It may be a small world, said comedian Steven Wright, 'but I wouldn't want to have to paint it'.

Small world:
the coming global contraction

'The digital planet will look and feel like the head of a pin. As we interconnect ourselves, many of the values of a nation-state will give way to those of both larger and smaller electronic communities. We will socialize in digital neighbourhoods in which physical space will be irrelevant and time will play a different role.'

Nicholas Negroponte, *Being Digital*, 1995

What do cravat-sporting actor David Niven and Manchester-born comedian Steve Coogan have in common? They both played Phileas Fogg getting around the world in 80 days – and both struggled to make it funny.[323] Though the two films are separated by almost 50 years, the actors shared a friend: Coogan was in *The Revengers' Comedies* (1998) with Liz Smith, who was also in *Curse of the Pink Panther* (1983) with Niven. Amazingly, most actors can be linked by just two or three intermediaries, even the two men who played Fogg's loyal French manservant Passepartout: Mexican comedian Cantinflas and Hong-Kong born stuntman Jackie Chan.[324]

To network theorists, this is called the 'small world phenomenon'. It gave birth to the cult game *Knowing Kevin Bacon*, where film-buffs try to guess how many links would connect their chosen actor to the star of *Footloose* (1984) and *Destination Anywhere* (1997). The small world phenomenon was first proposed in 1967 by the controversial psychologist Stanley Milgram (1933–1984). Milgram's experiment suggested that two random US citizens could be connected by just six acquaintances.[325] The idea of the small world has permeated the popular consciousness.

Signal beacons and Roman roads; vellum books and relays of horses; knotted Inca ropes and printing presses: all were radical technologies to gather, process and spread information faster than word of mouth and better than the human memory. These technologies had the potential to confer enormous military, commercial and cultural advantages to the groups that possessed them – to make the world small. We have noted the global impacts of the fifteenth-century package of maps, compass and long-distance sailing vessel. In the seventeenth and eighteenth centuries, the combination of printing, learned journals, reliable postal services, scientific openness and coffee-shop enabled the development of laissez-faire economics and botanical piracy. From the 1860s, it was the turn of the telegraph, railway, steamship, newspaper and passport to shrink the world. In the early twentieth century came the typewriter, telephone, telex, TV, radio and airplane.

In 1945, head of IBM Thomas Watson thought there could be a market for anything up to five computers worldwide. By the mid-1950s he was giving Regency portable radios to his engineers and telling them to put transistors into computers. Marshall McLuhan, looking at the telephone and radio, announced the birth of the 'global village'. At the time there were 69 simultaneous phone lines across the Atlantic. 'What the railroads and telegraph did a century ago,' said Arthur C. Clarke in 1971, 'jets and communications satellites are doing now to all the world.' A satellite launch was tantamount to signing 'the first draft of the Articles of Federation of the United States of Earth.'[326] In 1980 futurist Alvin Toffler predicted that many of us would soon be working in 'electronic cottages'.

Until recently, the fruits of global culture seemed to be reserved for an elite of youngish American and European men. 'A typical American yuppy drinks French wine, listens to Beethoven on a Japanese audio system, uses the internet to buy Persian textiles from a dealer in London, watches Hollywood movies funded by foreign capital and filmed by a European director, and vacations in Bali', wrote Tyler Cowen in *Creative Destruction* in 2002. Cultural globalization 'enriches our lives', claimed Philippe Legrain in *Open World*, published the same year. 'I [am] certainly much the richer for it. As, indeed, is anyone who can take holidays in Spain or Florida, have sushi or spaghetti for dinner, drink coke or Chilean wine, watch a Hollywood blockbuster or an Almodovar, listen to bhangra or rap, practice yoga or kick-boxing, read *Vanity Fair* or *The Economist*, have friends from around the world'.

These descriptions of the joys of cultural globalization sound remarkably like Keynes's description of the lucky Londoner calling up the world's riches on his telephone in 1914. It's an obvious point that this cultural feast is not on offer for the two and a half billion people living on less than two dollars a day. There are production limits to Persian textiles and shrinking natural resources available for sushi. But can modern technology at least share this cultural opportunity more equitably with the rapidly growing middle classes in Mumbai, Shanghai, Lagos and São Paolo? Can it offer a virtual equivalent for those who will never be able to afford the real thing?

The modern package of computer, email, world-wide web and mobile phone is now reaching an unprecedented level of global diffusion. In 2004 alone, over 600 million mobile phones were shipped – enough for a tenth of the world's population. Internet access has been growing rapidly, and is approaching a billion users. Over half the population in rich nations now uses the internet. The Pew *Global Attitudes Survey* found in 2002 that two-thirds of people worldwide think the internet is a change for the better. Mobile internet, open-source software and free online information projects like Wikipedia and Project Gutenberg have enormous potential to reverse the 'digital divide' between rich and poor.

As we have seen, cultural and technological packages have repeatedly offered the potential to create a small world. Each time, the world *did* shrink. But it remained stubbornly large and diverse. Will it be different next time? The coming global contraction must overcome two major challenges before this will truly be a small world. The first is our love of the local. The second is the limit to littleness.

Google, the internet search engine that has rapidly become a global brand, regularly publishes Zeitgeist, a list of the most popular searches around the world. Search behaviour provides some insight into the intellectual, moral and cultural climate. 'This flurry of searches often exposes interesting trends, patterns, and surprises', says Google. Only the CIA and spammers know more about global trends in internet use. In January 2005, millions of people searched for information on the Indian Ocean tsunami. But interest in the disaster came second to the football league in Spain, to online auctions in New Zealand, and to railway enquiries in France. The Irish were more interested in cheap flights, the Japanese in downloading local maps, the South Koreans in the Celebrity X-files TV show. The Norwegians wanted to known more about Britney Spears than the tidal wave.[327]

Surfers hunt for important information, checking out the latest on federal tax in Brazil or the smoking ban in public places in Italy. But many searches are frankly trivial: Canadian collectors of Japanese *inuyasha* cartoon characters or German fans of the cartoon crocodile *Schnappi*. Google does not report on pornography hunters, who are reputedly one of the largest groups of internet users.

Google's snapshot also provides evidence of how different cultures remain. From the table of top searches in early 2005, the Chinese emerge as entrepreneurial, and more interested in domestic martial arts movies or planning the spring festival than the remote tsunami. Indians plan their rail journeys assiduously, and prefer online university sites to catching up on the latest Bollywood gossip. They are more interested in sporting stars than actresses, and get their news not from CNN or the BBC but New Delhi TV. In Britain, concern for the tsunami vied with the cult show *Little Britain*. The British are into online and physical games, cars, mini-breaks, and, reluctantly, income tax.

Table: Top Google searches, January 2005

Rank	China	India	UK	USA
1	Business license information	Tsunami	Tsunami	Tsunami
2	*Kong Fu* (movie)	Indian Railways	*Little Britain* (TV show)	Britney Spears
3	*A World Without Thieves* (movie)	Sania Mirza (tennis player)	Games	Paris Hilton
4	Jay Chou (singer)	Trisha	Cars	Christina Aguilera
5	Andy Lau	Aishwarya Rai	Multimap	Pamela Anderson
6	Jingjing Wu (Olympic diving Gold medalist)	Anara Gupta (celebrity)	Paintball (game)	Angelina Jolie
7	*The Silence of the Witness* (TV series)	Ignou (open university)	Dictionary	Brad Pitt
8	Spring Festival	Bollywood	Currency converter	Games
9	Spring Couplets	NDTV	Ryanair	Carmen Electra
10	Tsunami	Australian Open	Inland Revenue	Dictionary

Source: Google.com zeitgeist, March 2005.

The USA, with by far the greatest concentration of internet users, turned to Nostradamus rather than the FBI for web information after 9/11. In January 2005, US humanitarian concerns overcame the usual obsession with shapely celebrities. Brad Pitt was outnumbered six to one by women, suggesting strong gender differences in surfing. Intriguingly, it is the Americans and British, not Indians or Chinese, who use online dictionaries.

For all the talk of the internet as a transformative globalizing technology, what emerges from Zeitgeist is how local most searches are. Enterprises like GeoURL and Quova recognise this, and are making 'geolocation' software to identify the physical location of websites and internet addresses. 'While any company of any size can deploy an economic presence online', says Quova, 'true e-commerce success has turned out to be a function of – and dependent on – the same business principles that determine success in the brick-and-mortar world. And one of those principles is geographic knowledge'.

IBM is betting on the rebirth of the local with WorldBoard, its proposed system to paste 'virtual information' notice boards onto physical places of interest. 'By one technological route or another, we are on the verge of being able to put information in its place on a planetary scale,' says James Spohrer of the IBM Almaden Research Center. 'This innovation could change our control over the environment, our notion of place, and our human relationship to information . . . We will map every metre of this planet. And not just this planet'.[328] Geography's premature obituary is also challenged by mobile phones and GPS, which despite all their potential are still mainly used to coordinate nightlife and monitor jogging. Martin Dodge at Imperial College London is a leading authority on mapping cyberspace. 'The idea that the internet liberates you from geography', he concludes, 'is a myth.'[329]

These local limits to further globalization are surmountable. After all, millions of people have already shaken off local shackles, broadened their horizons and embraced the globe. Could we all be on the way to becoming as well-connected as Kevin Bacon?[330] Or are there limits to littleness? The Small World Project at Columbia University decided to find out. Researchers Duncan Watts, Peter Dodds and Roby Muhamad asked 60,000 volunteers from 166 countries to try to get an email message to an unknown person. The targets ranged from a US academic to an Estonian archivist and an Indian consultant. Participants could choose any known intermediary they thought would be able to get the message closer.

The results of this twenty-first-century version of *A Message to García* offer important insights into the shrinking planet. The successful efforts succeeded with a chain length of between five and seven people – so the world certainly *can* be small. On the other hand less than two per cent of all attempts actually reached the target.[331] Is the world getting smaller? 'I don't think it is actually shrinking all that much', Watts told me, 'for the simple reason that the smaller the world gets, the more difficult it becomes to make it smaller still'. Watts believes the typical separation between people around the world is already near its theoretical minimum. 'I don't see it changing in a hurry. Furthermore, if such a thing did happen, and we lived in a world in which most interaction was virtual, there would be many more important and noticeable changes in our lives (like none of our friends knowing any of our other friends) than simply being another step or two closer'.[332]

Evolutionary psychologist Robin Dunbar at the University of Liverpool has also been looking at the limits to littleness. Bill Clinton and other 'connectors' are famous for their enormous networks of contacts, but Dunbar believes there are both cognitive and practical constraints to the number of close relationships we can have – people that we know as people, that we would rush up to if we happened to see them at Shanghai Airport. Our circle of friends is limited by the size of the human neo-cortex. To make matters worse, maintaining friendships requires time, and that is a finite resource for all of us.

In 2001, Dunbar and fellow anthropologist Russell Hill decided to test the size of people's social networks by asking how many Christmas cards they sent that year. The result? The typical respondent sent cards to 125 people.[333] Hill and Dunbar found that close proximity affects the frequency of contacts, but that people would go to extra efforts to stay in touch with friends who had moved overseas. The size of the network depends on all sorts of factors: gender and age as well as psychological, social and economic factors. But in Dunbar's view, most people have networks of between 75 and 250 people. This number remains remarkably similar to the networks of the earliest hunter-gatherers. 'People might *like* to increase their circle of acquaintances to well beyond the value of 100–200,' Dunbar told me, 'but they simply can't do it.' In other words, the planet can't get much smaller. If you don't already know Kevin Bacon, you probably never will.

8

THE INCREDIBLE
SHRINKING PLANET

*'The further backward you look, the further forward you
can see.'*

Winston Churchill (1874–1965)

'History is just one damn thing after another.'

Henry Ford (1863–1947)

Who was right, Churchill or Ford? The history of globalization can sometimes seem like one damn long-distance exchange after another. But look more closely, and patterns,
even lessons, start to emerge. As I proposed at the beginning of
this book, understanding the history of globalization matters,
because that history has been hijacked. It risks being caught in
a cross-fire between market fundamentalists and anti-capitalists. Both sides see themselves as the rescue team – always bad
news for the hostage.

'The thing that lives in history is not the event,' wrote
Elbert Hubbard in 1914, before he was torpedoed on the
Lusitania. 'It is the written account of it.'[334] Market funda-

mentalists have tended to evade awkward definitions, to airbrush out losers, and to use 'we' as shorthand for a tiny elite of globe-trotters. Anti-capitalists have been too ready to downplay the astonishing improvements in living standards and opportunities that have come with global exchanges. This brief history has shown that globalization is a highly complex set of phenomena. Nothing could be more foolhardy than making bold assertions about the imperative need to either support or reject globalization. It is a sort of Tasmanian Devil on the loose.

At the beginning of the book, we agreed that the history of globalization is different from a history of the world. A few kings, queens, emperors and peasants have appeared in these pages, but the heroes and villains of globalization are the rare individuals with the ability to see the globe in its entirety, as a piece of fruit ripe for the picking.

The early phases of globalization overlapped with imperialism and colonialism, but we have stressed the importance of Monsieur de Vogüé, the late nineteenth-century consumer who loved to travel and who went 'to the East and to the West for colours and ideas.' Unlike most imperialists, the interests of globalizers have been 'as wide as the universe'. Unlike globalizers, most capitalist entrepreneurs never think of exporting even to their neighbours.

The three other questions we posed are much more difficult: who has driven globalization; how far has the process gone; and is it a good thing or a bad thing? These are the questions to revisit after our review of the history of global trade, migration, finance and ideas. They might give us some clues about how to prepare for the next global contraction.

Will the real planet-shrinkers please step forward?

'Every sustained wave of technological progress and economic development everywhere has been fuelled by greed, profiteering, special privileges, and megalomania.'

Professor Theodore Levitt[335].

Many 'great' men and women in history never developed global intent, either by choice or circumstance. But the history of globalization features some remarkable mavericks – both individuals and organizations – with a global vision. Entrepreneurs, explorers, diplomats, inventors, footballers and intellectuals – have made globalization happen. Ptolemy and Columbus had it; so did Jules Verne, Jules Rimet and Roger Casement. Derek Vestey, H. J. Heinz and Sony's Akio Morita had it. But Sam Walton's early Wal-Mart and Celtic Football Club didn't.

You don't hear many radical voices like Levitt's in the academic debate on globalization these days. Yet planet-shrinkers *have* often been greedy, egotistical, rent-seeking profiteers. Columbus and the negotiators at Tordesillas were all that, and more. But Benjamin Franklin and the men who founded the modern Olympic Games and Football World Cup were animated by more generous universal visions. How can we fathom the motives of Hiram Maxim? Globalizers often swim against the tide, for better or worse. Two mavericks of huge influence on the globe were out of step with popular views: Woodrow Wilson, with his belief in a League of Nations, and George W. Bush, with his disbelief in global warming.

What does it take for powerful men like Alfred Nobel or George Soros to develop a benign world-view and the appetite to push it through? Should all *Fortune 500* CEOs, UN functionaries and national policy-makers 'traverse the ball round and round,' as Andrew Carnegie proposed, rather than flitting from summit to limousine to hotel suite? Today, all the talk is about global competitiveness, and the public discourse in Western nations is on how to improve national educational performance in science and engineering. But many citizens are ill-informed about global affairs, not least geography and history. Do we really need engineering skills more than global vision?

Globalization is not just the story of individuals with global intent. Countries and cultures develop it too. The idea of a 'Clash of Civilizations' was popularized in the 1990s by Samuel Huntington to explain the existence of enduring global fault-lines. Benjamin Barber wrote of the inherent tension between McWorld and Jihad. Thomas Friedman saw it as a primeval conflict between Lexus-loving globalizers and Olive tree-tending traditionalists. 'The Arab East still sees the West as a natural enemy,' wrote Lebanese novelist Amin Maalouf in 1983. 'Against that enemy, any hostile action – be it political, military or based on oil – is considered no more than legitimate vengeance.'[336]

In the minds of many, the destruction of the World Trade Center and Madrid, Bali and London bombings vindicated this view of long-lasting global incompatibilities. 'What has been believed now for a century in the Middle East is that the West, having lost the first round of the crusades in the Middle Ages, re-embarked on crusading in the late nineteenth century, using the techniques of commerce, banking, politics, diplomacy, backed of course by power,' observed Professor Jonathan Riley Smith of Cambridge University about the 2005 Crusader movie *Kingdom of Heaven*.[337]

The history of clashing civilizations should be treated with utmost caution. Politics, geography, disease and technology are, I believe, adequately convincing drivers of global competition, without recourse to ideological and cultural stereotypes. But you can bet on a new round of global clash books from political scientists. This time they won't be about Islam but about China, poised to lead in the early fifteenth century, quiescent for over 500 years, and now again a powerhouse of global exchange. Some US business journalists seemed to detect something underhand, almost vindictive in the spate of takeover bids by Chinese companies in mid-2005. What do Westerners know about how the Chinese think about their history? What, for that matter, do Dutch, British and French multinationals know about how the Indians and South-East Asians interpret the spice trade and East Indies Companies. There is already criticism in Southern India that talented graduates are taking up high-paying jobs in British and American call-centres that commandeer skills needed for social and economic development more broadly. Can we believe the assurance that if a country becomes part of Dell's supply-chain it will never harbour a grievance and go to war?

Civilizations should be handled with care, but can we at least identify nations at the forefront of globalization? The conventional view is that first came Anglobalization, then came Americanization. There is some merit in this. In the 1880s, Britain clearly dominated global decision-making, and there was something ruthlessly and systematically global about its acquisitions in Africa from North to South. And it is equally clear that US corporations were firmly on the profitable end of the global supply-chains established in the 1990s.

But this account leaves out important chunks of the story and a host of other historical globalizers. The Abbasids, Chinese and Scandinavians had many of the components of global intent. The Spanish and Portuguese first carved up the planet between them, and genuinely believed that they could enforce the deal. The French played a central global role, coining the word global, developing modern consumerism, and often pushing a universalizing yet still chauvinistic version of globalization – the metre, the Canaries meridian – at odds with the pragmatic, self-serving approach of the Anglo-Saxons.

France continues to play that role today, with a unique density of global corporations and a political vision of a multipolar world – provided one of those poles is Paris. But no country has a genius for globalization. It is not a baton passed from nation to nation through history. The British on a number of occasions opted out of global processes – like metrification and the promotion of world football – either temporarily or permanently. US isolationism is the single biggest obstacle to tackling global climate change today, as it was the downfall of the League of Nations.

Many other countries are at the forefront – or sharp end – of globalization today. The Irish have an enviable track record at the Eurovision song contest, if that is any guide. Irish singers have chalked up seven wins and were runners-up four times over the years. A Globalization Index is produced each year by *Foreign Policy* magazine and stockbrokers AT Kierney. When Ireland was ranked the world's most globalized country in the 2004 Globalization Index, Mickey Harte's song for the Eurovision contest was called *We've Got the World*.[338] Ireland has been at the very heart of the history of globalization. Irish troops formed a mainstay of the British imperial armies; the mass emigration after the potato famine gave a major boost to the population of the United States. In 2005, the Emerald Isle was toppled from its top position in the Globalization Index. Chris Doran's 'Song for Europe' was uncannily prophetic: *If My World Stopped Turning*.

The most globalized country in 2005 was another small island economic miracle: Singapore. After Ireland came the Netherlands in third place, ahead of the USA, which performed 'badly' on political, personal and economic factors but still came in fourth due to the heavy technological weighting of the index. The Scandinavian countries came in ahead of the UK (12th). Croatia and Israel are more globalized than France (18th). The Iberians have slipped further, from first place in 1492 to 22nd and 26th in 2005. China and India, the awakening global giants, are ranked 54th and 61st, respectively, out of 62 countries.

As we have found, measuring truly global exchanges is not an easy job. The problem with this index is that it measures a bunch of things that are international but not necessarily global, like exports and imports, international travel, foreign direct investment and secure internet servers. And it leaves out cultural exchanges altogether. What the global historian wants, of course, is such an index capturing inter-regional exchanges and going back in time.

Taken with a pinch of salt, however, the *Foreign Policy* index provides an interesting reality check. It tells us two important things. One is that countries have very different experiences of globalization. Global leaders from the past are no longer leaders now. Globalization is not an attribute that can be stored away, like gold. The other thing the index highlights is evident from the preceding chapters. There is a big difference between being a globalizer and being globalized. Countries and citizens need to be aware of this difference if they want to manage globalization.

Mavericks have also been important for the study of globalization, from Fuat Sezgin's valiant efforts to put tenth-century Baghdad back on the global map to Benoit Mandel-brot's remarkable theories linking stock markets and hurricanes. George Bernard Shaw claimed that the truly civilized person was deeply moved by statistics. Furnishing relevant data on global trends has been the hobby of a handful of passionate number-crunchers. We have to admire Simon Kuznets' work on GDP, Lewis Fry Richardson's obsession with deadly quarrels, and Angus Maddison's fascination with the economic long run. These iconoclasts developed new knowledge and data to inform the globalization debate. There is no shortage of globalization pundits today, but perhaps not enough people like Alan Rugman, prepared to put in the tedious legwork behind fresh insights.

The limits to globalization: how far has it got; how far can it go?

> 'There's so much that we share
> That it's time we're aware
> It's a small world after all'
>   Walt Disney World Magic Kingdom[339]

Every writer's nightmare is to see a book on the same subject hit the bookstands while grappling with final drafts. In my case, there were *two* history books on globalization. When I read them, I was entertained, puzzled and relieved. One said that a new era of globalization started in 2000. The other said globalism started to collapse in 1995.[340] Was US Presidential candidate Ross Perot's 'giant sucking sound' the sound of the planet shrinking in the early 1990s? Or did globalization get underway thousands of years ago, as world-system historians like the late Andre Gunder Frank maintain? Was Adam Smith correct to see 1492 as globalization's great leap forward? Or do we believe Kevin O'Rourke and Jeffery Williamson's claim that 'the 19th century contained a *very big globalization bang*.'[341] These histories are all good, but surely they can't all be right?

Let's review what we have found. In the past 1,000 years, against all the background noise, there were eight periods when a 'bundle' of slow-building globalizing influences looked set to create a global contraction.

Globalization: false labours and genuine contractions

Dates	Globalizing build-up	Galvanizing event
10th–14th century	Mongol conquests; European-Islamic crusades; growth of luxury; Baghdad world map; Chinese fleets.	
1490–1500	Maritime technology (sails, compass & maps); Portuguese Naval School; population pressure; Columbus & Da Gama; printing press.	1. Treaty of Tordesillas
1600–1700	Circumnavigations; Joint stock companies; intercontinental commodity trade; silver & gold from New World; botanical piracy	
1770s–1815	Mass consumerism; Industrious revolution; Joint Stock Companies; French & American revolutions; metre; newspapers; first abolitions of slavery.	
1880–1890	European emigration; indentured Asian labour & abolition of slavery; scramble for Africa; telegraph, steamship, Suez Canal; Gold Rush & Gold Standard; Maxim gun; *Red Rubber*	2. Meridian Conference
1920s–30s	League of Nations; Great Depression; aviation; US productivity surge; paperback books; Football World Cup; *Brave New World*	
1955–65	Decolonization; Third World; growth of multinationals; international tourism; pocket radio, rock'n'roll, TV; *Fistful of Dollars*; rise of environmentalism and the NGO	3. Sputnik orbit
1995–2005	Fall of Berlin Wall & collapse of USSR; Internet & world-wide-web, GPS; WTO; debt crises; rise of Wal-Mart; outsourcing & offshoring; year of the sweatshop.	4. Global supply-chains

Of these eight periods, half failed to leave the world markedly smaller. There was something missing, a galvanizing event that would surprise and shock participants. These galvanizing events – the Treaty of Tordesillas, the Meridian Conference, the orbit of Sputnik, the global supply-chain – were not always the highest-profile thing happening at the time, but they were all consciously globe-embracing, and seen as such by con-temporaries. There are two noteworthy features of these global contractions. The first is that the galvanizing events were all global fault-lines – often literally lines – that generated enough friction to throw up global shockwaves. Far from being a 'world without walls', as Bill Clinton called it, globalization has been forced along by divisions.

The other four periods appeared to have many of the pieces in place, but lacked such a galvanizing episode. In the seven-teenth century, the danger of long-distance shipping arguably prevented a global contraction. In the 1790s, the international metre could have done it, but was treated with suspicion by global gatekeepers. The 1920s and 1930s is a real puzzle, a period of 'phoney globalization' that saw key global institu-tions but where an emerging global vision shattered into pieces amid local turf wars where 'never again' became 'might as well'.

The other feature is that each global contraction had vociferous critics. These were not Luddites calling out 'Stop the world, I want to get off'. They were studiously modern, with an alternative vision of how the globe could work. From the Spanish Dominicans in the early sixteenth century to Roger Casement and E.D. Morel calling for more re-sponsible trade in the late nineteenth to the nascent envir-onmental movement of the early 1960s and the No Sweat campaigners of the mid-1990s, critical voices were listened to, not ignored.

Was there one contraction bigger than the rest? Each contraction built on the last, as well as on the factors from failed periods. But the years from 1955 to 1965 were an especially intense crucible for globalization. This formative decade saw Sputnik and Gagarin's orbit, and the US develop its domino theory of Cold War intervention. Over 60 countries were added to the family of nations, enhancing identity and giving globalizers a target free from imperial trammels. The decade saw the early burgeoning of US multinational corporations. The world's population grew at its faster ever rate, and the number of people travelling on international holidays grew by ten per cent each and every year, closely matched by international refugees. The teenager arrived as a cultural force, empowered by pocket radio, rock'n'roll and TV. The dollar took its place as the global reserve currency, but oil was steadily seeping into the global economy. In the early 1960s, according to the Worldwide Fund for Nature's *Living Planet Index*, American and European consumers began to outstrip the capacity of the environment to provide food, energy, materials and building land and act as a sink for pollution. The modern environmental movement was born. This period also saw the rise of globalizing institutions, ranging from McDonald's to the Eurovision Song Contest.

Historians are either 'lumpers or splitters', and splitters will object to this focus on four decades of global contraction. It is tempting to bundle Leonardo da Vinci's *Mona Lisa* into the first globalizing decade as the most ubiquitous global artwork. But the painting started life, ostensibly at least, as a portrait of a Florentine businessman's wife, and was in any case painted just outside the key decade (from 1503–07). The painting's universal fame as a symbol of feminine mystique only really began after Walter Benjamin became obsessed with her in the 1860s. Similarly, the Sputnik Decade misses out on the crucial year 1971, when Nixon cut the dollar loose from gold and campaigning NGOs were founded.

Where has this series of contractions got us to? Both market fundamentalists and anti-capitalists have reasons to exaggerate the extent to which the world is globalized. But the facts and figures are dramatic enough. Three-quarters of the world's capital market is international. Over half of the world's top 150 economies are multinational corporations. Half of international trade is between world regions. A fifth of all people old enough to use a keyboard are using the internet. One in ten people is a migrant, slave, international traveller or works for a foreign company.

Global goods and muscle are the longest established; ideas and culture followed. Relative to the other areas, global finance is the area that has globalized fastest. 'Among the three most important types of markets – those for capital, products, and labor – the global capital market is the farthest along the road to true global integration,' says Diana Farrell, director of the McKinsey Global Institute. Farrell leaves out the world of ideas. Ideas and culture move as easily as money – it's just that we don't know how to count them.

Looking at all the patterns together, we are reaching a stage that could be called *semi-globalization* – affecting very roughly half of all trade, labour, finance and ideas. How much further can globalization go? It can't go all the way. There are logistical, commerical and environmental limits to globalization. From global warming to hyper-mobility to consumer saturation to mutual incomprehension, exchanges will grind to a halt well short of a 'fully globalized' world.

A global grind may already be starting, as large corporations concentrate on key markets, travellers revert to safe and familiar destinations, local cultures gain new resilience, empowered migrant workers return home and immigration restrictions prevent others from taking their place. Complex global supply-chains are proving very difficult to 'clean up' in terms of labour standards. Local food production is fighting back against global sourcing.

On the other hand, there is no shortage of people with global intent. Global warming and economic competition will throw people into motion and see vast transfers of resources from one region to another. On the basis of past contractions, there looks to be at least one more global contraction to come. Some of the pieces are already in place. But history has its limits. There is no template as to where the next galvanizing event will come from, and what form it will take.

Is globalization a good thing? Winners, losers and the missing middle

> 'When a man's got money in his pocket, he begins to appreciate peace.'
> The Man with No Name, *For a Fistful of Dollars*, 1964

Neo-liberal historians currently command the heights of economic history. According to this school of thought, globalization is a long-established and basically progressive process. Where the British Empire was the prime mover of globalization from 1870 to 1913, today it is US and European corporate capitalism and its democratic vision that makes goods available for all, improves labour standards, increases wealth and shares cultural riches. A more recent account has the USA and Europe not as the drivers but as the intended victims of the new round of globalization. This time it's the vast 'armies' of educated entrepreneurs in China and India that will call the shots. If you think your job can't be outsourced halfway round

the world – it probably already has been. Both accounts are
self-centred claptrap.

As we have seen, there have always been many losers from
globalization. Downsized blue- and white-collar workers in
the West deserve sympathy and support – it could be me next.
But the modern counterparts of the brutalized Spice Islanders
are desperate Indian farmers killing themselves because they
see their livelihoods collapse, Eastern European women sold
into sexual servitude, Africans orphaned because providing
affordable retroviral treatments undermines a business model,
Andean villagers robbed of their resources.

One thousand years ago, almost every person on the planet
– all 268 million of them – was eking out an existence on
around $1.20 a day. In the year 2000, the average person was
living on $15.50 a day. But over one billion people – one in six
of the world's population and four times more than had been
alive in the year 1000 – was living on an income *even lower*
than that of their ancestors 50 generations previously. Income
inequality between regions has never been higher, and it is
growing. The scourage of AIDS has seen life expectancy – one
of the great success stories of the twentieth century – actually
falling for the first time in Africa. Obesity will do the same in
rich nations.

The world's nations set themselves the target of halving this
obscenely persistent world poverty by 2015. Note the realism
of halving – not eradicating – poverty. In September 2005,
they met to review progress towards the Millennium Development Goals. Their conclusion? The 'dollar a day' target
would not be met, despite the phenomenal growth in China
and India.

China and India will inevitably take their proportionate
place at the global table. This will impoverish some Western
workers. But globalization has served rich countries well and

they own nine-tenths of the world's capital assets. Brazil, Venezuela and Malaysia are steering paths towards globalization on their own terms. The real losers could be middling countries like Mexico, Argentina, Poland and Kenya, struggling to find a new role in world markets that favour either intellectual capital or cheap labour and raw materials.[342]

David Dollar and Aart Kraay, from the World Bank, are perhaps the leading experts on the impacts of globalization on poverty levels. What do they think? Dollar and Kraay concede the global trend towards rising inequality over the past two centuries or more. But, they claim, this peaked around 1975 and 'since then, it has stabilized and possibly even reversed. The chief reason for the change has been the accelerated growth of two large and initially poor countries: China and India.' They divide the developing world into two camps: a 'globalizing' group of countries that have welcomed trade and foreign investment over the last 20 years – and grown by five per cent a year as a result. The 'nonglobalizing' camp trades less than it did 20 years ago, and grew at just one per cent a year.[343]

The message seems pretty clear: it's better to be Croesus of Lydia – opening up to foreign investors – than Lycurgus, trying to keep Sparta out of the system. Growth may cause domestic income inequality, but globalization is good news because, it will bring absolute poverty down. Dollar and Kraay adopt a narrow definition of globalization: openness to foreign trade and investment, low tariffs, few capital controls. They don't factor in debt burdens, bank crises, irresponsible corporations and punitive commodity prices – effects as we have seen which come with the globalization package whether poor countries want them or not. Even so, their findings have been picked up and publicized as a global rule. The problem is, the global results are totally skewed by the huge populations and abnormal globalizing paths to globalization taken by India and China.

Elsewhere in the developing world the picture is less rosy. GDP is static or falling in many African countries; and income growth in Latin America is patchy and susceptible to sudden setbacks. 'Something is clearly wrong', says former World Bank economist Branko Milanovic, now senior associate at Carnegie's Global Policy Program. 'Maintaining that globalization as we know it is the way to go and that, if the Washington Consensus policies have not borne fruit so far, they will surely do so in the future, is to replace empiricism with ideology. This has been done before, but unfortunately the consequences were less than positive.'[344]

When the Pew *Global Attitudes Project*, chaired by Madeleine Albright, asked people from 44 countries around the world how they felt 'about the world becoming more connected through greater economic trade and faster communication', the answers were almost unanimously positive. When the researchers asked whether 'growing trade and business ties between our country and other countries is good for you and your family', one in five people in many countries said they disagreed, didn't know or didn't like to say. I started writing this book with a nagging feeling that there was already too much written, too much said, about globalization. If one in five people can't decide if globalization is a good thing or not, there hasn't been nearly enough debate. Perhaps the history of globalization – beauty marks, warts and all – can help people make up their minds.

Pro-globalizers wheel out Myanmar and North Korea in evidence of the risks whenever someone challenges 'globalization as usual'. But the nations in most serious trouble are in sub-Saharan Africa. These countries have not 'failed to embrace globalization' – far from it. They have massive international debts, are dependent on exports of primary commodities to world markets, and have adopted European languages in preference to local ones. However, they are small, landlocked, and have a high prevalence of HIV/AIDS.

As David Dollar and Aart Kraay admit, 'Our research shows that countries that grow faster or trade more are as likely to see inequality decrease as increase.'[345] Robust global data on the trends that affect the lives of billions of people – inter-regional exchanges in trade, people, finance and culture – should be a properly resourced undertaking. This was a job that earlier globalizers, for all their other faults, took seriously. Today we rely on government whim and under-resourced UN statisticians. Dollar and Kraay concede that the data of household income that have been used as evidence of the benefits of globalization are full of flaws, but 'they are the best we have, and so we use them.'[346] If Wal-Mart headquarters in Bentonville can know within seconds when a customer buys a tin of beans in Beijing, how is it that we still don't know what the impacts of global trade and investment are on poor people?

As China and India grow, world production and consumption will have to expand proportionately, other countries will have to forego growth, or the West will have to surrender existing income. Global trade and finance growth rates in the mid-2000s are an order of magnitude faster than anything that has been seen before. We are in uncharted territory and a GPS wristwatch or some dodgy multiple regression analysis are no guide to the future.

Can globalization be managed?

> 'Look at the world around you. It may seem like an immovable, implacable place. It is not. With the slightest push – in just the right place – it can be tipped'.
> Malcolm Gladwell, *The Tipping Point*[347]

100 years ago, Italian-born Frenchman Maurice Garin retired from professional cycling after he was disqualified from the second Tour de France. Garin, the winner of the first tour, had broken the rules by taking the train for a part of the second. There is a 'bicycle theory of globalization' – in fact like everything else to do with this contentious topic, there are two conflicting versions of the bicycle theory. To pro-globalizers, it means that you have to keep moving forward reasonably fast or you'll fall off. To global sceptics, by contrast, the bicycle theory says you *should* get off every once in a while to get your breath back and admire the view.

'The nation-state is just about through as an economic unit,' claimed Charles Kindelberger in 1969. Numerous commentators since then have made the same diagnosis. Japan, Brazil, India and Germany don't agree. They have lobbied hard to get into an expanded UN Security Council. Mexico and Indonesia want to join them, but there is no agreed basis for membership of the group or who should have a veto. Meanwhile, China and other large economies must soon be invited to join the outdated G8 group of 'advanced economies'. Whether the emerging group is a G20 or a G196 is an open question.

Nation-states are resurgent, empowered by global contractions and keen to find tipping points to help them manage global exchanges. Countries are prepared to regulate, engage in trade wars, raise taxes if need be. What is remarkable is that, unlike other periods in history, recent advances in information technology have not yet been applied to global governance and decision-making processes. Real time multinational voting by phone, text and email is perfectly feasible – just check the Eurovision Song Contest. So why is it so hard to imagine a global referendum about global warming in the near future?

Citizens are also empowered by globalization. From local food to fair trade to exerting pressure on the G8, there are a whole range of tools that were simply not available to activists in the 1890s or 1960s. 1995–96 was *The Year of the Sweatshop*. Why did US and European citizens become so obsessed with labour standards at this precise time – far more widespread than the Boycott South Africa movement of the early 1980s, or when rubber-tapper Chico Mendes was murdered (1989), or during the Congo and Putumayo scandals of the early 1900s? 1995 saw a concatenation of hitherto disconnected events: terrible industrial accidents like the 1993 Kader toy factory fire in Bangkok; the murder of Ken Saro-Wiwa; campaigning CEOs and companies like Anita Roddick and the Body Shop breaking ranks with the rest of their industries; the blatant untransparency of corporate environmental and social reports; the growing financial, technical and networking resources of NGOs; and the mainstream media's sudden interest in exposing sweatshop stories about wholesome companies.

History shows that tipping points can be maddening elusive. Despite all sorts of judicious levering, in all the obvious places, slave trading still persists, 200 years after the most powerful nation in the world decided to ban it. Global warming is happening, and the most powerful nation in the world refuses to accept it. Working conditions in the global supply-chain remain, as often as not, terrible. But the history of globalization also shows how global intent can persevere against the odds. People still have power to choose when, how, even whether they enter global exchanges.

As fans of *For a Fistful of Dollars* will know, The Man with No Name actually *did* have a name: Joe.[348] But there really is a person on the planet with no name. He is the last surviving member of a small tribe of Amazon Indians. Over recent decades every other member of his people has disappeared through disease and violence as cattle ranchers and illegal loggers have spread into Tanaru, in the south of the Brazilian state of Rondônia. The Brazilian government agency charged with protecting the interests of Amazon Indians has been making genuine efforts to assist the loneliest man on earth. But each time the expert trackers known as *sertanistas* identify his isolated camp, he abandons it and moves deeper into the rainforest. Although he has accepted the occasional gift left for him – a pot or machete – it is now clear to the *sertanistas* that he refuses further contact with the outside world.[349]

It is impossible to imagine the state of mind of someone whose name is unknown; someone who chooses, literally, to turn his back on the rest of the world. How do we feel about his tragic loneliness? Can we help feeling a sneaking admiration for his ability to pick and choose from the messy, exhilarating and dangerous process known as globalization?

FURTHER READING

Aczel, Amir, *The Riddle of the Compass: The Invention that Changed the World*, Harcourt Harvest, San Diego, 2002.

Agostino, Gilberto, *Vencer ou Morrer: futebol, geopolitica e identidade nacional*, Mauad, Rio de Janeiro, 2002.

Appadurai, Arjun, *Modernity at Large: Cultural Dimensions in Globalization*, University of Minnesota Press, Minneapolis, 1997.

Appadurai, Arjun (ed), *Globalization*, Duke University Press, Durham,NC.,2001.

Bairner, Alan, *Sport, Nationalism and Globalization: European and North American Perspectives*, State University of New York Press, Albany, NY, 2001.

Bairoch, P. & Kozul-Wright, R., 'Globalization Myths: Some Historical Reflections on Integration, Industrialization and Growth in the World Economy', UNCTAD Discussion Papers No 13, Geneva, 1996.

Bakan, Joel, *The Corporation: the pathological pursuit of profit and power*, Constable, London, 2004.

Barber, Benjamin, *Jihad Vs.McWorld: Terrorism's Challenge to Democracy*, Corgi, London, 2003.

Bauman, Zygmunt, *Globalization: The Human Consequences*, Polity Press, Cambridge, 1998.

Bayly, Christopher, *The Birth of the Modern World 1780–1914*, Blackwell, Oxford, 2004.

Beck, Ulrich, *What Is Globalization?* Polity Press, Cambridge, 1999.

Berger, Peter & Huntington, Samuel, *Many Globalizations: Cultural Diversity in the Contemporary World*, Oxford University Press Inc, USA, 2003.

Bergreen, Laurence, *Over the Edge of the World: Magellan's Terrifying Circumnavigation of the Globe*, HarperCollins, London, 2003.

Berman, M., *All That is Solid Melts into Air: the experience of modernity*, Verso, London, 1983.

Bhagwati, Jagdish, *In Defense of Globalization*, Oxford University Press, 2004.

Bourdieu, P., *Firing Back: against the tyranny of the market 2*, New Press, New York, 2003.

Buisseret, David, *The Mapmaker's Quest: Depicting New Worlds in Renaissance Europe*, Oxford University Press, 2003.

Burbach, Roger, Nunez, Orlando & Kagarlitsky, Boris *Globalisation and Its Discontents: The Rise of Postmodern Socialisms*, Pluto Press, London, 1996.

Burnet, John, *Early Greek Philosophy*, Kessinger, Whitefish, MT, 1892, (reprint, 2003).

Cain, Peter & Hopkins, Anthony, *British Imperialism: 1688–2000*, Second Edition, Longman, Harlow and New York, 2001.

Castells, Manuel, *The Rise of the Network Society, Vol. I. The Information Age: Economy, Society and Culture*, Blackwell, Oxford, 1996.

Castells, Manuel, *The Internet Galaxy: reflections on the internet, business and society*, Oxford University Press, 2002.

Cavanagh, John & Mander, Jerry, (eds), *Alternatives to Economic Globalisation: A Better World Is Possible*, Berrett-Koehler Publishers Inc., San Francisco, 2004.

Chua, Amy, *World on Fire: How Exporting Free-Market Democracy Breeds Ethnic Hatred and Global Instability*, Arrow, London, 2004.

Conn, David, *The Beautiful Game?*, Yellow Jersey Press, London, 2003.

Cookson, Gillian, *The Cable: The Wire That Changed the World*, Tempus Publishing, Stroud, 2003.

Cosgrove, Denis, *Apollo's Eye: A Cartographic Genealogy of the Earth in the Western Imagination*, Johns Hopkins University Press, Baltimore, 2003.

Crosby, Alfred, *The Measure of Reality: quantification and Western society, 1250–1600*, Cambridge University Press, 1997.

Davis, Mike, *Late Victorian Holocausts: El Niño Famines and the Making of the Third World*, Verso, London, 2002.

Diamond, Jared, *Guns, Germs and Steel: A Short History of Everybody for the Last 13000 Years*, Vintage, London, 1998.

Diamond, Jared, *Collapse: how societies choose to fail or survive*, Allen Lane, London, 2005.

Dicken, Peter, *Global Shift: Reshaping the Global Economic Map in the 21st Century*, Sage, Thousand Oaks, CA, 2003.

Dickson, Paul, *Sputnik: The Shock of the Century*, Berkley Publishing, New York, 2003.

Divine, Robert, *The Sputnik Challenge*, Oxford University Press, 1993.

Dorin, Jamie & Bizony, Piers, *Starman: The Truth behind the Legend*, Bloomsbury, London, 1998.

Ellis, John, *The Social History of the Machine Gun*, Random House, London, 1975.

Ellwood, Wayne, *No-nonsense Guide to Globalisation*, Verso, London, 2001.

Emmott, Bill, Crook, Clive & Micklethwait, John, *Globalisation: Making Sense of an Integrating World*, Economist Books, London, 2002.

Fergusson, Niall, *Empire*, Penguin, London, 2004.

Fergusson, Niall, *Colossus*, Penguin, London, 2005.

Fernández-Armesto, Felipe, *Columbus*, Oxford University Press, 1991.

Flandreau, Marc & Zumer, Frederic, *The Making of Global Finance 1880–1913*, OECD (Organisation for Economic Co-Operation & Development) Paris, 2004.

Foer, Franklin, *How Soccer Explains the World*, HarperCollins, London, 2004.

Frayling, Christopher, *Sergio Leone: something to do with death*, Faber & Faber, London, 2000.

Friedman, Thomas, *The Lexus and the Olive Tree: Understanding Globalization*, Anchor, London, 2000.

Friedman, Thomas, *The World is Flat: a brief history of the world in the 21st century*, Allen Lane, London, 2005.

Giddens, Anthony, *Runaway World*, Profile Books, London, 2002.

Gray, John, *False Dawn: The Delusions of Global Capitalism*, Granta Books, London, 2002.

Guedj, Denis, *The Measure of the World: A Novel*, Arthur Goldhammer (trans), University of Chicago Press, 2001.

Gunnell, Barbara & Timms, David, (eds.) *After Seattle: Globalisation and Its Discontents*, Catalyst Trust, London, 2000.

Gurney, Alan, *Compass: A Story of Exploration and Innovation*, W.W. Norton, New York, 2004.

Hardt, Michael & Negri, Antonio, *Empire*, Harvard University Press, Cambridge, Mass., 2000.

Harvey, P., *Medieval Maps*, British Library, London, 1991.

Held, David, McGrew, Anthony, Goldblatt, David & Perraton, Jonathan, *Global Transformations: politics, economics and culture*, Polity, Cambridge, 1999.

Held, David & McGrew, Anthony, *Governing Globalization: Power, Authority and Global Governance*, Polity, Cambridge, 2002.

Hertz, Norena, *The Silent Takeover: Global Capitalism and the Death of Democracy*, Arrow, London, 2002.

Hertz, Noreena, *IOU: The debt threat and why we must defuse it*, Perennial, London, 2005.

Hobhouse, Henry, *The Seeds of Wealth*, Pan, London, 2004.

Hobhouse, Henry, *The Seeds of Change*, Pan, London, 2002.

Hopkins, A.G. (ed), *Globalisation in World History*, Pimlico, London, 2002.

Huntington, Samuel, *The Clash of Civilizations? The debate*, W. W. Norton, New York, 1997.

Kelley, Kevin (ed), *The Home Planet*, Addison Wesley Longman, New York, 1991.

Klein, Naomi, *Fences and Windows: Dispatches from the Frontlines of the Globalization Debate*, Flamingo, London, 2002.

Klein, Naomi, *No Logo*, Flamingo, London, 2001.

Krugman, Paul, *The Great Unravelling*, Penguin, London, 2004.

Landes, David, *The Wealth and Poverty of Nations*, Abacus, London, 1999.

Launius, Roger et al., (eds), *Reconsidering Sputnik: Forty Years Since the Soviet Satellite*, Routledge Studies in the History of Science, Technology & Medicine, London, 2000.

Lechner, Frank & Boli, John, *The Globalization Reader*, 2nd edition, Blackwell, Oxford, 2004.

Legrain, Philippe, *Open World: the truth about globalisation*, Abacus, London, 2003.

Maddison, Angus, *Monitoring the World Economy 1820–1992*, OECD, Paris, 1995.

Maddison, Angus, *The World Economy: A Millennial Perspective*, OECD, Paris, 2001.

Maddison, Angus, *The World Economy: historical statistics*, OECD, Paris, 2004.

Maguire, Joseph, *Global Sport: identities, societies, civilizations*, Polity Press, London, 1999.

McBride, Stephen, Fraser, Simon & Wiseman, John, *Globalization and its Discontents*, Macmillan, London, 2000.

McLuhan, Marshall & Fiore, Quentin, *War and Peace in the Global Village: an inventory of some of the current spastic situations that could be eliminated by more feedforward*, Bantam Books/Random House, New York, 1968.

McMillan, John, *Reinventing the Bazaar: a natural history of markets*, W.W. Norton, New York, 2003.

Menzies, Gavin, *1421: The Year China Discovered the World*, William Morrow, New York, 2003.

Micklethwait, John & Wooldridge, Adrian, *The Company: A*

Short History of a Revolutionary Idea, Weidenfeld & Nicholson, London, 2003.

Micklethwait, John & Wooldridge, Adrian, *A Future Perfect: the challenge and hidden promise of globalisation*, William Heinemann, London, 2000.

Miller, Toby, Lawrence, Geoffrey, McKay, Jim & Rowe, David, *Globalization and Sport: Playing the World*, Sage, London, 2001.

Milton, Giles *Nathaniel's Nutmeg: How One Man's Courage Changed the Course of History*, Sceptre, London, 2000.

Monbiot, George, *Captive State: the corporate takeover of Britain*, Macmillan, London, 2000.

Moore, Mike, *A World Without Walls: Freedom, Development, Free Trade and Global Governance*, Cambridge University Press, 2003.

Munro, John, 'The Consumption of Spices and Their Costs in Late-Medieval and Early-Modern Europe: Luxuries or Necessities?', 1988 *http://www.economics.utoronto.ca/munro5/SPICES1.htm*, accessed January 2005.

Murray, Bill, *The World's Game: a History of Soccer*, University of Illinois Press, 1998.

Notes from Nowhere, *We Are Everywhere: The Irresistible Rise of Global Anti-capitalism*, Verso, London, 2003.

Osterhammel, Jürgen & Peterson, Niels, *Globalization: a short history*, Princeton University Press, Princeton, 2005.

Perrone, Charles & Dunn, Christopher (eds), *Brazilian Popular Music and Globalization*, Routledge, 2002.

Polanyi, Karl, *The Great Transformation: the political and economic origins of our time*, Beacon Press, Boston, 1957.

Pomeranz, Kenneth, *The Great Divergence: China, Europe and the Making of the Modern World Economy*, Princeton University Press, 2002.

Robins, Nick & Kumar, Ritu, 'Black Pepper Country' in: *Resurgence* **220** September/October 2003.

Roche, Maurice, *Mega-events: Olympics and Expos in the Growth of Global Culture*, Routledge, 2000.

RoperASW *National Geographic – Roper 2002 Global Geo-*

graphic Literacy Survey, National Geographic Education Foundation, *http://www.nationalgeographic.com/geosurvey/ download/RoperSurvey.pdf*, accessed February 2005.

Rosenberg, Justin, *The Follies of Globalisation Theory*, Verso, London, 2002.

Russell, Jeffrey, *Inventing the Flat Earth*, Praeger Paperback, New York, 1997.

Saul, John Ralston, *The Collapse of Globalism*, Atlantic Books, London, 2005.

Schivelbusch, Wolfgang, *Tastes of Paradise: A Social History of Spices, Stimulants, and Intoxicants*, Vintage, London, 1993.

Scott, James, *Seeing Like a State: How Certain Schemes to Improve the Human Condition Have Failed*, Yale University Press, New Haven, 1998.

Sezgin, Fuat, 'Arab Origins of European Maps' in: *Zeitschrift fur Geschichte der Arabisch-Islamischen Wissenschaften* 15, Frankfurt, pp. 1–23, 2003.

Siddiqui, Asif, *Sputnik and the Soviet Space Challenge*, University Press of Florida, Gainesville, 2003.

Silverberg, Robert, *The Longest Voyage: Circumnavigation in the Age of Discovery*, Bobbs-Merrill, Indianapolis, 1972.

Smith, Adam, *An Inquiry into the Nature and Causes of the Wealth of Nations*, Oxford World's Classics, 1776 (reprint 1998).

Sobel, Dava, *Longitude: The True Story of a Lone Genius Who Solved the Greatest Scientific Problem of His Time*, Walker and Company, New York, 1995.

Spate, Oskar, *The Spanish Lake: The Pacific since Magellan*, Volume I, 2nd edition, Australian National Library E-Press, 2004.

Spufford, P., *Power and Profit: The Merchant in Medieval Europe*, Thames & Hudson, London, 2002.

Steger, Manfred, *Globalization: a very short introduction*, Oxford University Press, 2003.

Stiglitz, Joseph, *Globalization and Its Discontents*, Penguin, London, 2004.

Stiglitz, Joseph, *The Roaring Nineties*, Penguin, London, 2004.

Traynor, John & Griffin, Tony, *A Season in the Sun: Celtic's wonder year 1966/67*, Lion Books, Kidderminster, 1992.

Veblen, Thorstein, *The Theory of the Leisure Class*, Prometheus Books, Amherst NY, 1998.

Veloso, Caetano, *Tropical Truth: a story of music and revolution*, Bloomsbury, London, 2003.

White, Andrew Dickson, *A History of the Warfare of Science with Theology in Christendom*, 1896, reprinted 1960, Dover, New York.

Wolf, Martin, *Why Globalization Works*, Yale University Press, New Haven, 2004.

Wright, Robert, *NonZero*, Abacus, London, 2001.

NOTES

1 Based on amazon.com, amazon.co.uk, amazon.fr and amazon.de book searches, December 2004.
2 *Global Transformations* (Polity, 1999), by Held, McGrew, Goldblatt and Perraton is the most even-handed and historical textbook. Giddens (2002) and Castells (1996, 2002) focus on sociological and technological aspects respectively. Huntington (1993) coined the phrase 'the Clash of Civilizations'; Barber (2003) and Friedman (2000) supplied the memorable metaphors.
3 Among the early bestsellers of the genre were Klein *No Logo* (2001) and Heertz *Silent Takeover* (2002). Monbiot (2000) focuses the anti-corporate approach on the UK. For academic takes, see also Grey (2002) and Bourdieu (2003). For a glossy book, try Notes from Nowhere (2003).
4 Micklethwait & Wooldridge *A Future Perfect* (2000); Legrain *Open World* (2003) and Wolf *Why Globalization Works* (2004) are entertaining variants of the genre. See Ferguson (2004 & 2005) for the free-market history; and Lal *In Praise of Empires: Globalization and Order*, New York: Palgrave Macmillan, 2004, for a rarer view from a non-Anglo-Saxon.
5 Perrone & Dunn (2002).
6 There is a fascinating collection of essays by Cambridge historians edited by Tony Hopkins (2002), which has sadly been allowed to go

out of print. Christopher Bayly has written an outstanding mono-graph covering the period 1780–1914 (Bayly, 2004). Thomas Friedman's new book *The World is Flat* (2005) is billed as 'a brief history of the globalized world in the 21st century'. It's highly readable, but as Friedman would admit, neither brief nor a history. Osterhammel & Petersson (2005) is a highly-distilled Germanic take on globalization's history.

7   Monbiot (2000), p. 10.

8   Micklethwait & Wooldridge (2000), pp. 332–42. Actually the reincarnated Marx would have been bemused rather than sur-prised, because Rolls-Royce was only founded in 1906, 23 years after his death. The previous images are from Friedman (2000) and Steger (2003).

9   Krugman (2004) p.365; Stiglitz (2002), p. *ix*; Friedman (2000), ch. 1; *http://www.ifg.org/about.htm*. The IFG suggests that globaliza-tion has the following key ingredients:
    • 'Corporate deregulation and the unrestricted movement of capital;
    • Privatization and commodification of public services, and re-maining aspects of the global and community commons, such as bulk water and genetic resources;
    • Integration and conversion of national economies (including some that were largely self-reliant) to environmentally and so-cially harmful export-oriented production;
    • Promotion of hyper-growth and unrestricted exploitation of the planet's resources to fuel the growth;
    • Dramatically increased corporate concentration;
    • Undermining of national social, health and environmental pro-grams;
    • Erosion of traditional powers and policies of democratic nation-states and local communities by global corporate bureaucracies;
    • Global cultural homogenization, and the intensive promotion of unbridled consumerism.'

10 Steger (2003) p.13.

11 'Embrace globalisation with vigour, says Sen', *The Indian Express*, February 21, 2001.

12 The Economist, *Globalisation: making sense of an integrating world*, London: The Economist/Profile Books, 2001, p.ix.

13 H.G. Wells, J.M. Roberts, Felipe Fernández-Armesto, David Landes and Jared Diamond have all produced entertaining and very different versions of world history compressed between two covers. Readers with more time on their hands could alternatively turn to the engrossing but incomplete 18 volume Blackwell history of the world for a more detailed, academic account.

14 Susie Dent alerted me to this early reference, from the OED database. *Harper's Magazine*, September 1892, 492/2. I have not

been able to trace M. Vogüé but presumably his family came from the small town in the Southern Ardèche of that name.

15 *Understanding Media*, pp.xii–xiii, quoted at *http://www.marshallmcluhan.com/faqs.html*. Marshall McLuhan's most famous phrase was originally inspired by a close reading of James Joyce's *Finnegan's Wake* and, says his son Eric, by discussions with writer and artist P. Wyndham Lewis.

16 Perhaps journalists are less interested in the new spirit of non-violence expressed in the annual anti-globalization meetings of the World Social Forum in Porto Alegre and Mumbai and the positive focus of the Make Poverty History campaign than they were in the smaller but more violent protests of the late 1990s.

17 Quoted in Klein (2001), p.439.

18 *History Today*, 2002, p.76.

19 *History Today*, 2002, p.76.

20 I am also going to stick with conventional BC and AD datings rather than the more politically correct BCE version. Apologies to non-Christians if they find this offensive – rest assured it is 'old habits die hard' rather than a hidden agenda to Westernize history.

21 Kurlansky, Mark *1968: The Year That Rocked the World*, Random House, (2005), p.*xix*.

22 Friedman (2005), pp.9–11.

23 Japan is the most aged country in the world. Half the population were born in 1963 or before, and witnessed first hand the emergence of Sony as a global brand. In China, most were born after 1973, when the Cultural Revolution was already running out of steam but when exports were at the lowest at any point in the 20th century. India is far more youthful. Over 500 million Indians are under 24. For them, the IBM PC and AIDS, both of which made their appearance in 1981, have always been a fact of life. Median ages for countries from Population Division of the Department of Economic and Social Affairs of the United Nations Secretariat, *World Population Prospects: The 2002 Revision*, *http://esa.un.org/unpp*; and CIA Fact Book, at *http://www.cia.gov/cia/publications/factbook/fields/2177.html*, accessed February 2005. Economic data from Maddison (2001), Appendix C.

24 Cited by Kolbert, Elizabeth 'The climate of man I', *The New Yorker*, 25 April 2005; *http://www.newyorker.com/fact/content/?050509fa_fact3*.

25 Wolf (2004), Legrain (2003), Klein (2002), Hertz (2005), Friedman (2005), Saul (2005).

26 David Held and colleagues have identified three groups in the globalization debate: hyper-globalizers, anti-globalizers and global sceptics. Other commentators have suggested globalization can be seen as either destructive, constructive or feeble. The history of globalization provides some support for all six perspectives.

27 *http://en.wikipedia.org/wiki/Image:Tasmanian_devil.jpg*.
28 Dreyer (1953).
29 Cavalli-Sforza, Luigi, *Genes, People and Languages*, Penguin, London, 2001.
30 As none of his writings survive, the later attributions by philosophers and churchmen should be taken with a pinch of salt.
31 Author's calculations.
32 This analysis of European mapmaking draws on Harvey, Paul *Medieval Maps*, British Library (1991), and Crosby, Alfred *The Measure of Reality*, Cambridge (1997).
33 Crosby (1997).
34 *History of the Warfare of Science with Theology in Christendom* (1896).
35 Harvey (1991).
36 Diamond (1998), Wright (2001).
37 *http://www.henry-davis.com/MAPS/LMwebpages/236mono.html*, accessed January 2005.
38 Wright (2001).
39 Peter Perdue cited in Wright (2001).
40 O'Connor, J. & Robertson, E. *http://geogdata.csun.edu/geog-courses/history_of_maps05.html*, accessed January 2005.
41 Recknagel, Charles, 'Historian Reveals Incredible Contributions Of Muslim Cartographers', Radio Free Europe, 15 October 2004. *http://www.rferl.org/featuresarticle/2004/10/4d691490–5295–4a17–b0cf-ccb542a013ab.html*, accessed January 2005.
42 'They All Laughed', lyrics by Ira Gerswin (1937), cited in Fernández-Armesto (1991).
43 Aczel (2002); Lane (1963).
44 Spufford (2002).
45 Fernández-Armesto (1999), pp. 35–8.
46 Fernández-Armesto (1991), p.174.
47 Fernández-Armesto (1991), p.174.
48 Slocum, Joshua, *Sailing Alone Around the World*, Century, NY (1899).
49 *http://www.petersworldmap.org/index1.html*, accessed April 2005.
50 'Redefining Nonviolence', speech, 5 April 1975, Boston College (published in *Our Blood*, ch. 6, sct. 2, 1976). Quote from *http://www.creativequotations.com*, January 2005. Friedman (2005).
51 Fernández-Armesto (1991), p.130.
52 *http://www.un.org/Overview/growth.htm*, accessed February 2005.
53 Between 1975 and 2002, more than 60 new national associations were accepted as members of FIFA. *http://www.fifa.com/en/organisation/na/index.html*, accessed February 2005.
54 'Treaty between Spain and Portugal concluded at Tordesillas; June 7, 1494', translation by The Avalon Project at Yale Law

School, *http://www.yale.edu/lawweb/avalon/modeur/mod001.htm*, accessed February 2005.

55 Spate (2004).

56 Crosby (1997), p.106.

57 Burgreen (2003); Gurney (2004).

58 'The Las Casas-Sepúlveda Controversy: 1550–1551', Bonar Ludwig Hernandez, *http://userwww.sfsu.edu/~epf/2001/hernandez.html*, accessed July 2005.

59 Tierney, Brian *The Idea of Natural Rights: Studies on Natural Rights, Natural Law and Church Law 1150–1625*, Emory University Studies in Law and Religion, No. 5, (1997).

60 Silverberg, Robert *The Longest Voyage: Circumnavigation in the Age of Discovery*, Ohio UP, (1997).

61 One of the few records we have of a *commercial* passenger travelling around the world is Giovanni Carreri, from 1693 to 1698.

62 Rogers, Everett *The Diffusion of Innovations*, 4th edition, The Free Press, (1995), pp.7–8.

63 Hobsbawm, Eric, *The Age of Revolution*, Weidenfeld & Nicolson, (1962), cited in Philippe Legrain *Open World*, Abacus, (2003), p.89.

64 Cited in Rothschild, Emma 'Global commerce and the question of sovereignty in the eighteenth-century provinces' in: *Modern Intellectual History*, 1, 1, 2004, Cambridge University Press, pp. 3–25.

65 Ferguson (2004), p.191.

66 Landes (1998), p.326; Held et al. (1999), p.93; Ferguson (2003), p.169; Braudel, Fernand, *The Identity of France: Volume One History and Environment*, Fontana, (1989), p.114–5.

67 Sobel (1995) is the best account of Harrison's obsessive mission.

68 Giovanni's offspring were all born at the observatory, and the Cassini clan lived to the ripe old ages of 87, 79, 70, and 98 respectively. It wasn't a good time for other Frenchmen to be planning a career in astronomy. The English astronomer royals may not have been so nepotistic. But they certainly knew they were on to a good thing – the post only changed hands twice between 1675 and 1762.

69 Brown & Duguid (2000), p.191–2.

70 Taylor, David 'Degree of Difficulty' in *Mercator's World*, May/June 1999, pp. 18–25.

71 In the late 1920s it was found that Maupertuis had made a series of errors that actually explained his finding of the equatorial bulge. Nevertheless, his answer was correct. Source: *http://www.roma-l.infn.it/~dagos/history/sm/node7.html*, accessed February 2005.

72 Bayly (2004), p.375.

73 Alder, Ken *The Measure of All Things: The Seven-Year Odyssey and Hidden Error That Transformed the World*, The Free Press, New York, (2002). Indeed, the story has been written in novel form:

Guedj, Denis *The Measure of the World: A Novel*, Arthur Goldhammer (trans), University of Chicago Press (2001).

74 Howse, Derrek *Greenwich Time and the Longitude*, Philip Wilson Publishers, London (1980); Blaise, Clark *Time Lord: Sir Sandford Fleming and the Creation of Standard Time*, Pantheon, London, (2001).

75 Murphy, Craig *International Organization and Industrial Change: Global Governance Since 1850*, Polity Press, London, (1994).

76 Palmer, Allen 'Negotiation and Resistance in Global Networks: The 1884 International Meridian Conference', in: *Mass Communication & Society*, 5(1), (2002), pp.7–24.

77 France finally bit the bullet at the International Conference on Time in Paris in 1912. Some countries such as India, Burma and Nepal are still not coordinated with the international time zones.

78 Sahr, Robert *Inflation Conversion Factors for Dollars 1665 to Estimated 2015*, Oregon State University, excel spreadsheet downloaded from *http://oregonstate.edu/dept/pol_sci/fac/sahr/sahr.htm*, February 2005.

79 Edney, Matthew *Mapping an Empire : The Geographical Construction of British India, 1765–1843*, University of Chicago Press, (1999).

80 Bayly (2004), pp.274–277.

81 'Top 50 Authors', Statistics on whole *Index Translationum* database, at *http://databases.unesco.org/xtrans/stat/xTransStat.a?V-L1=A&top=50&1g=0*, accessed February 2005.

82 Jones, Gordon, 'Jules Verne at Home' in: *Temple Bar* 129 (June 1904), pp.664–671.

83 Given that his prize money was £20,000 (equivalent to about £1.1 million), he pocketed £60,000 in today's money on the bet.

84 *http://www.julesverne.ca/nelliebly_pbs.html/*; *http://home.att.net/-gapehenry/BlyAdCards.html*. In all the furore, there was little coverage for a rival woman journalist dispatched by *Cosmopolitan* magazine who did it in 76 days.

85 *Laconia* was converted to naval service in the Second World War, and finally sunk by German submarine U-156 in 1942. After torpedoing the ship, the U-boat surfaced, sent out a signal and attempted to save passengers, which included many Italian prisoners of war. A US bomber flew over and ignoring a large red cross flag the U-boat had unfurled, bombed the submarine. Admiral Donitz as a result gave the fateful Laconia Order that U Boats were no longer to pick up survivors. Source: *http://www.cunardline.com/AboutCunard/default.asp?Active=Heritage&Sub=Get-Ship&ShipID=90*, accessed February 2005.

86 Officer, Lawrence H. 'Comparing the Purchasing Power of Money in Great Britain from 1264 to 2002.' Economic History Services, 2004, at: *http://www.eh.net/hmit/ppowerbp/*.

87 *http://en.wikiquote.org/wiki/Yuri_Gagarin*, accessed January 2005.
88 Launius, Roger (no date) 'Sputnik and the Origins of the Space
    Age', NASA history, *http://www.hq.nasa.gov/office/pao/History/
    sputnik/sputorig.html*, accessed January 2005.
89 The Vanguard satellite in still in space today and has been round the
    earth 180,000 times and counting. 'The grapefruit' has actually
    provided more useful information about the globe than the sput-
    niks, helping improve the accuracy of road maps, and also showing
    that the North Pole is slightly raised, while the South Pole is slightly
    flattened. According to Vanguard, both Newton and the Cassinis
    were wrong, and Columbus was right: the earth is more like a pear
    than an egg or an apple.
90 Ezell, Edward & Ezell, Linda *The Partnership: A History of the
    Apollo-Soyuz Test Project*, NASA Special Publication 4209, (1978),
    at *http://www.hq.nasa.gov/office/pao/History/SP-4209/ch1-4.htm*,
    accessed January 2005.
91 Dorin & Bizony, 1998.
92 Dallek, Robert, *John F Kennedy: an unfinished life*, Penguin,
    London, (2003), p.652.
93 Valeri Polyakov is arguably more impressive as a starman. This
    Russian cosmonaut holds the record for the longest space flight in
    history, staying aboard the Mir space station for more than 14
    months and orbiting the earth about 7,075 times.
94 Dallek.
95 Most recently and entertainingly in Scott, David & Leonov, Alexei
    Two Sides of the Moon: Our Story of the Cold War Space Race,
    Pocket Books, (2005).
96 The handshake had been scheduled to take place over Bognor Regis
    on the south coast of England but was slightly delayed.
97 Kleinrock, Leonard (no date) 'The History of the Internet', at *http://
    www.lk.cs.ucla.edu/first_words.html*, accessed January 2005.
98 RoperASW (2002), p.70.
99 Trivedi, Bijal, 'Survey Reveals Geographic Illiteracy', *National
    Geographic Today*, November 20, 2002, *http://news.nationalgeo-
    graphic.com/news/2002/11/1120_021120_GeoRoperSurvey.html*,
    accessed February 2005.
100 Earth Sciences and Image Analysis, NASA-Johnson Space Center. 8
    Nov. 2004. 'The Gateway to Astronaut Photography of Earth.'
    <*http://eol.jsc.nasa.gov/Faq/genEarth.htm#three*, accessed January
    2005.
101 Henry Hobhouse began his catalogue of plants that changed the
    world with *Seeds of Change* (1987) looking at quinine, sugar, tea,
    cotton and the potato. In 2003 came *Seeds of Wealth*, covering
    timber, grapes, rubber and tobacco. Hobhouse has also collabo-
    rated with London's Natural History Museum to produce a virtual
    book – *Seeds of Trade* – that covers more than 60 plant products.

102   *The Economist*, 'A taste of adventure: The history of spices is the history of trade', December 17th 1998; Vandana Shiva (no date) 'The turmeric patent is just the first step in stopping biopiracy', Third World Network, *http://www.twnside.org.sg/title/tur-cn.htm*, accessed April 2005.

103   There are three accounts of the spice trade as a whole, though they tend to finish up prematurely at a point in the eighteenth century where the trade – for a study of globalization – really gets interesting. See Schivelbusch, Wolfgang, *Tastes of Paradise: A Social History of Spices, Stimulants, and Intoxicants*, Vintage Books, (1993); Turner, Jack, *Spice: the history of a temptation*, HarperCollins, (2005); and Dalby, Andrew, *Dangerous Tastes: the Story of Spices*, University of California Press, (2002). For individual spices see Milton, Giles, *Nathaniel's Nutmeg: how one man's courage changed the course of history*, Sceptre, (1999); Ecott, Tim, *Vanilla: Travels in Search of the Luscious Substance*, (2004); Michael, Joseph and Meinen, Letta, *The Cinnamon Stick: Tales of the Spice Trade*, Booklocker, (2002); Pearson, M. (ed), *Perfumed Road: Spices in the Indian Ocean World*, Valorium, (1996).

104   Milton (1999) p.6; Schivelbusch (1993) Chapter 1.

105   Cited in Ferguson, (2004), p. 5.

106   Frank, Robert, *Luxury Fever: Why Money Fails to Satisfy in an Era of Excess*, Princeton University Press, (2000).

107   Skate, Oskar, *The Spanish Lake* (2004), *http://epress.anu.edu.au/spanish_lake/c04.pdf*.

108   Cipolla, Carlo, 'Pepe, vino (e lana) come elementi determinanti dello sviluppo economico dell'età di mezzo' in: *Allegro, Ma Non Troppo*, Mulino, Milan, (1988).

109   The phrase is from Robins, Nick (2004) 'The world's first multi-national' in *The New Statesman*, 13 December 2004.

110   Braudel, Fernand, *The Perspective of the World*, London: Phoenix, (2002), p.218.

111   Van der Wee, Hermann, *The Growth of the Antwerp Market and the European Economy, 14th-16th centuries*, II, (1963), p.127.

112   *Critical Review*, 1756, cited in Ferguson (2004), p.31.

113   John Munro of the University of Toronto has tracked the price of pepper and other spices from the Middle Ages to today – as much because he is a fan of Indian cookery as because of his expertise in medieval economics. Munro, John, 'The Consumption of Spices and Their Costs in Late-Medieval and Early-Modern Europe: Luxuries or Necessities?', (1988) *http://www.economics.utoronto.ca/munro5/SPICES1.htm*, accessed April 2005.

114   Micklethwait, John & Wooldridge, Adrian, *The Company: A Short History of a Revolutionary Idea*, Weidenfeld & Nicholson, (2003).

115   Chandler, Alfred, *The Visible Hand: The Managerial Revolution in American Business*, Harvard University Press, (1980).

116 Federico, Giovanni, *An Economic History of the Silk Industry, 1830–1930*, Cambridge University Press, (1997).

117 Robins, (2004).

118 Bakan (2004), p.10.

119 *http://www.fortune.com/fortune/subs/500archive/founded/ 0,19757,,00.html*, accessed February 2005.

120 Rothschild, Emma, 'Global commerce and the question of sovereignty in the eighteenth-century provinces', in: *Modern Intellectual History*, 1, 1 (2004), pp. 3–25; Berg, Maxine & Clifford, Helen, (eds), *Consumers and Luxury: Consumer Culture in Europe, 1650– 1850*, Manchester University Press, (1999).

121 Key sources for the history of global consumerism include Stearns, Peter, *Consumerism in World History: The Global Transformation of Desire*, Routledge, (2001); Bayly, Chris, *The Birth of the Modern World*, Blackwell, (2004); Berman, Marshall, *All That is Solid Melts Into Air*, Verso, (1983); Miller, Michael, *The Bon Marché: Bourgeois Culture and the Department Store, 1869–1920*, Princeton University Press, (1994); and Koehn, Nancy, *Brand New: How Entrepreneurs Earned Consumers' Trust from Wedgwood to Dell*, Harvard Business School, (2001).

122 Berman (1983), p.194. It was another 100 years before the idea of everyday luxuries returned to the Russian working classes, with the launch of Soviet Champagne in 1936. Gronow, Jukka, *Caviar with Champagne: Common Luxury and the Ideals of the Good Life in Stalin's Russia*, Berg Publications, (2003).

123 Whiteley's Shopping Centre, *http://www.mypaddington.co.uk/paddington/fashion-whiteleys.htm*, accessed July 2005. Other stores soon followed suit. London's Selfridges, inspired equally by Whiteley and by Chicago's Marshall Field flagship store, opened its doors in 1909. Tesco started life as a market stall run by Jack Cohen, mainly selling tea; Cohen opened his first shop in 1929. Outside the big cities, shopping as leisure took off more slowly, but first Sears store was opened n 1925, in Evansville Indiana. Prior to this the company has been exclusively mail order.

124 Fortune 500 Database, *http://www.fortune.com/fortune/subs/500archive/1955_2004rules/0,19786,,00.html*, accessed April 2005.

125 The classic works are by Roger Thevenot (1979), Oscar Anderson (1972) and Willis Woolrich (1967).

126 Fields, Gary, *Territories of Profit: Communications, Capitalist Development, and the Innovative Enterprises of G. F. Swift and Dell Computer*, Stanford: Stanford University Press, (2004).

127 Biography of America, *http://www.learner.org/biographyofamerica/prog14/transcript/page02.html*, accessed May 2005.

128 He was joined by spice trader Eugene Durkee, who drafted the first standards for spice purity under the U.S. Pure Food and Drug Act.

129 By the 1920s the company had 25 factories and over 200 smaller

operations; in 1946 it launched operations in Venezuela, Holland and Japan; and in the late 1950s began an aggressive programme of acquisitions. Today, Heinz is the quintessential multinational corporation with over 110 major locations worldwide, and market-leading brands on six continents. *http://www.heinz.com/jsp/history.jsp*, accessed March 2005; Lukas, Paul, 'H.J. Heinz: Shake It Up' in *Fortune Small Business*, April 2003. *http://www.fortune.com/fortune/smallbusiness/articles/0,15114,432279,00.html*.

130 Knightley, Philip, *The Rise and Fall of the House of Vestey: The True Story of How Britain's Richest Family Beat the Taxman – and Came to Grief*, London: Warner, (1993). For Evelene Brodstone see *http://www.superiorne.com/evelynbrodstone-ladyvestey.htm*.

131 'They did not live on their income; they did not live on the interest from their investments', wrote Knightley (1993), 'they lived on the interest on the interest.'

132 This and subsequent world economic statistics are from the indispensable Maddison (2001).

133 Keynes, J.M., *The Economic Consequences of the Peace*, (1919), pp. 9–10.

134 McCormick company website: *http://www.mccormick.com/content.cfm?ID=10116*, accessed January 2005.

135 Of the total, nearly $9 trillion was merchandise, and about $2.2 trillion was services. 'World Trade 2004, Prospects For 2005: Developing countries' goods trade share surges to 50-year peak', World Trade Organization, Press Release 14 April 2005, *http://www.wto.org/english/news_e/pres05_e/pr401_e.pdf*.

136 Frankel, Jeffrey and Romer, David, 'Does Trade Cause Growth?' *American Economic Review*, Vol. 89, (1999), pp. 379–99.

137 Among the critical responses to Frankel and Romer are Hallak, Juan Carlos & Levinsohn, James (2004) 'Fooling Ourselves: Evaluating the Globalization and Growth Debate', University of Michigan; Helpman, Melitz & Rubinstein (2004) 'Trading Partners and Trading Volumes', Tel Aviv / Harvard Universities; and Rodríguez, Francisco and Rodrik, Dani 'Trade policy and economic growth: A skeptic's guide to cross-national evidence,' in Bernanke, B. and Rogoff, K. (eds.), NBER Macroeconomics Annual 2000, MIT Press, Cambridge, MA, 2001. Some academics even tried to explain countries' economic growth by looking at how long European colonists survived in the eighteenth century.

138 Network of world merchandise trade by region, 2001–03, Table A2, *World Trade Statistics 2004*, World Trade Organization, Geneva. Since this report, the WTO has changed its definition of the seven regions, including Mexico in North America (where it has always been) and joining Western Europe with the Baltic and Central and Eastern Europe. These two changes actually reduce the amount of extra-regional trade.

139 The data is too patchy to identify trends, but there is some evidence that the amount of local trade in the European Union and NAFTA has actually *increased* in the last decade.

140 The double y-axis is a masterpiece of what Darrell Huff called '*How to Lie with Statistics*' (Penguin, 1991), an unfortunate tendency among both pro- and anti-globalization books.

141 UNCTAD *GlobStat: Globalization and Development Facts and Figures*, at: *http://globstat.unctad.org/html/index.html*, accessed March 2005.

142 Anderson, Sarah & Cavanagh, John *The Rise of Corporate Global Power*, Institute for Policy Studies (2000).

143 Klein, Naomi, *No Logo*, Flamingo, (2000), pp. 339–340; De Grauwe, Paul & Camerman, Filip, *How Big Are The Big Multinational Companies?* University of Leuven, Belgium, (2002), accessed February 2005; Legrain, Philippe *Open World*, Abacus, (2002), p. 139.

144 I used De Grauwe & Camerman's methodology, with the World Bank's *World Development Indicators Database* for 2004 GDP (July 2005), and *Fortune* magazine's Global 500 listing for corporate sales (July 2005), and an average value added figure of 32.8 per cent derived from 600 leading European corporations from UK Department of Trade and Industry *Value Added Scoreboard*, 2004, at: *http://www.innovation.gov.uk/value_added/analysis.asp?p=analysis*, accessed March 2005.

145 MacGillivray, Alex, Raynard, Peter & Oliveira, Cris, *Towards Responsible Lobbying*, AccountAbility for UN Global Compact, New York, (2005).

146 Slogans from corporate websites of IBM, LVMH, Coca-Cola, Canon and Yum (complete with misplaced apostrophe), as at 30 March 2005. IBM is not currently using its 'Solutions . . .' registered trademark.

147 Transnational corporations (TNCs) are 'incorporated or unincorporated enterprises comprising parent enterprises and their foreign affiliates', according to UNCTAD. 'A parent enterprise is defined as an enterprise that controls assets of other entities in countries other than its home country, by owning an equity capital stake (normally 10 per cent or above)'. Transnational is preferred to the common term multinational, because the latter implies multiple countries of operation, whereas only two countries are needed.

148 UNCTAD (1992–2004) 'The Top 100 TNCs, Ranked By Foreign Assets', in *World Investment Reports*, 1992–2004, Geneva.

149 Rugman covers the geographical origin of sales, but not supplies or staff. He also leaves out Africa. A major problem in tracking global corporations is that reporting requirements are not the same in different parts of the world.

150 In 2002, France had 14 top 100 transnationals, the UK 12 and the USA 26, according to UNCTAD (2004).

151 Bakan, Joel, *The Corporation, the pathological pursuit of profit and power*, Constable, (2004); Micklethwait & Wooldridge (2003).

152 *http://www.greenevents.fsnet.co.uk/features/art057.html*.

153 'Hottest chilli sauce launched', *BBC News*, 9 May 2005. *http://news.bbc.co.uk/1/hi/world/americas/4530739.stm*.

154 *http://www.oligopolywatch.com/stories/2003/04/17/definingThe-NewOligopoly.html*, accessed February 2005.

155 Marks, Stephen & Pomeroy, Jacqueline, 'International Trade in Nutmeg and Mace: issues and options for Indonesia' in: *Bulletin of Indonesian Economic Studies* 31(3), December 1995, pp. 103–18.

156 Cited in *The Economist* (1998).

157 United Nations Comtrade database. *http://unstats.un.org/unsd/comtrade/ce/ceSnapshot.aspx?px=S3&cc=075*, accessed April 2005.

158 Boyle, David, *Authenticity: brands, fakes, spin and the lust for real life*, Flamingo, (2003).

159 *The Socio-Economics of Geographical Indications: a Review of Empirical Evidence from Europe*, Centre for the Study of Globalisation and Regionalisation, Warwick University for UNCTAD & ICTSD, May 2004.

160 Forstater, Maya, MacGillivray, Alex & Raynard, Peter, *Responsible Trade: implications for SMEs in developing countries*, UNIDO, Vienna, (2005).

161 'Britain blamed for India suicides', BBC News World Edition 16 May 2005. *http://news.bbc.co.uk/2/hi/uk_news/4548927.stm*, accessed May 2005.

162 Robins, Nick & Kumar, Ritu, 'Black Pepper Country' in: *Resurgence* 220 September/October 2003.

163 Shiva, Vandana, (no date) 'The turmeric patent is just the first step in stopping biopiracy', Third World Network, *http://www.twnside.org.sg/title/tur-cn.htm*, accessed April 2005.

164 'Clear off! We don't want you to help us', Sunetra Chakravarti, *The Times*, 6 January 2005.

165 Data and dates on migration draw on Cavalli-Sforza, Luigi, *Genes, Peoples and Languages*, Penguin Books pp.54–95, (2001) and Diamond, Jared, *Guns, Germs and Steel*, Jonathan Cape (1997), pp.35–52.

166 The third species has been named *Homo floresiensis*, and nicknamed the Hobbit. See *http://www.nature.com/news/specials/flores/index.html*, accessed July 2005.

167 The phrase is Jared Diamond's (1997).

168 Zeldin, Theodore, *An Intimate History of Humanity*, Penguin, 1999, p.78.

169 Lovejoy, P. (2000) *Transformations in Slavery*, Cambridge University Press argues that 2.2 million Africans were enslaved and shipped to Asia in the years between 650 and 1500 while another 4.3 million were transported across the Sahara.

170 The numbers are still debated by historians. These are mid-range figures drawn from Klein, H., *The Atlantic Slave Trade*, Cambridge University Press, (1999) and Lovejoy, P. *Transformations in Slavery*, Cambridge University Press, (2000). Numbers are lower in the classic work by Curtin, P. *The Atlantic Slave Trade*, University of Wisconsin (1969).

171 Hobhouse, H., Knapp, S., and Lowndes, *Seeds of Trade*, (2004). *http://internt.nhm.ac.uk/jsdml/seeds/*. For recent monographs on sugar see Macinnis, Peter *Bittersweet: The Story of Sugar*, Allen & Unwin, Australia, (2003); O'Connell, Sanjida *Sugar: The Grass That Changed the World*, Virgin Books, (2004). Another two million Africans, mostly female, went to slave markets in the East over this same period. European population figures from Maddison (2001) p.241.

172 The phrase is Ferguson's (2004).

173 Conversion of £20 million to 2002 value by Economic History services – How Much is That Worth Today? *http://eh.net/hmit/ppowerbp/*.

174 Some historians are beginning to address the legacy of these commodities. See Moxham, Roy *Tea: addiction, exploitation and empire*, Constable & Robinson, (2004), and Wild, Anthony, *Black Gold: The Dark History of Coffee*, Perennial, (2005).

175 Rothschild (2004), p.14.

176 Torpey, John, *The Invention of the Passport*, Cambridge University Press, (1999), p. 9.

177 Bayly (2004), p.173.

178 O'Rourke, Kevin *The Era of Migration: Lessons for today*, Centre for Economic Policy Research Paper DP4498, July 2004.

179 Asian numbers from Held, David *et al.*, *Global Transformations*, Polity Press, (1999), p. 293–295. Income estimates from Maddison (2001) who says the per capita income of India fell in real terms from US$550 to $533 between 1700 and 1870. In China the fall was from $600 to $530 over the same period (all in constant 1990 dollars).

180 Fearing the threat to its established routes to India, the canal was vehemently opposed by the British – until they grabbed an opportunity to buy out the Egyptian half-share from a heavily-indebted Isma'il Pasha in 1875 for a knock-down price.

181 Pakenham, Thomas, *The Scramble for Africa*, Abacus, (1991).

182 Diamond, p.210–212; Ferguson, p. 65–66.

183 The bike won 62 per cent of the votes, way ahead of electricity (20 per cent), vaccination (nine per cent) and the web (seven per cent).

The panel of experts assembled by *The Times* voted for electricity –
but were overruled by the popular poll. Exactly the same thing
happened with a 2002 poll organised by Radio 4 to celebrate 150
years of the Patent Office. In that exercise, the bicycle garnered 70
per cent of votes from all continents, thrashing numerous worthy
inventions that *do* find their way into the index of books on
globalization. Seven per cent of voters actually said the mobile
phone was the *worst* invention in 150 years, while only one person
in twenty voted for the radio (5.5 per cent of votes) or the computer
(4.5 per cent) and even fewer for the internet (3.5 per cent), the
telephone or television (just 1.5 per cent of votes each). Henderson,
Mark, 'So is it the computer? Electricity? No, pedal power makes
the bicycle our favourite invention', *The Times*, November 27
2004, *http://www.timesonline.co.uk/article/0,,18069-1376728,00.*
html, accessed March 2005; *http://www.bbc.co.uk/radio4/today/*
reports/archive/science_nature/inventions.shtml.

184 Jones first made the claim in his *Language of the Genes* (1994), and
has stuck by it. 'Human Evolution has Stopped', The Truth Will
Out, BBC/Open University, *http://www.open2.net/truthwillout/*
evolution/article/evolution_jones.htm, accessed May 2005. Some
epidemiologists and geneticists disagree, citing HIV as an example
of a disease which still exerts formidable selective pressure on
people, especially in the developing world.

185 *http://archives.econ.utah.edu/archives/pen-1/1999m08.d/msg00074.*
htm, accessed July 2005.

186 Montesquieu, *The Spirit of Laws*, Book XXVI.

187 Hobhouse (2003), p.141.

188 Araña's company only folded in 1920, the victim not of moral
outrage but of global competition from Malaysian plantations
tapped by Indian coolies. Hobhouse, pp.125–185; Loadman, John
'The Putumayo Affair', Bouncing Balls: everything you ever wanted
to know about rubber, *http://www.bouncing-balls.com/in-*
dex2.htm, accessed May 2005.

189 *The Economic Consequences of the Peace*, Harcourt, Brace &
Howe, NY, (1920).

190 Casement himself was executed for treason in 1916 for his part in
supporting the Irish rebellion. Morel was imprisoned for sending
pacifist tracts to Switzerland, and only rehabilitated some time after
the war, standing as a Labour candidate for Dundee and beating
Winston Churchill in 1922. Disappointed not to be appointed
Foreign Minister by the victorious Ramsay MacDonald, Morel
died of a heart attack while nominated for the Nobel Peace Prize.
He didn't win it.

191 The Armenian massacres took the lives of 1.5 million people
between 1915 and 1923. Wilson quote from *http://www.sparta-*
cus.schoolnet.co.uk/FWWleague.htm; Stalin quote from Emott

(2003), p.9; Hitler quote from Bardakjian, Kevork *Hitler and the Armenian Genocide*, Cambridge, MA, (1985), p.6.

192 Richardson, Lewis, *Statistics of Deadly Quarrels*, Pittsburgh: Box-wood Press, (1960). For an entertaining account of Richardson's work and efforts to update it, see Hayes, Brian, 'Statistics of Deadly Quarrels', *American Scientist*, 90 (1), January–February 2002, pp.10–15.

193 According to Rudy Rummel at the University of Hawaii, the devastating death toll of the 20th century includes 29 million troops and 37 million civilian victims of world war. Including civil wars and civilian deaths inflicted by their own governments in the periods of upheaval surrounding these two great wars, notably in Turkey (1909–18), the USSR and China, we arrive at a death toll of 170 million people up to 1987. The Spanish Flu could only have happened in a time of global conflict, and should be included – taking the total well past 200 million. Rummel's estimate for pre-twentieth-century deaths is 133 million people. Rummel, Rudolph, *Death By Government*, New Brunswick: Transaction Publishers, (1994) & 'Democide since World War II', (1998). *http://www.ha-waii.edu/powerkills/POSTWWII.HTM*, accessed May 2005; *http://www.hawaii.edu/powerkills/SOD.FIG23.2.GIF*.

194 The classic story is Ellis, John, *The Social History of the Machine Gun*, Random House, (1975). See also Kelly, Jack, *Gunpowder: The Explosive That Changed the World*, Atlantic Books, (2004); Diamond, Jared, *Guns, Germs and Steel*, Jonathan Cape, (1997).

195 Davies, Norman, *Europe: A History*, Oxford University Press, (1996), pp.565–568.

196 'I haven't slept very well,' Palin admitted of his night at the Welcome Guest Lodge in Qingdao. 'It wasn't the maotai as much as the awareness that some of the most ruthless men of this century have slept beneath this roof and, for all I know, on my very bed . . . Ho-Chi-Minh of Vietnam, Prince Sihanouk of Cambodia, Mao's foreign minister Zhou Enlai and two general secretaries of the Albanian Communist Party all stared up at my ceiling. Though not at the same time.' *http://www.palinstravels.co.uk/book-364*, accessed May 2005.

197 The term 'democide' is Rudy Rummel's. The Nazis are responsible for at least 25 million deaths in a six-year period. Courtois, Stephane *et al.*, *Le Livre Noir du Communisme: crimes, terreur, répression*, Robert Laffont, Paris, (1997).

198 More US soldiers died in the Civil War (620,000) than in all America's foreign wars from Independence to Korea, according to David Reynolds (in Hopkins, ed., 2001, p.246).

199 Arguably Wilson's stroke cost him the battle to convince the Senate, although he had underestimated the strength of isolationists like Henry Cabot Lodge. Cooper, John, *Breaking the Heart of the World: Woodrow Wilson and the Fight for the League of Nations*,

Cambridge University Press, (2001); Knock, Thomas, *To End All Wars: Woodrow Wilson and the Quest for a New World Order*, Princeton University Press, (1995).

200 Maddison (2001), Table 3–4, p.128; James, Harold, *The End of Globalization: Lessons from the Great Depression*, Harvard University Press, (2002).

201 Nehru quote from *http://www.globaltraveltourism.com/site/wttc_india/LalitS.asp*; Veblen quote from *http://www.quotationspage.com/quotes/Thorstein_Veblen/*.

202 WTTC (2005) *Travel and Tourism: sowing the seeds of growth 2005*, executive summary, World Travel and Tourism Council, London.

203 'Only 11% of U.S. citizens even hold passports,' writes Ed Readicker-Henderson. 'Three times that number of people watch NASCAR races, and if there's a better definition of anti-travel – endless circling, trapped in a lower ring of hell – I don't want to know what it is.' *Nos Patriam Fugimus*, Motionsickness, Summer 2003.

204 Sebald, W.G., *On The Natural History of Destruction*, Penguin, London, (2003).

205 UN, *Trends In Total Migrant Stock: The 2003 Revision*, United Nations Department Of Economic And Social Affairs Population Division, New York; *International Migration Report 2002*.

206 Pew (2003), pp.34 & 106.

207 This includes 11.3 million forced labourers in Germany. United Nations High Commissioner for Refugees, *The State of the World's Refugees 2000: Fifty Years of Humanitarian Action*, Oxford University Press, (2000), Ch.1.

208 United Nations High Commissioner for Refugees, *The State of the World's Refugees 2000: Fifty Years of Humanitarian Action*, Oxford University Press, (2000), Ch.11.

209 *The World's Stateless People; questions and answers*, Geneva: UNHCR, April 2004.

210 'UNICEF Official Cites "Largest Slave Trade in History",' UN Wire, 20 February 2003.

211 ILO (2005) *A Global Alliance Against Forced Labour, Report Of The Director-General*, Report I (B), International Labour Office, Geneva.

212 *http://news.bbc.co.uk/1/hi/world/europe/4531123.stm*, accessed 12 May 2005.

213 UNGA (2005) *Progress made in the implementation of the Declaration of Commitment on HIV/AIDS: Report of the Secretary-General*, UN General Assembly A/59/765, April 2005, New York.

214 'UN calls for action to halt Aids', BBC News World Edition, 3 June 2005, *http://news.bbc.co.uk/2/hi/americas/4605413.stm*.

215 World Health Organization (2005) 'Summary of Probable SARS

cases', *http://www.who.int/csr/sars/country/table2004_04_21/en/ index.html.*

216 Saul, John Ralston, *The Collapse of Globalism*, Atlantic Books, (2005), p.269.

217 WTO *World Trade Report 2004*, World Trade Organization, Geneva; Friedman, Thomas *The World is Flat: a brief history of the 21st century*, Allen Lane, (2005). Friedman (2005) traces the development to the era of cheap global telecommunications beginning in 2000.

218 Colvin, Geoffrey, 'America isn't ready', *Fortune*, 152(3), (2005), pp.22–31.

219 *http://www.un.org/esa/population/publications/longrange2/World-Pop2300final.pdf*, accessed December 2004.

220 Cited in Saul (2005), p.78.

221 Estimates of the world's above the ground gold stock are around 120–150,000 tonnes. A tonne of gold would set you back about $13.8 million in July 2005. Source: *http://www.galmarley.com/ framesets/fs_commodity_essentials_faqs.htm*. Estimated world oil reserves are 1,050 billion barrels. *http://www.eia.doe.gov/pub/in-ternational/iea2003/table81.xls*

222 Evans, David & Schmalensee, Richard, *Paying with Plastic: The Digital Revolution in Buying and Borrowing*. MIT Press, (2005).

223 The classic history of money is Davies, Glyn *A History Of Money From Ancient Times To The Present Day*, 3rd edition, Cardiff: University of Wales Press, (2002). For an entertaining and thought-provoking alternative, see Boyle, David, *The Little Money Book*, Alastair Sawday Publishing, (2004), and Buchan, James, *Frozen Desire: an enquiry into the meaning of money*, Picador, (1997).

224 Base but not precious metal coinage appeared in China at this period.

225 Cited in Standish, David, *The Art of Money: the history and design of paper currency from around the world*, Chronicle, San Francisco, (2000), pp.20–21.

226 Spufford (2002), p.95.

227 Dunnett, R.E. *Gentlemanly Capitalism and British Imperialism: The New Debate on Empire*, Pearson Books, (1999).

228 'The Relentless Contrarian: Peter Drucker' in Wired: *http://wired-vig.wired.com/wired/archive/4.08/drucker.html?pg=2&topic=&to-pic_set=*, accessed April 2005.

229 Cited in Buchan (1997), p.82–83.

230 Maddison (2001), p.64.

231 World Gold Council, *http://www.gold.org/value/reserve_asset/history/ monetary_history/vol1/1667jun12.html*, accessed January 2005.

232 Cited in Buchan, (1997), p.268.

233 Mundell, Robert, 'Uses and Abuses of Gresham's Law in the History of Money', *Zagreb Journal of Economics*, 2(2) 1998.

234 Dale, Richard, *The First Crash: Lessons from the South Sea Bubble*, Princeton University Press, (2004).

235 Chancellor, Edward, *Devil Take The Hindmost: a history of financial speculation*, Plume, (2000); Kindelberger, Charles, *Manias, Panics, and Crashes: A History of Financial Crises*, Wiley, (1978).

236 Garber, Peter, *Famous First Bubbles: The Fundamentals of Early Manias*, MIT Press, (2000). James Surowiecki at *The New Yorker* has also argued that stock markets have been fairly effective price-setting mechanisms relying on the 'wisdom of crowds', at least most of the time.

237 Bakan, Joel, *The Corporation*, Constable, (2004), pp.6–8.

238 Based on Kikochi, Masotoshi, *An Infocommunications Bubble?*, Daiwa Institute of Research, Tokyo, (1999), supplemented from Surowiecki, James, *The Wisdom of Crowds*, Abacus, (2004).

239 Green, Timothy, *Central Bank Gold Reserves: an historical perspective since 1845*, World Gold Council Research Study 23, London, (1999).

240 Maddison (2001), Table 3–1a, 3–1b, p.126. All sums in 1990 international dollars.

241 Maddison (2001), Table 3–3, p.128; Table 2–6a, p.99. All sums in 1990 international dollars.

242 *The Economic Consequences of the Peace* (1920).

243 Legrain (2002), p.102.

244 Reynolds in Hopkins (2002), p.249.

245 The Real Ponzi, Social Security Online, *http://www.ssa.gov/history/ponzi.html*; *http://www.explore-biography. com/biographies/C/Charles_Ponzi.html*, accessed June 2005.

246 McDougall, Walter, *Freedom Just Around the Corner: A New American History: 1585–1828*, HarperCollins, (2004).

247 Keynes, J.M., *The General Theory of Employment, Interest and Money*, New York: Harcourt, Brace and World, (1936), p. 159.

248 'Money Matters', IMF, *http://www.imf.org/external/np/exr/center/mm/eng/mm_cc_01.htm*, accessed June 2005.

249 Alexander Field 'The Most Technologically Progressive Decade of the Century,' *American Economic Review* 93 (September 2003): 1399–1414.

250 Maddison (2001), Table 3–3, p.128. All amounts in 1990 US dollars.

251 GPO, *Public Papers of the Presidents, Richard Nixon, Containing the Public Messages, Speeches, and Statements of the President, 1971*, Washington: Government Printing Office, 1972, pp. 886–890.

252 Schlesinger, Stephen, *Act Of Creation: The Founding of the United Nations: A Story of Superpowers, Secret Agents, Wartime Allies and Enemies, and Their Quest for a Peaceful World*, Westview Press, 2004.

253 Despite repeated efforts to devise better indicators of national progress, GDP remains the paramount indicator today. MacGillivray, Alex & Zadek, Simon, *Accounting for Change*, New Economics Foundation, London, (1995).

254 Some 1,090 Kikuyu were hanged, 12–20,000 killed in combat, and up to 100,000 died in detention, while there were 32 white deaths, according to Anderson, David, *Histories of the Hanged: Britain's Dirty War in Kenya and the End of Empire*, Weidenfeld, (2005), and Elkins, Caroline, *Britain's Gulag: The Brutal End of Empire in Kenya*, Cape, (2005).

255 *Fortune*, **151**(10), June 13 2005, p.31.

256 The Roaring Nineties is Joseph Stiglitz's phrase. McKinsey Global Institute, *$118 Trillion and Counting: Taking Stock of the World's Capital Markets*, (2005), p.19.

257 Yergin, Daniel, *The Prize*, Simon & Schuster, (1991).

258 Stiglitz, Joseph, *Globalization and its Discontents*, Penguin, (2002).

259 'The Twin Crises: The Causes of Banking and Balance-of-Payments Problems' draft for: *American Economic Review*, downloaded March 2005 from *http://www.puaf.umd.edu/faculty/papers/reinhart/bank3.pdf*.

260 The global supply of gold scrap normally averages about 600 tonnes a year. In 1998 it shot up to 1,100 tonnes, thanks to this 'dishoarding'. GFMS *Gold Survey 2004*, cited by World Gold Council, *http://www.gold.org/value/markets/supply_demand/recycled.html*, accessed June 2005.

261 Shiller, Robert *Irrational Exuberance* 2nd edition, Princeton University Press, (2005). Meriwether is quoted in Mandelbrot & Hudson (2004), p.107.

262 Janis, Irving *Groupthink: psychological studies of policy decisions and fiascos*, Houghton Miffin, (1982), Stiglitz (2002), p.230–231.

263 *http://www.huppi.com/kangaroo/L-chinobel.htm*; *http://www.right-livelihood.org/recip.htm*, accessed June 2005.

264 The G8's GDP was $26.4 trillion in 2004, according to the World Bank's *World Development Indicators database*, released on 15 July 2005. Note that the IMF debts are not all owed to G8 countries anyway.

265 McKinsey Global Institute (2005); *Financial Times*, 25 May 2005. *http://news.ft.com/cms/s/dc7572ba-ccba-11d9-bb87-00000e2511c8.html*, accessed 25 May 2005. Much of the US capital stock is actually debt, which is now approaching the $1 trillion mark.

266 'Disarming the markets', *http://mondediplo.com/1997/12/leader*.

267 Assuming 250 currency trading days a year.

268 As at April 2004. The percentages come to more than 100 per cent because there are two currencies in every exchange. McKinsey Global Institute, 2005, p.21.

269 'A theory of roughness', Edge, December 2004, *http://www.edge.org/*

3rd_culture/mandelbrot04/mandelbrot04_index.html, accessed May 2005.

270 'Oil Industry', Readers Companion to American History, Houghton Mifflin, *http://college.hmco.com/history/readerscomp/rcah/html/ah_066100_oilindustry.htm*.

271 Carbon emissions from 1750–2002 from Marland, G., Boden, T.A. and Andres, R. J., *Global, Regional, and National CO2 Emissions.* In *Trends: A Compendium of Data on Global Change.* Carbon Dioxide Information Analysis Center, Oak Ridge National Laboratory, U.S. Department of Energy, Oak Ridge, Tenn., U.S.A., 2005; crude oil prices in 1999 $ from *http://www.eia.doe.gov/pub/international/iealf/BPCrudeOilPrices.xls*, accessed May 2005.

272 Davis, Mike, *Late Victorian Holocausts: El Niño Famines and the Making of the Third World*, Verso, (2002), Le Roy Ladurie, Emmanuel, *Times of Feast, Times of Famine: A History of Climate Since the Year 1000*, Farrar, Strauss & Giroux, (1988); Fagan, Brian, *The Long Summer: How Climate Changed Civilization*, Granta, (2004); Fagan, Brian *The Little Ice Age: How Climate Made History 1300–1850*, Basic Books, (2002).

273 MacGillivray, Alex, *Rachel Carson's Silent Spring: words that changed the world*, Barrons, (2004).

274 Environmental Defense, *Global Warming: The History of an International Scientific Consensus*, *www.environmentaldefense.org/documents/381_FactSheet_globalwarming_timeline.pdf*, (2005).

275 Munich Re's latest report predicts that eco-system losses, including mangrove swamps, coral reefs and coastal lagoons, could run at over $70 billion by 2050. Europe's biggest climate-related losses will be in higher levels of mortality and health costs, which are estimated to reach $21.9 billion by 2050. In the US, the additional cost of health-related measures and more intensive water management may reach nearly $30 billion by 2050.

276 Simms, Andrew *Ecological Debt*, Pluto, (2005) London.

277 Cited in Agostino, Gilberto, *Vencer ou Morrer: futebol, geopolitica e identidade nacional*, Mauad, Brazil, (2002).

278 One of the best accounts of football fanaticism's local/global tensions is Foer, Franklin *How Soccer Explains the World*, HarperCollins, (2004). See also Murray (1998 & 2003) or Maguire, Joseph, *Global Sport: identities, societies, civilizations*, Polity Press, (1999), for a more academic treatment.

279 The Football Association was formed in 1863 and over the next 15 years slowly gained agreement for a single set of rules. 11 players a side became the norm in 1870 and crossbars were introduced in 1875. Floodlights and referees' whistles were in use by 1878, but the controversial concept of the penalty was not agreed until 1891.

280 *http://www.learnhistory.org.uk/football/GCSE%20Football%20-Coursework.ppt*, February 2005.

281 In 1885 paying players was formally legalized in England; previously clubs had had to keep false accounts to hide the wages. The first League members were Accrington, Aston, Blackburn, Bolton, Burnley, Derby, Everton, Nottinghamshire, Preston, Stoke, West Bromwich and Wolverhampton. Half the original member clubs were from Lancashire and none of the five clubs which today dominate English football was included.

282 'Ten dates that changed the game (1902–25)', FIFA, *http://www.fifa.com/en/news/feature/0,1451,74407,00.html?articleid=74407*, accessed June 2005.

283 Lowrey, James, Neatrour, Sam & Williams, John, *Fact Sheet 16: The Bosman Ruling, Football Transfers and Foreign Footballers*, Sir Norman Chester Centre for Football Research, University of Leicester, (2002).

284 *http://www.footballculture.net/teams/feat_bilbao.html*, accessed February 2005.

285 'Dein attacks "home-grown" quotas', Jon Brodkin, *The Guardian*, 4 February 2005.

286 Hindley, Geoffrey, *The Crusades: Islam and Christianity in the struggle for world supremacy*, Robinson, (2004).

287 Manguel (1996), pp.133–138.

288 Bayly (2004), pp.325–365.

289 By then the British work ethic was lackadaisical – Weber was not translated into English until 1930.

290 Bayly (2004), p.110, 314.

291 There have been other proposals, such as Kenneth Searight's *Sona* (1935), the International Auxiliary Language Association's *Interlingua* (1951), and more recently *Lingua Franca Nova* (1965) and *Mondlango* (2002).

292 Gunn, Geoffrey, *First Globalization: The Eurasian Exchange, 1500–1800* Rowman & Littlefield, (2003).

293 A recent scholar has disputed the story of the lost arm, although my father Ian MacGillivray had it directly from the son of the Turkish official who permitted the French to take the statue. See Curtis, Gregory, *Disarmed: the story of Venus de Milo*, Sutton Publishing, (2005).

294 Bayly (2004), p.366.

295 Manguel, Alberto, *A History of Reading*, London, Harper Collins, (1996), pp.134–44.

296 Roche, Maurice *Mega-events: Olympics and Expos in the Growth of Global Culture*, Routledge, (2000).

297 Cowen (2002), p.133.

298 Brown, J.S., & Duguid, P. *The Social Life of Information*, Harvard Business School Press, (2000).

299 Gordon, John Steele, *A Thread Across the Ocean: The Heroic Story of the Transatlantic Cable*, Perennial, (2003); Cookson,

Gillian, *The Cable: The Wire That Changed the World*, Tempus, (2003).

300 Diamond, Jared *Guns, Germs and Steel*, Jonathan Cape, London, (1997), p.243.

301 *http://www.atlantic-cable.com/CableCos/ComPacCable/*, accessed March 2005.

302 Cushing, Lincoln *Centennial of the Spanish-American War 1898–1998*, *http://www.zpub.com/cpp/saw.html*, accessed March 2005; 'How I Carried the Message To Garcia', Colonel Andrew Summers Rowan, *http://www.foundationsmag.com/rowan.html*, accessed March 2005.

303 Bayly, (2004), p.461.

304 Its value as motivational literature may be more limited today than it was 100 years ago. 'My manager at work gave [the *Message to Garcia*] to all his employees a few years ago,' wrote an anonymous reviewer on amazon.com. 'As soon as I finished reading it, I decided to start looking for another job.'

305 Trumpbour, John, *Selling Hollywood to the World: U.S. and European Struggles for Mastery of the Global Film Industry, 1920–1950*. Cambridge University Press, (2002).

306 Tragically, it also saw the return of art theft under the Nazis.

307 Eurovision historical milestones, *http://eurovision.tv/archive_2004/english/611.htm*, accessed May 2005.

308 For some recent samples, see Cowen (2002); Perrone, Charles & Dunn, Christopher *Brazilian Popular Music and Globalization*, Routledge, (2002); Taylor, Timothy *Global Pop: world music, world markets*, Routledge, (1997); Condry, Ian, 'Japanese Hip-Hop and the Globalization of Popular Culture'; in: *Urban Life: readings in the anthropology of the City*, George Gmelch and Walter Zenner (eds), Prospect Heights, IL, Waveland Press, (2001), pp. 357–387.

309 Today it is a major tourist attraction for film-lovers, with several theme parks based on 1960s film-sets.

310 A prison warder, played by Harry Dean Stanton, releases the Man with No Name from prison on condition that he sorts out the violence in San Miguel. This extra footage gave The Man with No Name a slender moral mission but was unauthorized by Leone and has not survived except in poor quality bootleg copies.

311 'The "Hilltop" Ad: The Story of a Commercial', Library of Congress, *http://memory.loc.gov/ammem/ccmphtml/colaadv.html*, accessed May 2005.

312 See *http://www.diacenter.org/km/web/web.html* for the world's most and least liked paintings, according to Kumar and Melamid, and decide for yourself. Pinker, Steven, *The Blank Slate*, Penguin, (2002), p.408–409.

313 Abley, Mark, *Spoken Here: Travel Among Threatened Languages*, Arrow, (2005).

314 Gordon, Raymond *Ethnologue: Languages of the World*, 15th edition, SIL, (2005). In the 14th edition of 2000, there were 6809 languages listed. See also Steger (2003), p.85.

315 UNDP, *Human Development Report 2004*, UNDP, New York, p.33.

316 Accounting for 53 per cent of cultural exports and 57 per cent of imports, according to UNESCO, *Study on International Flows of Cultural Goods, 1980–98*, Paris, UNESCO, (2000).

317 They were: *Confessions*, Usher; *Feels Like Home*, Norah Jones; *Encore*, Eminem; *How To Dismantle An Atomic Bomb*, U2; *Under My Skin*, Avril Lavigne; *Greatest Hits*, Robbie Williams; *Greatest Hits*, Shania Twain; *Destiny Fulfilled*, Destiny's Child. Source: IFPI, *http://www.ifpi.org/site-content/press/inthemedia16. html*, accessed June 2005.

318 'How to Look at Globalization Now', Harvard Business School, 10 June 2002, *http://hbswk.hbs.edu/item.jhtml?id=2970&t=globaliza-tion&noseek=one.*; 'Semiglobalization and international business strategy', *Journal of International Business Studies* (2003) **34**, 138–152.

319 *http://www.loc.gov/folklife/ryko.html*, accessed March 2005.

320 Brown, Andrew *The Guardian Wrap*: 'A worm's eye view', 6 June 2005.

321 *Prospect* Magazine, 2004.

322 Pew Global Attitudes Survey (2003).

323 Niven starred in the 1956 version directed by Michael Anderson; Coogan in the 2004 remake by Frank Coraci.

324 Cantinflas was in *Around the World in Eighty Days* (1956) with Frances Fong, and Frances Fong was in *Rush Hour* (1998) with Jackie Chan. Try the game for yourself using *Star Links*, the brilliant website of the University of Virginia Department of Computer Science at *http://www.cs.virginia.edu/oracle/star_links.html*. If you prefer rock music, try *http://bandtoband.com/index.php*. The Kevin Bacon game can be accessed at The Oracle of Bacon, at *http:// www.cs.virginia.edu/oracle/center_list.html*.

325 Milgram, Stanley (1967) 'The Small World Problem', *Psychology Today*, May 1967, pp. 60–67.

326 Cited in Staple, Gregory (1993) 'Telegeography and the Explosion of Place: Why the Network That Is Bringing The World Together Is Pulling it Apart', in: *TeleGeography*, October 1993, pp. 49–56. *http://www.telegeography.com/ee/free_resources/essay 06.php? PHPSESSID=009d2bb7cee69a2c7b1c354366c68451*, accessed March 2005.

327 *http://www.google.com/press/intl-zeitgeist.html*, accessed March 2005. Experienced web users save their most popular websites as favourites, so using search behaviour is only a partial guide to what people are doing on the web.

328 Spohrer, James (1999) 'Information in Places', *http://www.research.ibm.com/journal/sj/384/spohrer.txt*, accessed June 2005.

329 *www.quova.com*; *www.geourl.org*; *www.cybergeography.org/atlas/atlas.html*.

330 Bacon's fame is actually undeserved. Rod Steiger is the world's most connected actor, according to The Oracle of Bacon.

331 Dodds, Peter, Muhamad, Roby & Watts, Duncan, 'An Experimental Study of Search in Global Social Networks' in *Science*, Vol **301**, 8 August 2003, pp.827–829.

332 Duncan Watts, personal communication, April 2005.

333 One Scrooge sent cards to fewer than 25 friends. At the other extreme a super-networker sent yuletide cheer to more than 350 friends. Hill, R. A. & Dunbar, Robin 'Social Network Size In Humans', *Human Nature*, Vol. **14**, No. 1, 2003, pp. 53–72.

334 Hubbard, Elbert *The Philistine*, (1914) cited at: *http://www.bigeye.com/ehwork.htm*, accessed March 2005.

335 'Historical perspective: Levitt shaped the debate', Harvard Business School Working Knowledge, June 2003. *http://hbswk.hbs.edu/item.jhtml?id=3542&t=globalization&noseek=one*

336 Maalouf, Amin, *The Crusades through Eastern Eyes*, Saqi Books (1983, 2001).

337 Marcus, Jonathan (2005) 'A small matter of Crusade history', BBC World Service, 14 May 2005, *http://news.bbc.co.uk/2/hi/middle_east/4544173.stm*, accessed May 2005.

338 In the event, he came in 11th, a victim, as Irish TV host Terry Wogan likes to say, of 'tactical voting'.

339 Music and lyrics by Richard M. Sherman and Robert B. Sherman.

340 Friedman, Thomas *The Earth is Flat*, Penguin Allen Lane, (2005); Saul, J.R., *The Collapse of Globalism*, Atlantic Books, (2005).

341 *http://rrojasdatabank.info/agfrank/reorient.html*, accessed March 2005. See also O'Rourke, Kevin & Williamson, Jeffrey *Globalization and History: The Evolution of a Nineteenth-Century Atlantic Economy*, Cambridge, Mass: MIT Press, (1999); and O'Rourke, Kevin & Williamson, Jeffrey, 'When Did Globalization Begin?', National Bureau Of Economic Research Working Paper No. 7632, April 2000.

342 *Foreign Affairs*, November/December 2004, http://www.foreignaffairs.org/20041101faessay83608/geoffrey-garrett/globalization-s-missing-middle.html, accessed May 2005.

343 Dollar, David & Kraay, Aart 'Spreading the Wealth', *Foreign Affairs*, January/February 2002.

344 'Revisiting "Good" and "Bad" Globalizers', World Bank Transition Newsletter. *www.worldbank.org/transitionnewsletter/janfebmar03/pg512–15.htm*, October 2005

345 *http://www.foreignaffairs.org/20020701faresponse8543/david-dollar-aart-kraay/inequality-is-no-myth.html*.

346 'Inequality Is No Myth', *Foreign Affairs*, July/August 2002. *http://
    www.foreignaffairs.org/20020701faresponse8543/david-dollar-
    aart-kraay/inequality-is-no-myth.html* accessed June 2005.
347 Gladwell, Malcolm *The Tipping Point: how little things can make a
    big difference*, London: Abacus, (2001), p.259.
348 In the prequel, *The Good the Bad and the Ugly*, he is called Blondie
    as well as Joe. *http://www.imdb.com/title/tt0058461/fullcredits*,
    accessed January 2005.
349 *http://www.socioambiental.org/pib/english/howtheylive/isol.shtm#t3*,
    accessed December 2004.

INDEX